P9-DCI-226

A FRESH LOOK
at
PSYCHOANALYSIS

The View from Self Psychology

A FRESH LOOK
at
PSYCHOANALYSIS

The View from Self Psychology

Arnold Goldberg

THE ANALYTIC PRESS

1988   Hillsdale, NJ   Hove and London

Copyright © 1988 by The Analytic Press.

All rights reserved. No part of this book may be reproduced in any form, by photostat, microform, retrieval system, or any other means, without the prior written permission of the publisher.

The Analytic Press.
365 Broadway
Hillsdale, New Jersey 07642

Set in Garamond type

Library of Congress Cataloging-in-Publication Data

Goldberg, Arnold, 1929—
    A fresh look at psychoanalysis.

    Includes bibliographies and index.
    1. Psychoanalysis. 2. Self. I. Title. [DNLM: 1. Ego.
2. Psychoanalysis. WM 460.5.E3 G6175f]
RC506.G65   1988   616.89'17   87[27000

First paperback edition 1992

ISBN 0-88163-156-6

10 9 8 7 6 5 4 3

Contents

I

THEORY

II

EMPATHY

III

CHARACTER

IV

CLINICAL PAPERS

Acknowledgments

I once edited a book of clinical cases in which it was necessary that the authors of the chapters remain anonymous. A call from the very efficient and knowledgeable copy editor informed me that one chapter was so obviously written by Heinz Kohut that it would have to be further disguised. The language and style were so unmistakenly his that only a fool could be deceived. When I assured the editor that Heinz Kohut had had nothing to do with the writing of that case, she was less than congenial about what seemed to her to be a further effort to deceive her. The conversation did, however, give me cause to wonder whether self psychologists, or perhaps even all psychoanalysts, sound so much alike that our jargon has gained mastery over us. My temporarily stilled wonder came alive once again when I was assembling this book. Since the book consists of both previously published and unpublished work written over several years, I am not surprised that some of it sounds familiar. But I was upset by the way some of the articles seemed to borrow freely from some of the others, even though I was guilty only of plagiarizing from myself. I ask the reader's indulgence over these seemingly innocent thefts, which may lead to a certain repetitiousness. Rather than correct this minor annoyance, I have left those few articles fairly intact save for editing changes and owe thanks for permission to adapt the following chapters.

Chapter 2: *Psychoanalysis: The Vital Issues* (1984), Vol. 1, ed. J. Gedo & G. Pollock. New York: International Universities Press.

Chapter 3: *The Annual of Psychoanalysis* (1984/85), Vol. 12–13. New York: International Universities Press.

Chapter 4: *Psychoanalysis and Contemporary Thought* (1984), 7(3).

Chapter 6: *Psychotherapy and Training in Clinical Social Work*, ed. J. Mishne (1980). New York: Gardner Press.

Chapter 8: *The Annual of Psychoanalysis* (1983), Vol. 11. New York: International Universities Press.

Chapter 11: *The Future of Psychoanalysis* (1983), ed. A. Goldberg. New York: International Universities Press.

Chapter 12: *Contemporary Psychoanalysis (1986).* Vol. 22(3).

Chapter 14: *The Psychoanalytic Quarterly* (1987), Vol. 56.

Chapter 17: *The International Review of Psychoanalysis* (1987) 14:409–417.

I would also like to express my gratitude to my secretary, Chris Susman; Dr. Paul. E. Stepansky and Eleanor Starke Kobrin, of The Analytic Press; and my very supportive family.

Introduction

The essays collected in this volume have a unifying history that allows them to be offered as part of a singular event in psychoanalysis: the origin and development of psychoanalytic self psychology. They reflect my personal involvement with that history as I met self psychology, embraced it, and struggled with it over a period of years. They represent my own waxing and waning uncertainties about its significance, along with my equally strong certainty about its value and impact. Essentially they have been my way of working out the many questions and doubts that self psychology brought to me. I remember Heinz Kohut telling me that his tombstone should somehow bear the inscription of a man who worried ideas to death. I certainly have joined him in that enterprise and therefore am continually astonished at the two opposing camps of self psychology: the true believers and the determined nonbelievers. My astonishment comes not from a lack of membership in either camp—I have wholeheartedly belonged to one or the other several times, sometimes in but a single day. Rather, it stems from the very nature of an allegiance that asks of us that we know something for sure. Self psychology has raised so many questions, opened up and torn apart so many settled issues, and itself been so fragilely constructed that I am now convinced that the serious student must necessarily live through an extended period of worry and befuddlement before he or she can possibly make a declaration of faith either as a true believer or a determined opponent. I have little doubt that this is equally true of many other psychoanalytic movements, and I sympathize with the incredible effort required to lay Lacan, Bion, Winnicott, and all the others to a proper rest. The easiest roads to follow are those of total dismissal or full-fledged allegiance; the most difficult is the struggle to find an appropriate place to fit the new ideas. It is especially a struggle because our kind of science clearly demands a wholehearted clinical trial of new ideas to gain conviction of their worth. To function as an analyst, one cannot only tentatively believe in an unconscious, and one cannot expect to see a selfobject transference unless and until one believes in its existence.

Perhaps no other field of science would respond to confessions of ignorance in the same way that psychoanalysis does. I have frequently heard well-known and respected speakers happily answer questions about selfobject transferences by saying that they have no idea what they are. But I am just as guilty as they, since I am equally ignorant of, for example, the work of Bion. I do part company, however, on the issue of complacency since each new idea in psychoanalysis is a challenge to us all. The dividing line for accepting the challenge must be an appeal to the test of clinical usefulness. As long as we see patients whom we cannot understand or cannot help, we are charged with the obligation to learn more. The only analysts and therapists who can readily dismiss Heinz Kohut's work are those happy few who help and understand everyone they treat. The same holds true for those adherents of self psychology whose smug complacency allows them to criticize others and ignore the failures in their own practice and the gaps in their own understanding. So much remains unfinished and unknown in psychoanalysis that we are most secure only in a continuing effort to learn more.

When it became clear to me that psychoanalytic self psychology did not easily fit into the usual set of psychoanalytic theories, I decided to go back to try to see just what a theory is and what a science is. I soon learned that a lot of what I had been taught was wrong. We do not make impartial observations and then develop a theory; on the contrary, we do just the opposite. The marvelous and convenient list of Waelders (1962) that asked us to move up the scale from our clinical observations to our theories and on to our values really had to be turned on its head. We *start* with our values and our theories, and only then can we see a fact. When I first urged this (and it is by no means an original idea of mine) my colleagues simply could not comprehend the theory—impregnation of facts; but over the years it seems to have gained a much more established place in our thinking. However, once one realizes that theory precedes observation, then one must confront the awful worry of competing theories. Allegiance to one theory seems to commits you to the data gathered by that theory, and so you might soon be chasing your tail and proving what you assumed in the first place. Alas, that seemed to be true of much of psychoanalysis, and so next I had to retreat to examine just how scientific was the field to which I was committed.

The first chapter in this book addresses that question and asks us to challenge the assumptions about just what scientific thinking ought to be. We have so long been intimidated by what a friend of mine calls "physics envy" that, sadly, we join hands with those who deride analysis as being unscientific (Von Eckardt, 1981). Once we recognize the postempiricist stance of science, see the historical and hermeneutic dimension of psychoanalysis, and cease our devotion to the hypo-thetico-deductive method, we can see our science as a legitimate member of the scientific community. This is not a plea for complacency as much as that we stop insisting that analysis prove itself to be what someone else said it is supposed to be. With that ceasefire in place, we can attend to the relative merits of one theory over the other.

The second chapter introduces the task of such comparative assessment. It is written as a response to a movement to put self psychology in its place. That phrase is meant to have a double meaning, since it evokes a problem of just where self psychology belongs as well as the sense of its being a mischievous upstart. Part of the movement to evaluate self psychology in an open-minded manner assigned it to a niche within the field and correspondingly restricted it to that area. I was an early adherent of that movement until I learned from Popper (1959) that that was the worst thing that could happen to a new idea. Any worthwhile new concept should really be at odds with the established order—it should be revolutionary. Chapter 2 outlines the necessary, even obligatory, differences between the ideas of classical psychoanalysis and psychoanalytic self psychology and asks that we recognize that we are really dealing with different theories. Now, we know that many sciences live for a long time in an atmosphere of pluralism up until one set of theoretical ideas manages to triumph over its rivals; and this could well be the case for the different set of analytic theories. Such pluralism regularly leads to efforts at integration, and this too became an activity of some psychoanalytic scholars. Thus this chapter also attempts to respond to this effort, as well as to lead to the next one, which addresses one method of integration—translating one theory back into the other.

Chapter 3, on translation, is an exercise to see just how compatible the different theories are. A word at this point may be warranted about the audacity of dissident theories that challenge Freud. It is sometimes said (Guttman, 1985) that we must not lose sight of the basic tenets of psychoanalysis in our zeal to expand the field. This caution naturally assumes a certain foundation to psychoanalysis that serves as a basic ground from which theories move out. It would be nice if we could all agree on such a set of basic tenets and even nicer if they were immutable. Rather than argue if such a set of basic tenets does exist, we need first to recognize that absolutely everything in our field is alterable and even dispensable. The only way a science advances is by questioning everything. Even our philosophical brethren (Rorty, 1982a). recognize that an unchanging foundationalism no longer can be assumed. Once we put that challenge to Freud aside, we can be free to examine any set of ideas and especially to see if they are readily absorbable from one into another. The translation task that is examined in this chapter tries to establish the futility of such efforts and makes a case for the free standing of different theories in order to see just what they can do, how far they can go, and when they seem to have exhausted their potential. It then leads naturally to the challenge of relativism, which is a worrisome problem in our field and is taken up in the next chapter.

The fourth chapter, on Realism and Relativism, addresses the problem that haunts every analyst who wants to know things "for sure" and is seemingly condemned to live with perpetual uncertainty. The anxiety that relativism brings seems to exist primarily because it is felt to lead to a sort of intellectual chaos that licenses all explanations and interpretations, and these are constrained only by personal taste or tolerance. The chapter discusses the comparative status of realism and relativism in our clinical practice. It seems to be true that most psychoanalysts do manage to function quite well in an atmosphere of relativism and even to insist on it in their general practice. We naturally want to see events from different points of view, and we realize that different realities are a part of every encounter between patient and analyst. So too must we realize that our different, and often very personal, realities are equivalent to our different and personal theories. We are, however, held together in a commonality of belief by our joined practices and our common training. In that way we manage to achieve the foundationalism (albeit temporary) that seems necessary for us to have a place on which to stand.

This first section also addresses the controversy over the hermeneutic status of psychoanalysis. Each chapter touches the problem, which for me is probably one of the great unnecessary controversies in our field. I appeal to a personal conversation with Paul Ricoeur as a foundation for my own position and an equally significant one with Adolf Grünbaum for my sense of conviction. In a nutshell, it appears to me that every science is hermeneutic, and this in no way deprives psychoanalysis, a special case of hermeneutics, of its scientific status.

This does not mean that it no longer remains a task for us to decide on one interpretation over the other. It does mean that the science of interpretation is a proper and lasting concern of psychoanalysis.

Part II, on empathy derives from Heinz Kohut's claim that empathy defines the field of psychoanalysis. He clearly meant this to apply to any form of depth psychology and not to restrict it to self psychology. The range of initial response to this claim travels from the complete dismissal of empathy as a reliable method (Brenner, 1985) to a partial acceptance of it provided we note and include the other forms of significant data (Cath, 1986) to an insistence among some of its adherents that only self psychology enjoys a privileged place in its application of this unique form of data gathering. It is not difficult to respond to these positions as long as one can maintain clarity in the scope and definition of empathy. The claim to its reliability stems from the equation of subjectivity and unreliability (Brenner, 1985). Though the gathering up of introspective data may present difficulty, this hardly means that it is to be discarded. We do strive to determine the subjective feelings of our patients, and we simultaneously aim to be objective in our efforts. Objectivity means to work with a minimum of bias or prejudice and naturally should apply to all efforts in all science. But when it is applied to subjective states, it is hardly a hopeless task because it is a difficult one. Kohut's (1959) definition of empathy as vicarious introspection is an effort to circumscribe the method and so clearly states that the patient's associations are read as clues to the feelings or subjective state of the patient. Associations cannot be considered as inviolate pointers to unconscious fantasies without this primary consideration of what they mean to a particular patient. This naturally directs a response to the second challenge about empathy, which insists on the presence and validity of other forms of data. For Kohut as well as for anyone else these would no doubt consist of exteroceptive data, such as the particulars of the patient's developmental history, the elements of the physical appearance and demeanor of the patient, and even some extra-analytic information about the real-life situation of the patient. Certainly these are all important and meaningful to an understanding of a patient. But the crucial word is "meaningful." We need to know what being short or fat or the son of an alcoholic father or the head of the department of psychiatry means to the person. These are not data that can be comprehended in their pure form; they need to be recast in terms of what they mean to the patient, that is to the subjective state. Every observation and every association is perceived by the analyst in terms of what it does to the patient, what it means to the patient, what it feels like to the patient. We learn these things through a very objective process of vicarious introspection—prolonged empathic immersion.

The first chapter in this section on empathy attempts to position our area of investigation in terms of the old problem of intrapsychic versus interpersonal. It is an elaboration of the stance that states that all events or happenings or observations must be read back to see what they mean to the patient. Essentially this is a very Freudian posture that over the years has been eroded by all the considerations about the meaning and nature of real events. Since there seems to be a repeated misunderstanding about the one- or two-person psychology involved for an understanding of Kohut (Modell, 1984), this chapter strongly urges that self psychology is definitely about but one person and all the data of self psychology are gathered from a point inside of that person. That is why it is empathic data, and that is why empathic data is introspectively gathered and is confined to the inner world of others. Selfobjects are parts of persons and thus should not be seen as interpersonal issues.

Chapter 6 was originally written some time ago in order to differentiate empathy as an objective method. It separates it off from common misunderstandings involving sympathy and positions it on the road to understanding. The latter is not achieved without a guiding theory (this point is elaborated in chapter 8, on the scientific status of empathy). There no doubt remains a host of problems associated with the process of achieving understanding with another person, and some of these are addressed later in the volume. Chapter 8 also takes up the question of empathy's being unique to psychoanalytic self psychology and shows that we have no exclusive rights save for our allegiance to our theory which, in the words of Rangell (1985), is felt to be "the most informed." Once again we must rely on the particulars of the theory that we use to confirm our observations since we all should share a common methodology. It is a collosal conceit for anyone to claim that only self psychologists are empathic, but that does lead to the question of why some people communicate empathy so much better than others. And here self psychologists do claim an edge. Chapter 7 is a necessary preparation for the conclusions of chapter 8 since it serves to demonstrate the interplay between our theory and our data.

Chapter 9 investigates just how the capacity for empathy develops and is employed. The accusations of self psychology's overuse of empathy certainly demand that we examine the term in its multiple assignments, the main two being its role in data gathering and its function as a therapeutic agent. Too often we have made empathy sound like the be-all and end-all of all of our analytic efforts and thereby have assigned all failure to simple lack of empathy. This chapter aims to differentiate empathy and its possession from the state of mental health, as well as to assess how a diminution of psychopathology could possibly result merely from an environment of empathy, i.e. how can empathy per se cure and/or are empathic people free of pathology? It seems safe to say that much more work is needed to fill out the developmental line of empathy and to see how it correlates with our views of other developmental stages. We need to navigate a neutral course between the total dismissal of empathy and the liberal attribution of just about everything wholesome to its presence.

Part III, which starts us on a clinical course, does somewhat paradoxically begin with a theoretical paper, one that attempts to present the structure of the self as the object of our study. Kohut always avoided a definition of the self as a part of his effort to avoid closure in many areas of investigation. He cautioned us to do the same, since he felt that concentrating efforts at definition could stifle creative work. No doubt it is frustrating to read about something that defies being a "thing" and insists that it may offer different meanings to different people. Some of the impetus to outline the structure of the self comes from a debate (Grossman, 1982) about whether we should consider it a fantasy or a structure. The wish to restrict the self to a fantasy and to limit the structures of psychoanalysis to the known agencies of the structural theory—the ego, the id, and the superego—is a perfectly legitimate way of organizing analytic material. The price that one pays for such a restriction is to limit the objects of study to these particular psychic structures; hence, considering such concepts as the self to be but the products of these agencies, that is, the ego, generates the fantasy of the self. To follow this reasoning, one cannot study the self as a structure in its own right, and so one cannot *explain* anything in the psyche as caused by or resulting from the self. One may study the hallucinated demons of a patient as the product of a deranged psyche, but one cannot explain the psychopathology as being due to the demons. Concepts such as self-esteem or explanations involving selfobjects would seem out of place in terms of their explanatory role. Rather, we are constrained to use our structures—the ego, id and superego—as the sole categories of explanation. If, on the other hand, we wish to explain psychological phenomena as a result of the self and its disorders (as with any other structure), we must allow it the status of structure. Chapter 10 offers this option using the conceptual framework of structuralism and illustrates how seeing structure as pattern enables one to explain a host of psychological phenomena. It especially emphasizes the consideration of the dimensions of the self structure as extending over time and space. It is seen as a system that is open and stable yet capable of growth and change and alterability. The concept of the self as structure allows us in turn to formulate a nosology of self pathology. The two chapters (11 and 12) on character are a start in this direction.

Chapter 11 is a study of character, a kind of categorization that is in contrast to the nosology suggested by Kohut and Wolf (1978). They listed character disorders on the basis of behavior or experiences of persons suffering from self-disorders: mirror-hungry, ideal-hungry, alter-ego-hungry, merger-hungry, or contact-shunning personalities. This classification directs attention to enactments that would repair the structure of the self or else defend against further rejection. My own examples stress the temporal dimension of the self and aims to correlate it to developmental processes of childhood. Kohut and Wolf also used their ordering to direct the therapist's attention to the sort of activities that should guide the treatment. My two forms are suggestive of a stable configuration usually true of character. I hoped not to illustrate a wide-spread pathology, but rather to describe a form of self-selfobject relationship that is rigid and archaic and unable to change easily. These people's hunger is overridden by the inability to move away from their archaic relationships.

There seems to be a certain appeal in the names of these character disorders, and when the papers have been read there is usually a sympathetic resonance in the audience. Interestingly the paper on The Wishy-Washy Personality was rejected by one leading psycho-analytic journal with the claim that the readers were unanimous in not feeling such a personality could be delineated or even existed. It certainly is hard to explain why such a different view of patients would prevail, since it seems evident that many clinicians feel that these are distinct forms of pathology. It may show how our theoretical biases extend into what we would like to feel are fairly obvious observations and so strengthen the points in the first section of this volume. I do feel fairly certain that as we expand and deepen our knowledge of the development of self-selfobject relations, we will be able to delineate even more such forms of character organization.

The final fourth of the book is totally clinical and begins with a chapter on rules. The chapter is applicable to both psychoanalysis and psychotherapy but is clearly more relevant to those therapies where rule change can be utilized and practiced. It was written before the one on negotiation, but they are companion pieces in that, the latter stresses these issues in psychanalysis where rule changes are considered more of an interference than an important part of the treatment. The two chapters are efforts to focus attention on the linkage between self and selfobject. One should caution that as much as this can be seen as an interpersonal phenomena, the negotiation process is a convenience of description. We remain centered on the inner world of the patient.

The concentration on the structure, i.e., the nature of the relation between self and selfobject allowed Kohut to delineate the selfobject transferences and enable us to more carefully explain these relations in their developmental course. Thus we can, for example, study the mirror transference not merely as an overall persistent pattern but as a series of exchanges. The chapter on the mirror is such an attempt. It tries to stress the originality of Kohut in describing the oft-noted occurrence of the mirror in analytic material as part and parcel of a transference, i.e., a re-enactment of an infantile situation. It then expands this configuration as it develops over time with an unfolding series of matches and disjunctions. Thus a mirror transference is a dynamic unfolding that should be analogous to the normal developmental process.

If self psychology wishes to lay claim to being a definitive psychoanalytic theory and not just a minor emendation to classical theory, then it must explain as much as does classical theory. We should try to push it as far as it can go, and we ought to re-examine a number of classical explanations in light of the new theory. One such issue is that of guilt. Selfobjects are too often talked about as supportive and sustaining, and we neglect the achievement of self control that comes from selfobjects. The chapter on selfobjects and self control tries to explain the attainment of these self-regulating functions and goes on to a study of the pathological results of such control. It will come as no surprise to the sophisticated reader that the hard-won truths of analysis in terms of psychodynamics are maintained in this discussion, but an attempt is made to incorporate them within the conceptual framework of self psychology.

The next chapter is both an effort to balance a misreading of self psychology as well as a plea for a reading of it. There seems to be a mistaken belief that parental errors in upbringing recreate themselves in analysis, and there they can be corrected and made good. Kohut's emphasis on the empathic failures of parents is too easily translated into parental blame, and this often rapidly gets transformed into analyst blame. Analysts and therapists in some logical sequence based on the parallel failures of treatment are instructed to apologize for their misdeeds and, to my mind, they make a mockery of the analytic process. On the other side of the scale we see the weight placed on the patient's impossible demands and the associated unrealizable fantasies. Thus we erroneously engage in patient blame. The chapter on apology is an effort to balance these exaggerated postures.

The last chapter says little about self psychology save that it alerts us to the fact that our theories determine the manner in which we continue to think about our patients. The aim of this essay is less that of a specific emphasis on self psychology and more of an effort to underscore that psychoanalysis remains open to much further debate and discussion. We have much more to learn.

Several volumes have been published in the years since Kohut's first discoveries were introduced, and these routinely attempt to explain self psychology in a simplified or elementary form. Without going into the relative worth of these offerings, on the whole they do not seem to me to have much advantage over reading the original work of Kohut. On occasion they may distort or oversimplify the ideas of self psychology, but even the most generous reading of these efforts fails to yield much more or different than Kohut originally wrote. These are primarily exercises in familiarization which reflect the authors' enthusiasm for the ideas. The more pressing need is to go beyond the commonplace and to struggle with advancing self psychology. I am sure that Heinz Kohut felt that he left a very unfinished body of work behind, and that he hoped for a multitude of investigative efforts to fill out his ideas, to push them further, to challenge and to modify them. Such challenges are not in the spirit of debunking, but rather are efforts to stretch the theory as far as it can go. I think it safe to say that we will not be well served by more work that repeats the tried and true in self psychology, but rather that we need more imaginative and questioning efforts.

There are more questions raised by self psychology than answered by it. That would seem to be the hallmark of a worthwhile new idea, i.e., it opens up areas to be looked at and studied and worried over. Psychoanalysis has had a very mixed reaction to the arrival on the scene of these new ideas and part of this has been a failure to soberly and critically evaluate its worth. Much too much time and effort has been expended in a defense of self psychology against all sorts of calumnies: that it is unoriginal, that it is psychotherapy, that it is wrong, that it is unscientific, that it is unseemly in its adoration of Kohut, that it is overly ambitious and even that it is leading impressionable young students into dangerous paths. It would be ideal if one could devote his energy to an expansion of the ideas without the distraction of these criticisms. I suppose, however, that one of the best and most forceful spurs to curiosity is the need to answer all sorts of unimagined and unimaginable questions, and, for this, we must be grateful to our critics. The wholesale embrace of self psychology has been noted as being equally toxic to its health and well-being, and so a nod of appreciation in that direction is needed as we work to correct the grandiose claims that are sometimes made for it. The essays in this volume have been written on a course midway between unbridled enthusiasm and forlorn hollowness—with a lot of zigzags. They are offered as part of an effort that seems to be the natural heir of new ideas: the search for more.

I

THEORY

1

The Three Theories
of Psychoanalysis

The enormous number of scholarly efforts designed to investigate, explain, and settle the status of psychoanalysis as a science make it unlikely that a new and original approach is possible. Periodically, we witness a wave of inquiries that once again strive to evaluate if psychoanalysis *is* really scientific (Von Eckardt, 1982) if it *can be* really scientific (Edelson, 1984), or if it *need be* scientific (Barratt, 1984). Like a wound that never will heal, there seems to be a recurrent worry about whether analysis belongs in the ranks of true science or should be positioned somewhere in the netherland between art, history, and perhaps mysticism. Solutions to the quandary have been to urge analysis to correct itself and become a proper member of the scientific community (Luborsky and Spence, 1978), to reconcile itself to the impossibility of achieving such credentials (Popper, 1959), to accept the cultural conclusion that it is really more of an art form (Breger, 1981), or to boldly declare itself a "different kind of science" (Barratt, 1984). When that range of arguments is viewed against the background of at least one conviction from the philosophy of science that there simply is no "scientific method" (Putnam, 1982), a certain wariness must be entertained not only as to whether a new approach is feasible but whether we should look at the problem at all.

But even lacking originality, one may still venture an appraisal in order to see if the many partial truths can be brought into a coherent whole.

As the title of this chapter suggests, this particular revisiting of the problem is aimed at the sorts of theories that have been employed in and about psychoanalysis; and so perhaps it may be properly called a study of metatheory—a theory about theories. It reexamines the three efforts to position psychoanalysis scientifically (1) as belonging to the large group of so-called empirical sciences that follows the usual scientific method, (2) as part of the group of investigations that are best approached as studies in historical science or, (3) as a particular form of hermeneutic exercise. Our thesis is that psychoanalysis rightfully enjoys a place in all three areas of scrutiny and that much of the confusion about its scientific status has been around a point of misapplication. To pursue this goal, we shall review the demands of each approach or theory and see where analysis can join as a proper member.

EMPIRICISM, LOGICAL EMPIRICISM, AND POSTEMPIRICSM

Inquiry that relies on observation to ascertain facts is called empiricism. It has several forms, but its link with experimental science probably derives from the British empiricist school of John Locke, David Hume, and Francis Bacon (Flew, 1979). It asks that we (more or less) reject preconceived ideas and allow experience to give our ideas to us. Acquiring knowledge thus is a slow, self-correcting process limited by experimentation and observation. It is, of course, assumed that the observations or the facts that we gather have status that allows them to be gathered with a high degree of consensus; for example, we would all agree on what the temperature on the thermometer indicated or that a patient exhibited a certain kind of behavior. Disagreements about facts become resolvable by the consensus of a community of observers that determines definitions, categories, and the like.

The logic of empiricism has to do with syllogistic or deductive reasoning and therefore a series of "if-then" or causal statements. The now familiar hypothetico-deductive method aims to explain subsequent observations. A set of observations is put together under a covering law (Hempel, 1942), which permits the construction of a theory that completes the "if-then" statement to form a causal explanation. All sorts of physical laws are designed to allow us to explain and predict what happened or will happen. Indeed, one prerequisite of scientific knowledge, unlike most other forms of knowing, is that it should allow one to predict and so to master the world. Predictions of hypotheses are said to need verification, a requirement that has been the center of much controversy. It has been argued (Popper, 1959) that rather than verify theories we should strive to falsify them. Empiricism and logical positivism, the systematization that stresses verifiability, have become whipping-boys of much of the modern philosophy of science. Not only is it said that science does not—indeed need not—operate in this fashion, but it is also claimed that the concepts of causation so dear to the heart of logical positivists are likewise without merit. But before abandoning the pursuit of empirical knowledge, we should note that the conflict over whether theories are verifiable or falsifiable reflects a very basic proposition: a theory is changeable. Unless the set of ideas one subscribes to is very fixed and absolute, there should be some mechanism for one to revise beliefs. Likewise we find that scientific scrutiny of the psychological life of people invites us to declare a position somewhere between "everyone is exactly alike" and "everyone is unique." Laws allow us some forms of generalization about psychology.

To illustrate the lawlike form of inquiry that psychoanalysis has taken since its beginnings with Freud, we can examine his seminal work, "Mourning and Melancholia" (1917), and subsequent work involving the loss of loved ones. In his 1917 work Freud developed two categories of response to loss—the normal and the pathological—while admitting that he lacked enough empirical observation to satisfy the latter grouping. The two categories of response were based on the external event of loss, but the crucial ingredient of reaction was felt to be the premorbid personality. Later work on loss tended to make the event itself, the more significant issue, especially in its timing. Such statements as "if a child loses his or her mother before age three . . ." or "the inability to mourn properly will result in . . ." are propositions that generalize over a large group of similar incidents. If the critical fact of melancholia lies in the narcissistic object choice of the patient, then the problem becomes one of determining why a person makes such a choice. Sooner or later, some interplay of biological environmental factors makes people different. If the critical factor is the loss itself, then once again we have delineated a subgroup, this time weighted more heavily on environment. Regardless of the emphasis, a lawlike generalization is generated.

Bowlby's (1984) later work attempted to bring the study of loss into the realm of natural science. Bowlby's theory does however falter on the particulars of the loss since its emphasis on biology seems quite at odds with Freud's. That discrepancy puts into question the accuracy of observations and points to revisions of our lawlike statements. Were Bowlby and Freud operating from the same data base? If they had examined the same patients, why would they have disagreed?

Attending once again to the issue of empiricism, we can reexamine a common conundrum about observation and theory. To begin with, it is now a commonplace that there are no observations without theory, there are no facts that are obtainable without preconceptions, and there are no unbiased observers. Gellner (1974) says of the empiricist insistence "that faiths must not fill out the world, but must stand ready to be judged by evidence which is not under their control, which is not pervaded, interpreted by them to the point of being forced to confirm the faith in question" (p. 206). This possible threat to empiricism raised by a fixed belief system such as psychoanalysis or any other theory is sometimes handled by dividing the world of observables into theory-laden and theory-neutral data. This wish for objectivity demands some neutral place to stand if one is to see if one's theory can be judged. Empiricism has always asked that the observer observe without bias, but the breakdown in the now discarded separation between subject and object shows that we bring a host of fixed capacities and prejudices to whatever we investigate.

The idea of theory-neutral observation attempts a remedy by asserting that there must be a body of common observations and acceptable words to refer to those facts which are beyond argument or simply are not subject to interpretation. Who would dispute the death of a parent as a real fact or a real event? Are there not many such facts that are consensually accepted and from which we can then make particular or individual interpretations? Between the extreme position that no word or event means the same thing to everyone and its polar opposite that anything either can be clearly categorized and defined or else must be eliminated as meaningless, we usually settle on some reasonable midpoint. Thus we can treat mourning as a response to loss in a general sense, until we try to pinpoint just what constitutes a loss. Our experience with children who have lost parents through death does not always enable us to differentiate them from children who have lost their parents in a psychological (i.e., the withdrawn parent) rather than a physical sense.

We soon see that we must define our words in terms of the particulars of our theory. It may well be that the hope for theory-neutral observations is really a hope for a community of investigators who are like-minded enough to agree on what they see, and Bowlby and Freud probably could be shown to operate from differing theoretical positions. This exposure of theoretical position is essentially what Spence (1982) asks for when he suggests a naturalization of data. It is an effort to reach consensus on the language employed. Thus there is no fundamental claim to neutrality save within that given community. Some psychoanalysts (Bowlby, 1984) feel that psychoanalysis should be considered a biological science and that then we shall achieve a higher degree of consensus. The special problems that result from this effort to make analysis more like a natural science are discussed later in this volume. Our struggle over the failure to achieve agreement highlights a problem of empiricism that revolves around the achievement of agreed upon, or neutral, or naturalized data in the face of the theory impregnation of facts, the lack of a clear division between subject and object, and the essential failure of words to refer adequately to the objects they denote. Thus empiricism has become an unrealizable ideal.

POSTEMPIRICISM

Mary Hesse (1980), a noted philosopher of science, has summed up the work since Kant, elaborating how every empirical assertion must be seen in light of the contributions of the observer. She lists the five postempiricist accounts of natural science as follows:

1. Data are not detachable from theory, and so facts are to be reconstructed in the light of interpretation.
2. Theories are not models externally compared to nature in a hypothetico-deductive schema but are the way the facts themselves are seen.
3. The lawlike relations are internal because what counts as facts is constituted by what the theory says about their interrelations with one another.
4. The language of natural science is metaphorical and inexact, and formalizable only at the cost of distortion;
5. Meanings are determined by theory and are understood by theoretical coherence rather than by correspondence with facts.

These principles apply to all of natural science and recognize how scientists develop theories and gather data. They are congenial to the method that all psychoanalysts employ, but they probably, though not necessarily or universally, demand a kind of proof different from verifiability or falsification. A number of guidelines have been developed to determine such evidence of proof, among which are "the coherence and best fit" theses (Goodman, 1978). Essentially these guidelines say that we employ the theory that seems to fit the material and to hold together with other material and other theories. That theory, then, has a greater depth and breadth of explanation than others and also is the most pragmatic one employed. Pragmatism in this sense is indeed the effort that works best, predicts most accurately, and articulates with maximum ease with other theories and disciplines. Added to these principles of postempiricism, complex, open systems also introduce feedback cycles that are concerned with such issues as purpose or goal. Later we consider how this feature adds a dimension to historical explanation by the entrance of personal agency in the form of reasons and motives. All in all, postempiricism is considered to present a new model for scientific knowledge.

Rather than pursue the problem of psychoanalysis as an empirical science under an outmoded model of physics, we can more profitably recognize that no science really follows that model any longer. The enormous efforts expended by psychoanalysts to show how analysis is different from physics or other natural sciences are really misplaced. Yet we need not abandon those fundamental tenets of empiricism which look for causal explanation and prediction. What empiricism asks is the ability to predict and control, and no matter how theory impregnated our observations may be, we still aim at these features. Where can we find a theory that will allow for the observation of predictable sequences and have a fair degree of likelihood in establishing a vocabulary of some consensus? One candidate is the arena of development, which Freud certainly championed as the underpinning of analytic theory. It is a place for a theory that, in one very clear sense, sits outside the analytic situation and has the potential of scientific verifiability or falsification outside analysis. To be sure, there exists no unitary theory of development, and the aforementioned points of postempiricism suggest that a long period of negotiation may be needed before that is achieved. The triumph of one theory over its competition is a topic for another study and may ultimately settle the Bowlby-Freud disagreement.

If we do achieve an overall theory of psychological development, it will be one of the tools that the analyst brings into the consulting room, and it will direct the observations, the facts, and the meanings that postempiricism suggests. There may indeed be other theories, such as developmental theory, that qualify, and this expands the base of postempirical scrutiny. All of science should have matured to approach this postempiricist stance, and so one task is to ascertain how much of psychoanalysis centers on such an approach. Theory becomes primary, and the theory that exemplifies a view of psychoanalysis that satisfies the demands of community agreement probably has to do with development. Later we shall differentiate the particulars of individual treatment in terms of theory and its potential to be empirically valid. Each form of theory may be different, but therein lies the potential for empirical substantiation. In developmental theory we see causation, generalization, possibility of falsification, and the variety of demands placed upon us by empiricists. It has the potential for an overall theory of pathology as well as treatment. In it we also see the potential for change in theory, Freud's original ideas about instinctual discharge and psychic energy, for example, having been eroded (Basch, 1975) by a growing community consensus. Here, too, we have an opportunity for articulating with other disciplines such as neurophysiology and cognitive psychology. Sooner or later one adopts a certain theory or set of theories about development and then moves on to individual development and finally to individual treatment, where we turn next.

PSYCHOANALYSIS AS HISTORY

Say Johnny lost his father at a vulnerable age and later became depressed. If we collected data on many such occurrences we could form a lawlike causal sequence about loss and depression—a generalization. If Jimmy were depressed but had not lost his father, we would revise our generalization about depression but not necessarily about parent loss and depression. And yet we would not be unduly surprised if one or more of our parent-loss subjects turned out *not* to be depressed and consequently threatened even that generalization. We apparently do not form our generalizations from or about large numbers of individuals; lack of correspondence with our thesis is a lack in the same way as we make predictions about, for example, a volume of gas without knowing the random movements of a single atom or molecule (Bowlby, 1984). Our generalizations are about individuals, not about groups, and they usually derive from single cases; every deviation demands a reappraisal and an explanation. We may make statistical generalizations, but ultimately we strive only to explain a particular patient. We must explain Johnny in a different manner than we explain Jimmy.

The unreliability of our generalizations is usually attributed to an enormous number of variables and the openness of the system. The hope is that with enough knowledge of other variables about the boy who does not become depressed we will be able to show what crucial factor lies within the event of depression, and that deep enough study of the depressed boy who has not lost his father will enable us to sharpen our definition of loss beyond the mere physical disappearance of a loved one. Thus, we attempt to work back from an event like depression to determine its antecedents. Since psychoanalytic work is devoted to reconstructing the events of a life and since we both take and make a history, the scientific approach in psychoanalysis is said to be like that of any historical discipline—not only those directly concerned with history per se but also geology, anthropology, and much, if not most, of biology, the last because it is a result of evolutionary (historical) processes.

Hempel (1942) states that general laws have analogous functions in history and the natural sciences. He claims that one can deduce events by following the flow of prior conditions and the rules of a regular law. His argument is examined in detail by Ricoeur (1984), who feels that history is a mixed case of causal and quasi-causal explanation, the latter exemplified by a statement like "The people rebelled because the government was corrupt." This is not a lawlike connection (many corrupt governments manage not to have rebellions), and there has now been introduced an element of purpose or teleology. Any examination of causality reveals an extended causal network of relations rather than a linear sequence of causes. Since "causes cause causes to cause causes" in a circle of relations (Wilden, 1972), we are often unable to separate cause from effect and to differentiate external causes from internal reasons or motives. Quasi-causal explanation (Ricoeur, 1984, p. 141) introduced complexity into the usual sequence of cause and effect because of the human agent, who at any point in the sequence interferes with a subjective appraisal of the situation. This evaluation of the way things are going and the way people thereby change the way things go makes the historian inquire into human intentions and add these to the mix of the causal network. The need to incorporate the goals or the teleological segments of the scheme into an overall model does not allow for a picture of a smoothly deterministic system.

Psychoanalysis as an historical investigation is retrodictive rather than predictive. It asks "How did this come about?" A new branch of applied mathematics may help to differentiate such investigations from those of predictive physical systems (May, 1976). It is the study of apparently chaotic systems, those that appear to be random but are really extremely sensitive, albeit deterministic. Initial conditions and the slightest of environmental perturbations completely defy the usual methods of analysis of these systems and cause conditions that seem chaotic or indeterminable. This perspective may help us to understand that such questions as "What might have happened?" are unanswerable or irrelevant. The combination of the retrospective view and the inherent potential chaos of the system that seems to defy the "laws of nature" forces us to include in each individual's history the overall generalizations, the personal motives of the person, and the particular events of that person's life. Apparently random open systems need to be described differently from hypothetico-deductive systems. A narrative or a story has been proposed as the way to do all this in a meaningful manner (Sherwood, 1969; Ricoeur, 1984). One may feel that this is less scientific than the hypothetico-deductive system, but it is perhaps merely a more reasonable method of telling or explaining a history.

Freud undoubtedly felt that a psychoanalysis consisted of filling in the bits and pieces of a patient's life that had been repressed and that a complete reconstructed history was the sine qua non of treatment. This raises questions of what is curative about such an enterprise and whether one story is as good as any other. Eagle (1984) tells us to separate theory from therapy in psychoanalysis, to look for events that are generalizable, and to recognize that interpretations are judged effective in a different manner than the construction of a good history. He joins many others in decrying the move to make psychoanalysis into a hermeneutic discipline (see final section of this chapter) and thereupon to lose its tie with science.

Sherwood (1969) was the first of a significant group of those who seemingly conflate the construction of the life story with its therapeutic effectiveness and thereupon come into conflict over whether we must indeed construct true histories or merely those that are accepted as true by the patient (Bellin, 1984). A most vocal critic of the problem of the validity of interpretations is Grünbaum (1982), who has discussed Freud's statement that interpretations must "tally with what is real" in terms of the "tally argument" that demands correct connections between past and present. Of course there is no knowing if Freud meant "real" to mean "what really happened." This leads one to the complex issue of whether history records real events as a camera might or reveals real meanings as a person might experience them (Goldberg, 1984). To discover what happened is to determine truth. It is a problem in every historical investigation that is subject to different interpretations by different historians who see the past differently. It is, of course, a separate issue from the determination of the curative factors in analysis.

If we carefully reconstruct the history of Johnny, we may find that he fits the premises of melancholia. A psychiatric epidemeologic study might show a significant correlation between parent loss and depression and between any loss and melancholia. This study could lump Johnny together with others, but our effort to better determine just what loss amounts to must nevertheless always focus on the individual history, and there we confront a particular quandary that is very problematic for psychoanalysis, that is, registration and remembering. We base our reconstruction of the history on its reemergence in the transference. Putting aside for a moment our own theoretical bias, we necessarily are limited by what the patient represents to us in the treatment situation. But we know that the capacity to register events is variable and (at least) based on developmental stages, and the ability to recall events regardless of repression is likewise limited. The accuracy of the reports of the experience is judged entirely within the analysis, save for those rare exceptions involving diaries or journals. We do not have the tools that other forms of history have for gathering corroborative evidence. To be sure, there are analytic devices that seem to point to the soundness of a history, but they remain within the confines of the analysis. The narrative that we construct will not be just any story, its truth will be restricted by the beliefs of the participants. It remains to be seen if the curative factor lies in the story, the retelling, or something else. This supposed resting point has led many to claim the status of psychoanalysis not as an objective study of facts but as a subjective dialogue of hermeneutics, and to this we turn next.

PSYCHOANALYSIS AND HERMENEUTICS

All knowledge is hermeneutic. We might once have thought that the world was delivered intact to our mind by our senses, but we now recognize that such things as, for example, light photons are organized and categorized, enhanced and rearranged by the retina and the rest of the visual system. A neurophysiologist might claim that the brain interprets these light waves, whereas a psychologist might say that the person or the mind does—but the very act of interpretation brings us squarely into the camp of hermeneutics.

Hermeneutics—the word is derived from the god Hermes the messenger—is the study of interpretation and was originally applied to biblical exegeses. The famous "Thou art Peter and upon the rock I shall build my church" is a nice example of how one can interpret the rock as referring to the man Petros (Greek for rock) or to the place where the church will stand. Depending on one's interpretation or translation, one reaches different conclusions. And, of course, Schliermacher's dictum that "there is hermeneutics where there is misunderstanding" (Ricoeur, 1981, p. 46) soon becomes evident. Since psychoanalysis is preeminently involved with interpretations, it is no surprise that it came to be seen as part and parcel of this field, but it soon became embroiled in a host of its own misunderstandings. These seemed to take the form of insisting that hermeneutics is subjective, untestable to the point of being capricious and thereby totally unscientific. The alliance of hermeneutics with the philosophical schools of Dilthey, which stressed Verstehen as a different form of data gathering, and Heidegger and Gadamer, who seemingly moved hermeneutics from a theory of knowledge to a mode of being (Ricoeur, 1981) made it even more worrisome.

One should at the start separate hermeneutical theory, which is the method of interpretative understanding practiced as a science, from hermeneutic philosophy, which has to do with the inquiry into the preconditions of understanding, and from critical hermeneutics, the study of unrestricted communication. If we confine ourselves to the theory or method, we must return to the plea for a set of theory-neutral standards from which to initiate inquiry. As Toulmin (1982) said, "All critical analysis and explanation begins at a point where some interpretive (theoretical, conceptual) standpoint has already been adapted" (p. 93). We move to misunderstanding only from some initial understanding, however limited it may be. The process involves the interpreter's making a preliminary projection of the sense of text or the other person and then revising, considering new proposals, and testing new projections. This circular process, called the hermeneutic circle, has the goal of achieving an interpretation of the whole into which the detailed parts can be integrated (McCarthy, 1973). Preconceptions on the part of the interpreter are unsuitable insofar as they collide with the material. Psychoanalysis has a particular form of this hermeneutic method, as we shall see in the chapter on realism and relativism.

The two parts of the hermeneutic method involve an awareness of the prejudices, cultural and historical antecedents, and theory that one brings to the task and a recognition of the above-mentioned collisions with the material. The first has to do with the acceptable set of theories of the scientific community, and these derive from the empirical studies that we noted earlier. We subscribe to certain beliefs, for example, about development, and these constrain and direct our inquiry. Therefore, not only is it not true that "anything goes," but in truth very little goes, because the range of creative ideas in psychoanalysis is not very impressive. Hermeneutics insists that we be aware of what we bring to the consulting room, and that is part of the basic system of every school of psychoanalysis. The second part has to do with the process of inculcating the patient with our ideas, and here Freud warned from the very first that we cannot simply impose ideas. In the case of the Wolf Man, Freud (1918) himself exemplified this when he made an interpretation and then dropped it because the analytic material "did not react to it" (p. 80).

To say that hermeneutics is merely subjective is to disparage the term, to dismiss it out of hand. We strive to be objective without blind bias in our study of subjectivity, but every form of investigation is subjective to the degree that individual concepts and percepts are brought to bear. Toulmin (1982) says that "to choose an interpretive standpoint . . . does not mean to condemn the results to the second class status of mere subjective opinion [since it] leaves open all sorts of questions about the objective considerations that are available as rational supports for those opinions" (p. 100). But once we recognize the need for objectivity, we return to the problem of the built-in theoretical bias of our observational stance. If we all entered the analytic situation with different theories, then indeed we would be constructing alternative narratives that bear no relation to the real world. Our empirical studies hope to expand the theory-neutral area of observations so that we attain some consensus about the inarguable parts of our field. These are necessarily a network of beliefs that move from individual histories to extra-analytic studies to considered reactions of the patient in treatment. These beliefs hold together because the stories that are reconstructed in analysis come from the emerging transference seen by the analyst within the confines of his theory and worked through in the analysis by the reactions of the patient. Narratives have their own standards of coherence and fit, and problems of reckless interpretations are no more tolerated in psychoanalysis than in physics (Bruner, 1984; Bellin, 1984). However, the emergence of new and unexpected moments is one of the creative aspects of this, as of any, science. To see what has never been seen before must be incorporated into every scientific endeavor to permit the movement from one set of beliefs to another. Unfortunately, the conceptual location of creative issues seems available only to certain minds at certain times (Simon, 1977).

Hermeneutics in psychoanalysis is not a fixed text being interpreted by a reader but is a dialectic. Dialectics has its own history (Flew, 1979) and comes from a Greek word that means "to converse". It is most prominent in the ideas of Hegel (see Flew, 1979), who felt it was the logical pattern of all thought, which proceeds by contradiction and its reconciliation—or thesis, antithesis, and synthesis. The disparagement of dialectics as "a jazzed up solution to the barren disjuncture of mentalism and behaviorism" (Barratt, 1984 p. 209) probably fails to appreciate the laws of dialectic (Lana and Georgoride, 1983; Gould, 1984) that move us in the historical direction of complex systems and the inevitable change inherent in a dialectic. Inasmuch as dialectics also involves the inextricable interdependence of components, we must likewise recognize that patients change in a relationship, and this in turn cannot leave the analyst unchanged. We discuss this at length in chapter 14. If psychoanalysis were but a fixed theory that allowed for alteration of another person by the analyst, then we would certainly be locked in "the boundaries of tradition" (Barratt, 1984, p. 209). We not only reveal the concealed, but we also allow the developmental process to pursue its interrupted path in both participants. Development, however is never fixed, and the process of evolution speaks for the new, the unexpected and the creative.

PSYCHOANALYSIS AND SCIENTIFIC CHANGE

Most scientists like to feel that they are not merely filling in the not yet articulated or defined parts of an accepted paradigm, as Kuhn (1970) has suggested, but rather are making new discoveries. Popper (1959) insists that any real discovery would have to be revolutionary and overthrow the old ideas. This seems to define a struggle between the construction of a new paradigm, which Kuhn says is a rare event, and the emergence of a new idea, which science claims as its very lifeblood. The scientist needs an immutable foundation in order to develop and create new concepts, and this is essentially the neutral theory that empiricists insist we accept. By expanding the area of this data base, we allow the undiscovered to become part of the accepted and agreed upon. The problem that arises in this process of enlargement of the accepted is the heart of our attitude toward scientific knowledge: that no concept, no idea, no truth is immune to change. The revolutionary discord of Popper must be tempered by the pressures of insisting that we not change everything all at once, and simultaneously balanced by our recognizing that every theory-neutral bit of knowledge is a candidate for disposal. Thus, when a community of scholars says "let us agree that loss means . . . ," they always parenthetically note "until we agree otherwise." This becomes tantamount to change by consensus and truth by agreement rather than the correspondence theories that are so appealing to us. We would rather point to the data to prove our point instead of asking for a vote. However, we seem always to return to some agreed upon or negotiated "reality" to which our facts correspond. Truth is also hermeneutic since it is a product of our understanding and interpretation, and so is not a "given."

The distinction between the work of agreement and that of change is said to be that between the context of justification and the context of discovery (Edelson, 1984, pp. 70–71). Such demarcations point to a different psychological set between times of "normal science" and those of scientific breakthroughs. Some psychoanalysts work with a feeling of reaffirming the accepted tenets of analysis and some with a conviction that nothing can be assumed until the patient so indicates. Both groups are in error. The more conservative group must necessarily not see a reservoir of undiscovered data, while the supposed liberal group seems not to see its own preconceptions. Psychoanalytic theory is not capable of encompassing everything since "everything is dependent on a multitude of theories" (Goldberg, 1985, p. 131). Nor can patients expose us to elements that we have no tools to explore. The logic of discovery (Popper, 1959) is different from that of justification for complex psychological reasons: However psychoanalysts join with all scientists in pursuing the puzzle of creativity: a mental phenomenon that allows for change and discovery. We do not have times for justification and other times for discovery, but rather seem to have a mind for one and a mind for the other.

DISCUSSION

The question whether or not psychoanalysis is scientific can be answered only if one has a clear definition of science. If we limit it to the successful pursuit of knowledge, then it can be achieved in many ways. No one has an absolute hold on licensing any activity as scientific or unscientific. Though any member of the community of psychoanalysts may practice in a capricious manner, the group as a whole is bound by a network of beliefs that are tested and confirmed by community consensus. The confirmation of these beliefs can occur at any point during the process of verifiability, falsification, or pragmatic fit. Thus, if we were, for example. to learn that homosexuality is a genetically determined disorder, then the attitude toward its treatment would be changed. If we were to hear that a certain way of seeing the history and development of homosexuals would lead to interpretative work that was particularly telling, so too would our therapeutic stance be altered. We conclude that psychoanalysis is an empirical science, but one constrained by all of the revisions of postempirical philosophy.

Psychoanalysis, in its pursuit of individual histories, can be compared to doing inverse problems in mathematics wherein one works backward from a finding to determining initial conditions (Eisenberg, 1984). There are many answers or solutions to these problems, and, if chaotic processes are involved, then a great deal of information is needed to understand the process since the smallest unobserved or unknown variable can deflect the entire subsequent development. All of biology is involved in this sort of problem, and much of biology avoids the question of reconstructing the history of "Why did it get that way?" because it is so forbidding; or, if the problem is chaotic, it is impossible to answer these questions accurately. If we recognize the influence of personal agency in these histories and add the person's reasons or teleology for doing one thing rather than another, we likewise settle for quasi-causal explanations rather than the strictly causal networks that we may prefer. The total constructed explanation takes the form of a story or narrative, but one constructed out of the available plots that our science allows, whether Freudian, Kohutian, or Mahlerian.

Most important, psychoanalysis is hermeneutic not only because every science is, but because we must be especially attuned to what we bring to our work. The hermeneutic circle of understanding demonstrates the continual trial and error process of seeing what ideas work best, fit best, and best allow for integration of the whole. The unfortunate abuse of the word hermeneutics is perhaps the result of popularization rather than of an appreciation of what it has meant to some major aspects of philosophy. Since psychoanalytic science is one of uncovering unconscious material by way of talking, we add to the complexity of understanding another in depth and in dialogue. When we study an object separate in space, such as a tree or a bird, we may have an easier time of it than when we study another person with whom we are necessarily involved, and we do so in a different manner. Though some (e.g. Habermas, 1971) may want to divide science according to this category of stance, I suspect this is really too simple and too easy. Certainly psychoanalysis is different from physics but perhaps every science is different from every other. We may need much time to return from "There is no scientific method" to recognizing that there are many ways to expand our knowledge. There is simply no justification for condemning any effort to learn how we learn about others. Psychoanalysis needs critics, but it probably is most in need of greater creative efforts and, in this regard, is certainly no different from any other science.

CONCLUSION

Psychoanalysis is an empirical science in that, like every science, it relies on observation to expand and advance and substantiate its concepts. But it, like every other science, belongs to the postempiricist principle that all observation is theory laden and our conceptual schemes depend on a community agreement that is, in entirety, capable of reevaluation and change. As a network of empiricism, we have causal or sequential explanations, such as we see in development, as well as quasi-causal ones that are part of historical explanation. Psychoanalysis is an historical discipline like all of biology. It seeks to explain individual development and history by way of reconstruction of lives. If it is seen as a chaotic system, then the slightest of perturbations can lead to widely varying and seemingly unpredictable results. This leads to an erroneous portrait of analysis as either nondeterministic or unpredictable. The necessary retrospective position of explanation lends itself to the production of stories or narratives as the vehicle best suited for historical concepts. The focus on the observer or the historian highlights the fact that psychoanalysis, again like all of science, is hermeneutic. It seeks to interpret the dialogue between patient and analyst and to consider primarily the unconscious productions of the patient. It is thus a unique form of dialectic. But as much as the analyst is constrained by his own history, values, and theory in the pursuit of the patient's inaccessible memories and history, there can be no absolute truth or limit to what is revealed. Analysis must always be open to creative moments that allow for the above-mentioned capacity for change.

The three theories or methods of psychoanalysis hold together in terms of their own network of applicability; they are not competitive but alternate ways of looking at the field. They support one another and become one, which in turn supports the certain picture of psychoanalysis as science.

2

One Theory or
More?

Pioneers in psychoanalysis, as in any field of scientific inquiry, are few and far between. In fact, our science may still be too young for us to determine who the significant leaders are, since it is often only in retrospect that one can assess the meaningful contributions in the history of a science. So many of the seemingly great chemists and physicists of their time have faded into obscurity that it will be little surprise to our future historians to note that the many, to us, meaningful figures of today will have contributed little of lasting significance to our science of psychoanalysis. As regards our own pioneers, only the future will reveal if their contributions will continue to take hold on our minds as the edges of psychoanalysis are further explored. This chapter examines some facets of the reception of new ideas before history can make a more reasonable assessment.

One of the very great difficulties in the establishment of new ideas in the field of psychoanalysis, perhaps more than in other scientific pursuits such as physics and mathematics, is the heritage of our ideas from one man, Sigmund Freud, and a form of trusteeship of his ideas that seems to carry on from generation to generation. Trustees are usually assigned the role of guardian, and at times they feel a necessity to decide issues of truth or falsehood in terms of the reigning ideas. I have been particularly interested recently in the impact of the new ideas of self psychology on the overall field of psychoanalysis, and I have often been struck by the wave of responses that these new ideas have evoked. Although some of these responses are quite challenging and provocative, a number of them seem to fail to meet the minimum demands for scientific theory and inquiry. One that struck me was a statement in a book review in a psychoanalytic journal (Gedeman, 1980) that said that Kohut's ideas were incorrect. I should like to expand upon that seemingly innocuous matter of opinion in order to pursue what I think is an erroneous form of criticism of scientific ideas, one that stems from a conviction that there is a "correct" theory that one must protect and guard and that new ideas are to be judged in comparison to such correctness.

The criticisms of self psychology at times seem confined to a mere protest that all of these ideas are not very new or different, that they are no more than every good analyst has adhered to all of the time and thus need no particular attention to be paid to them. I suspect this is more of a problem in sociology than in psychology since there seems to be no consensus among analysts about the originality or popularity of the ideas. Some seem to see them as revolutionary or deviant or dangerous; and this hardly squares with the old wine in new bottles thesis. Of course the best example of such a criticism was the one that followed the publication of "The Two Analyses of Mr. Z." (Kohut, 1979). It dismissed that report by saying these two inadequate analyses should have really been one adequate one. That these analyses were at times contradictory and that the central dream was interpreted quite differently in the separate treatments seems to have escaped these readers (Rangell, 1981). But, more important, the question arises what guiding theory would allow one to see these two analyses as one, or would compel one to face the conclusion that the theories, though perhaps compatible are really quite different?

Do we have one theory or do we have two or more? If we have one theory that is essentially the correct one, should we work toward translating supposedly new ideas back into the old language, and should we make minor changes or adjustments in our accepted theory in order to accommodate new findings? This, of course, is what Kuhn (1970) felt was the job of normal science. On the other hand, we might have to face a problem of different theories, which, by certain standards, are necessarily what some philosophers of science have called "incommensurable" or seemingly lacking in any basis of comparison. Popper (1963) feels that any theory worth its salt would necessarily overthrow the old one because it must be, by definition, revolutionary. Thus, a really new finding cannot long exist in the confines of on old theory. Yet another school of philosophy (Feyerabend, 1975) believes in a multiplicity of theories that coexist for a time until the best survives.

It is important for any proper evaluation of the pioneers of our field to try to determine whether these are political movements character- ized by schools and personalities, whether they are significant addi- tions within the realm of normal science, or whether they have presented us with a vision that challenges the basic "facts" of our old theory. But, especially in these evaluations, we should pursue as ob- jective and scientific a course as is possible. I think we are now witness to such an inquiry into the theoretical status of self psychology, and I believe we can profit from relinquishing a preoccupation with cor- rectness in favor of one of usefulness, i.e., that of the breadth, depth, and elegance of the explanatory yield of the theory.

THE CONTROVERSY

At a conference on self psychology several years ago, Kohut started a discussion of the "one theory or two problem" by likening it to the dim appearance of a figure of a man who approached the viewer from far away down a road. At first, one could not make out whether it was the one or the other of two men. As the figure came closer, there was more of a tendency to commit oneself to a decision; and, finally, as he came clearly into focus, there would be no doubt who the per- son really was. So too, it was felt, most of the questions that confronted the either-or problems of psychoanalytic psychology could be likened to that stage in our scientific investigations at which a certain level of uncertainty necessarily dominated our perceptions. A resolution and an absolute conviction of the one truth remained beyond our ken. At least at that point in our scientific study, most of the controversy seemed to be posited around seemingly rivalrous positions. That is, either it was a problem of narcissistic pathology *or* it was one of a struc- tured neurosis; either it was an oedipal or a preoedipal problem; either the analyst was a real object or a selfobject, and so on.

It is also important at the outset to realize that an appeal to a resolu- tion of any controversy can only fall on willing ears. If all of one's cases do well and there exists little or no sense of dissatisfaction with one's theory, then it is pointless to hope to enlist one even to con- sider a controversy. Recent literature has revealed a posture wherein authors (Richards, 1981; Tyson and Tyson, 1982) attempt to demon- strate that they do just fine with their cases and the existing theory. They unfortunately tend to denigrate the supposed opposition by coin- ing such words as pseudonarcissistic (Tyson and Tyson, 1982), which are used to expose a lack of fidelity to the correct theory. One must necessarily feel a certain awe toward analysts who have achieved such contentment. They are not to be disabused of that state.

I should like to take this opportunity to pursue this matter of supposed rivalry since I think there remains a good deal of ambiguity in these controversies. There are at least three different opinions that can be considered.

(1) One school of thought, best articulated by Wallerstein (1981, 1983) holds that it is not a question of either/or but of both/and. Essentially this orientation pays close attention to the deficits of developmental arrests but claims that analytic material is too fluid to make a sharp dichotomy between deficits and regression. It especially espouses what is felt to be a variant of Waelder's multiple-functions principle by stressing multiple vantage points in assessing clinical data. Although this approach seems most flexible and liberal, it tends to evolve into its own either/or question, i.e., the question of the crux of pathology as being due either to deficit *or* to conflict, and the latter does seem to win the day. Therefore, there remains a tendency to subsume the new findings of self psychology under the rubric of classical findings and to stretch the umbrella a bit in order to define conflict as "any opposition of any kind involving any aspect of psychic functioning in any form." I think that is worth pondering.

(2) The second approach to the either/or problem takes a much firmer stand. It divides the world of psychoanalysis into narcissistic pathology and structured pathology and only occasionally allows oedipal pathology to have narcissistic features. There is a marvelous convenience to this kind of strict dichotomy: one can even separate analytic practitioners into those who treat narcissistic disorders and those who do not. But, these somewhat political considerations stem from the early writings of self psychology, and they resist the encroachment of self psychology into the area of classical psychoanalysis. They admit of a category of narcissistic disorders, but they are strict segregationists. While the first position is all inclusive, this one treats self psychology as an aberration of sorts.

(3) The third position is the most radical one. It posits self psychology as subsuming classical oedipal pathology as but one form of aberrant self development. It states that the natural culmination of normal self development is oedipal resolution, but that failures in such resolution always reflect underlying problems in the self-selfobject matrix. And although it allows for a focused concentration on the oedipal conflict in a neurotic, it always looks beyond this to a developmental defect. In a rather obvious way, this is also the most radical point of view in terms of development. It states that oedipal problems are developmental ones that are not inevitable but are determined by the vicissitudes of normal development.

There are other positions to be sure. They range from utter dismissal of the existence of any of the findings of self psychology to an equally absurd embracing of the primarily clinical material in every possible encounter, whether psychoanalytic, therapeutic, or social. Such severe stances, which liken self psychology to a cult or claim it to be some sort of gratification exercise, are probably best classified as unscientific efforts that are, fortunately or otherwise, themselves capable of being understood only by a self-psychological approach. But leaving these exaggerated poles aside, I offer these three positions as being at the heart of the controversy.

Now initially I want to sidestep these different stances to say a few more words about theories in general since the three positions of both/and, either/or, or entirely one are essentially three different clinical theories.

To begin with, we must accept that all scientific theories are underdetermined. That is to say, there is never a one-to-one correspondence between theories and fact; but rather we know that any given theory allows us to see some things and to miss others and to make of many things what we wish them to be. Our theories do pretty much direct our perceptions, and, unfortunately, they probably belong in the category of "preconceived ideas." This is not so unfortunate as long as we retain a certain flexibility to recognize a misfit when it occurs and realize that a theory is valuable only in terms of its usefulness as a kind of map or visual aid. The remarkable beauty of Freud's discovery of the Oedipus complex, a clinical theory in itself, was its enabling us to see, understand, and explain a host of disparate phenomena that had previously made no sense. The phobia of Little Hans is now revealed in a way that was not previously possible. And, of course, once one can see phenomena in a new light, then they will never be the same as before. Similarly, the theory of selfobjects makes for a perception of relationships and transferences that is also like a new map of foreign terrain, and this allows for a kind of explanation of patient-analyst relationships that was heretofore lacking.

The other point about theories that I want to emphasize is that they are always wrong and are waiting for a better one to come along. Any good and new theory should be revolutionary and should overthrow the old one. This certainly does not mean that rival theories do not coexist for long periods of time, but ultimately one of them manages to dominate because of the aforementioned points of simplicity, elegance, and explanatory yield. But theories that continue to live side by side either explain different phenomena or are waiting for a single theory to replace each of them. In the history of any scientific enterprise one sees periods of relative agreement about the value of a theory followed by the introduction of a new set of ideas. This is often accompanied by a form of social and/or political dispute until the practitioners of the science reach some sort of consensus on how they do their work. This sequence may not be clearly demonstrated or easily observed, but a few salient periods do seem to stand out. One of these is the task of revising the old theory to incorporate the findings of the new one. I think we see this in the first position outlined, wherein the usual and customary tenets of classical psychoanalysis are modified to accommodate self psychology. These efforts are praiseworthy since old theories should never be abandoned without extremely good reason. However, ultimately there occurs an eroding of the old theories. Certainly Waelder's Principle of Multiple Function (1930) had nothing whatsoever to do with multiple vantage points of observation except in the most generous of interpretations. And if conflict theory is allowed to equal any sort of opposition that one experiences, including conflict over developing further because of the lack of sufficient structure, then it probably can embrace just about everything and thus runs the risk of trivializing its original meaning.

Let us focus on the conflict issue. We all know that it enjoys a narrow definition, such as that offered by Brenner (1979), who confined it to the instinctual wishes of childhood, or a more broad and inclusive one, such as that of Anna Freud (1965), who includes conflicts between the child and his environment, between the ego and the superego, and between drives and affects of opposite quality. The latest to be enlisted in this stretching exercise is conflict between ideals (Tyson and Tyson, 1982). The direction of the extension of a definition of conflict is certainly outward; for Sandler (1976) it includes an adult use of a childhood defense in a particular circumstance.

I am reminded of an analytic case, that of a homosexual, who for the first time was entering into heterosexual activity. I suppose one could say that he was filled with conflicts of all sorts. Perhaps one could say that he had a conflict between being homosexual or heterosexual. One of his major problems was a need for a response to his masculine strivings. He had had a childhood of ridicule in this regard, having been dressed in girl's clothing. His penis was an object of scorn for his sister and mother, and he had been ashamed of his body all of his life. Much of the period in his analysis had to do with the emergence of exhibitionistic fantasies of his masculine self and the concomitant need for a reflecting selfobject. My own way of conceptualizing the new developmental achievement (his entering into heterosexual activity) is that I am simply not able to consider this as much of a psychoanalytic conflict situation.[1] It is a matter of ongoing new experiences being con-

---

[1] A recent criticism of the case was directed against me as an "environmentalist" (see chapter 5). It is true that some childhood incidents show marked parental pathology while others remain quite subtle. But the parental response is a necessary part of the ecosystem, which we examine in the transference, and we no longer are able to distinguish the child from the parents in the sense of a proper selfobject milieu.

fronted. I have no doubt that some heroic stretching of classical theory could make it a conflict, but it seems at some point to have lost its moorings in Freud's original sense. Making it a conflict is, I think, a fine example of theory tampering and is probably reason enough to say that theory really cannot do the task assigned it. To say that conflict should embrace what are essentially conscious *decision* problems i.e., a movement into a new state of affairs versus maintaining the old—should I do this or should I do that?—is, to my mind, no longer a psychoanalytic effort. Even the material of child and infant observation can remain on a descriptive and superficial level if one reports that the child departs and returns for refueling because of a conflict over separation. Psychoanalysts must ask exactly what the child communicates to the mother and vice versa. Of course, going back and forth is a conflict of sorts, but it is not quite what Freud had in mind about the clashing of forces. If everything is "conflict," then conflict is nothing.

Another step in the historical sequence of theory ascendancy is the attempt to isolate the new theory by admitting its value but assigning it to a different domain of inquiry. Sometimes we see the development of new methods of investigation in this manner. At other times, however, these efforts are doomed to failure because new theories are, as emphasized, essentially incompatible and revolutionary. I think we see this dilemma within self psychology in the very concept of the selfobject. Either one grows out of such a relationship, leaves it behind, and advances to clear and permanent self and object differentiation, or else a whole new way of conceptualizing normal growth and development must be entertained in order to comprehend the existence of lasting and mature selfobjects.

Let us compare the clinical situation to an analyst listening to a patient who is upset or concerned about a pending separation. If one listens with a theoretical assumption that normal development involves movement toward individuation and gradual independence, then one would probably concern oneself with the struggle over such freedom and the conflict over leaving the libidinal object to whom one is attached. The typical sequence of behavior seen in separation-individuation conflicts, and translated back into fantasies about the relationship with and the ties to the analyst or parent, may or may not lead to different analytic results from those derived from an alternate theory. But a typical statement like "The analyst continued to sense the patient's need to evoke the hated and wanted intrusiveness in the transference, followed by resistive withdrawal" certainly sounds as though the theory is dictating the kind of information one obtains from a patient (Kramer, 1979). Other elaborations of the need for the patient to experience rage (Rothstein, 1979) insist that one does a disservice to a patient by neglecting a consideration of the patient's sadism and aggressiveness. This seems to support the position of most philosophers of science that one cannot separate observation statements from theoretical statements (Grandy, 1973) and to confirm that we see what we look for, as noted in chapter 1.

If one contrasts this guiding theory with one that states that the individual needs continuing relationships with his selfobjects and that individuation is not separation but rather a change in the nature (controlling versus being controlled) of the relationship, then a new and different form of data emerges. Rage is not a necessary condition of separation but rather a reaction to selfobject failures. Termination is not a working through of particular individuation conflict but rather the attainment of empathic connections (Kohut, 1979). Much, if not all, of the material elicited sounds and looks different, and even the technical interventions become changed. But this soon is seen *not* as a matter of translating one theory back into the other, but rather as facts that are so theory laden as to defy comparison.

The significant point about incompatibility of the two ways of looking at separation is not that one is right and the other wrong. This is simply not the case with theories, and for any critic to show incorrectness by stressing incompatibility is merely to underscore the obvious. The question is a much more difficult one and has to do with a lengthy examination of the value of one theory against the other. If one examines a new set of ideas and finds them in conflict with established ones, this is not an occasion to write a critique. It is a call for the curiosity to ascertain if certain old unanswered problems may now lend themselves to better understanding. Of course, all new theories are "incorrect." That is as they should be, or one would only relearn what one already knows.

This, of course, brings us to the final position of the three, the one that posits a psychoanalytic theory of self psychology that includes and replaces that of the primacy of the oedipal conflict. Again, without making a claim for its correctness, I can suggest what we must expect of it: it must encompass everything we already know, and more. If it fails to do this, then it indeed is but a minor variation on a theme that will ultimately be absorbed into our existing views of psychoanalysis without any fundamentally radical upheavals. This is where we are today, and that is the problem that confronts us.

To return to some clinical material, I would like to reconsider a point that we are all familiar with which demonstrates the seeming paradox of good analytic work followed by depression and despondency. A patient, for example, gains insight into a phobic avoidance and instead of feeling better, feels worse. There are many ways to talk of this: certainly as one variant of a negative therapeutic reaction. Either the patient felt guilty about getting better, or was afraid to get better, or the correct interpretation undid repressions, which released aggression, which was turned inward. Yet another way of seeing what happened is quite different. It is that the very act of interpretation takes place within a self-selfobject matrix and that one must subsequently respond to the patient to confirm him or her, to mirror an achievement positively, much as one must respond to the oedipal achievements of the developing child. Inasmuch as some analysts might agree with this technical advice, it still is necessary to recognize that there is a significant theoretical difference between the insight itself making the change and the insight also serving as the expression of a developing self. There should be no question that one must interpret the need for confirmation in turn; but there is a distinct difference between the two clinical theories in terms of levels and breadth of the interpretive work. The introduction of so-called structure-building features in psychoanalysis is neither new nor confined to self psychology.

Two points may illustrate how the psychology of the self can go beyond what we know in this regard. The first is that selfobject transferences enable one to conceptualize, to see, the unfolding of how the self as structure becomes increasingly able to be self regulating. This is a more congenial and more clinically relevant picture than an abstract concept such as "ego repair." The second feature that needs our careful consideration suggests that interpretations per se are structural alterations that proceed by transmuting internalization; and the interpretation of the meaning of an interpretation might therefore be a necessary activity of every analysis. Every interpretation is capable of eliciting a new feeling about oneself.

Since theories are underdetermined as to facts and since alternative theories seem to handle the data equally well at a certain level of investigation, how are we to decide which one to follow? It is certainly not a case for an indiscriminate choice of theories, yet the answer (and there is one) may be hard for some to take. In order to decide which theoretical approach is of maximum utility, one must commit oneself to it and use it in a nonprejudicial way for a period of time. Only a test of usefulness is worthwhile, and only a complete understanding of the theory will allow such a test. Unfortunately and incredibly, so many of the criticisms of self psychology are based on those basically irrelevant comments which range from a claim that selfobject transferences do not exist to the insistence that the conduct of these analyses is no different from what everyone has been doing all along.

The final acceptance of one theory over another is not arbitrary.

No matter how long parallel theories may coexist, there are criteria for choosing one over another. Philosophers of science (Harre, 1972) sometimes suggest two poles of the epistemology of science: phenomenalism and realism. Some sciences, like anatomy, are more suited to realism, and some, like physics, more suited to phenomenalism. So, too, are some theoretical statements directed to real things and some to "fictions" that have a degree of plausibility. But regardless of how we position psychoanalysis in our consideration, some of these same philosophers list criteria for choosing one theory over another (Popper, 1963). Until we come to grips with the essentials of our analytic observations, with "true facts" of psychoanalytic evidence, which may never be agreed upon, we must content ourselves with criteria of comprehensibility and coherence in our selection of theories. But the first and essential step is to use the theory to see just what we can learn.

The person who claims never to have seen an idealizing transference must learn what to look for. The person who claims he has known this all along or has been doing this all along, as in the typical critiques of Mr. Z., betrays both a suspect honesty and a glaring misconception of the basis of scientific theory. One can guess just what would be the psychoanalytic explanation behind a statement of the need to confirm the patient's accomplishments in dealing with a phobia—one that could be communicated to others and is part and parcel of a classical approach. Niceness, kindness, support—those are not answers since even these social amenities are capable of being explained. The claims of doing what every good analyst does are both foolish, because we simply do not all do the same things, and insubstantial, because the next generation of analysts needs a framework for operations. I, for one, do not see a place in classical psychoanalytic theory for this particular kind of intervention except perhaps in the usual effort of expanding the theory.

It might be worthwhile to examine just what so many of the so-called pioneers in psychoanalysis do offer us. I think it is an opportunity that allows us a choice to see if our old map is as good as ever or if we can go further with a new one. Theories are never right or wrong. No theory can be conclusively refuted. No theory is absolutely acceptable (Hesse, 1978). The criterion of pragmatism is the best guide to adopt; and this certainly calls for a maximum of tolerance and a minimal conviction of certain truths (Rorty, 1982a).

DISCUSSION

Self psychology has presented psychoanalysis with a challenge by allowing certain observations to be made. These include a theory of self development that uses the concept of maturing relationships with selfobjects. It is a holistic theory that posits an overall open system of the self and suggests continuing relationships with one's selfobjects. It likewise places at the center of treatment the development and resolution of the selfobject transferences.

Psychoanalysts must come to grips with the ideas of self psychology by testing their utility in the service of explanation. Such an inquiry involves an acquaintance with and understanding of the working through of these selfobject transferences. Unfortunately, most critics of self psychology seem to restrict their activities to citing deviation and difference. This is not the proper avenue for the critique of new ideas. On the other hand, to neglect a careful study of the contributions of pioneers is to rob ourselves and our patients of a chance to advance our science. This is hardly tolerable in any effort that aims to help and is equally unfair to our wish to know.

New ideas are not new paradigms. That unfortunate word has been so abused that its greatest popularizer (Kuhn, 1977) has now modified it. His intent seems to have been to describe an event in the sociology of knowledge. But pioneers who present new ideas essentially offer us epistemological tools, and the reactions to these changes in perception are not necessarily an accurate gauge of their value. To change a set of convictions is always an effort, but psychoanalysts should be *more* rather than less capable of this task. Freud was as ''incorrect'' in his time as Kohut (1979b) was in his. We owe our gratitude to that pioneer who has the courage to be wrong.

3

Translation
Between
Psychoanalytic
Theories

Translation is a part of every psychoanalyst's life. It began, of course, with the translation of Freud's words from German to English and other languages (and that debate over the accuracy of the effort still engages many scholars (Bettelheim, 1982; Mahony, 1982). It extends to the daily work of translating the language of dreams and the unconscious to the common sense terms of the analytic consulting room. It lives in the mind of every analyst who tries to explain an idea in words that will be "understandable" to a patient or a colleague, and it struggles for life with all of those feelings and images that never or hardly ever, seem to gain access to the communication that translation hopes to achieve.

Anyone who translates knows that the simple exchange of word for word or word for image will never do. Good translation requires conceptual bridges that encompass whole sets of ideas and feelings, and bad translation can be dangerous as well as uninformative. To translate is to carry or convey and therefore to bear the burden of information moved from one locale to another. So much has been written on translation (e.g., Steiner, 1975) that it might be well to acknowledge at the outset, that some people feel that translation is always inadequate and in some cases is impossible (Quine, 1969). The intent of this chapter is, however, to examine the exercise of translation between psychoanalytic theories. It assumes that people do succeed in conveying information to one another, do manage to feel understood and to operate as if they comprehend what was intended by another. The crucial question is whether our present sets of theories are easily, or even with difficulty, understood in terms of other theories. Does a word or an idea mean approximately the same thing to, say, Mahler as it does to Winnicott? Does perhaps a similar idea lay buried in an altered vocabulary and could a simple act of uncovering aid in translation? The basic premise of our inquiry is that the theories in psychoanalysis are interchangeable. How much of analytic theory is a monolithic entity albeit with numerous variations and branches? How much of its is a wilderness of unconnected paths?

The answers to these questions begin with a political and social set of positions. One school of theorists takes the "one big happy family" approach. It says that the fundamental tenets of psychoanalysis are firm and set, and all theory extends from these tenets (of uncertain number). Thus, every new idea must be an offshoot or an elaboration of a basic tenet. An example of this would be the Hartmann (1964) addition of the ego's own energy, which is derived from the libido theory by way of additional views involving neutralization and the like. His elaboration builds on the basic theory and in no way clashes with it—although some purists may feel that it does depart from Freud's original intent. Nevertheless, this basic approach is an all-embracing one that wholeheartedly espouses a translation that connects what seems to be alienated with Freud's aims. Thus adherents of the unitary approach will therefore expend time and effort explaining what Fairbairn or Adler or Winnicott "really mean" in terms of the given and acceptable theory.

It should be evident that everyone at some time is a member of this group, for we all tend to approach new findings by exchanging them for old ones. Our private thoughts and public forums are filled with phrases like "That is no more than . . ." or "That is just another way of saying . . ." or "Isn't that really the same as . . .?" We are inclined to reduce things to the tried and true as a necessary part of weeding out what is essentially trivial novelty. Our fallback position is that there is a sort of basic program for psychoanalysis. This assumes that some findings or new positions may be included or integrated into the extant theory, some must be discarded as clearly nonanalytic, and some must be held suspect until they can be integrated. This last immigrant group is the one that evokes accusations of "not being understood" or of being distorted. Translation is strained mightily in this area.

A radical position that lies in sharp opposition to the one-big-happy-family group encourages diversity and insists that translation is impossible between different theories. It states that the words and sentences of Winnicott, Kohut, Mahler, and the like are part of separate theoretical systems that share only common areas of interest and not common vocabularies. At its most extreme, this position probably concedes that even individuals have singular theoretical perspectives that may not easily be mapped onto one another. Analysts from different training programs often seem unable to agree on what different terms stand for, and indeed the field itself is often ridiculed for being unable to come up with an agreed upon definition of the word "psychoanalysis." This position does not deny that persons share ideas and reach agreement, but it does say that essentially we deal in approximations of meaning with many of them being negotiated during discussion. It also seems to claim that theories in science are not clearcut systems of logical structures but rather are clusters of propositions. In regard to this point, we can recall that theories are usually thought of as hypothetico-deductive systems in which observations are tied to hypotheses by correspondence rules. Hypotheses are assumed, but laws are generated and are in turn verifiable. Statements or facts can be predicted and follow from the general laws. Theories, therefore, are examples of deductive logic—or at least this is the customary definition (Suppe, 1974).

The contrasting position holds that a theory is but a cluster of accepted problem solutions (Barnes, 1982) and there is no basic logical structure behind the application of any theory. Scientific inference therefore is not deductive but is derived by analogy. This cluster theory of theories allows for a diversity of positions that need not share any common fundamental structure. It is an unhappy resolution for many scientists who dislike the ad hoc application of theories and who feel such freedom of theory erodes the status of a science. Thus it is no surprise to note how a third, or compromise, position has emerged.

The compromise between diversity and unity has to do with carving out a family of connected and similar theories that overlap in some areas and separate in others. Therefore, for example, Mahler and Winnicott would fundamentally agree on a wide area of findings (i.e., observations and conclusions) but would diverge in others. The job for the integrationists would be to bring more of the divergents back into the family by way of translation. The task for the anarchists would be to sharpen differences by emphasizing the failure of translation. The compromisers hold out promise for the arrival of an all-inclusive umbrella theory. It will provide a vocabulary that will permit translation of what has heretofore been untranslatable. For example, Hartmann's (1964) efforts to extend psychoanalysis to a general psychology had, as one goal, the inclusion of certain social phenomena in the overall theory of psychoanalysis. It was a bigger, more expansive theory and thus gave new hope to the integrationists. It was also condemned by some as being nonanalytic, by others as changing the meaning of the words of psychoanalysis—such as ego—and thus as essentially being another analytic theory entirely (Klein, 1968).

The implications of these positions are not insignificant for they direct attention to the activities of our scholarly contributors. If translation from one theory to another is feasible, then one can profitably work in this area to aim for an integrated whole theory. Of course, this may be achieved by contraction as well as by expansion, but it does require a standard of correctness for judgment. For example, one judges whether such words as splitting, countertransference, or self are being used legitimately or whether there is an idiosyncratic usage that goes beyond what is considered to be normal. So, too, does one decide whether parataxic distortion is "really" transference or counter-transference or whether it falls outside the realm of reasonableness. If, however, such translation is not feasible, then it might be well to accept that fact and for the efforts in this direction to be understood as reflecting an entirely different sort of phenomenon, that is, a social or political problem that will need a different kind of solution. An exercise is in order.

AN EXERCISE IN TRANSLATION

Any comparison between terms and concepts in different theories will undoubtedly provoke controversy. Thus, when we compare the *part-object* of traditional Freudian theory with the *transitional object* of Winnicott (1953) and the *selfobject* of Kohut, we invite argument that these are unequal or of incompatible significance and meaning. Even if we compare the exact same word in each theory, we might expect difficulty since many words are used differently in different theories. There are always large areas of fuzziness of definition. Inasmuch as some authors (Gedo and Goldberg, 1973, p. 62) seem to feel that these three terms are capable of translation, a reasonable exercise would be to test the feasibility of any translation. Thus, we are not in this exercise aiming for accuracy but rather to stake out the possibility of reasonable translation.

1. *Part-object:* The part-object is defined as follows (Laplanche and Pontalis, 1973):

> A type of object toward which the component instincts are directed without this implying that a person as a whole is taken as the love-object.

> In the main part-objects are parts of the body, real and phantasied (breast, feces, penis) and their symbolic equivalents. Even a person can identify himself or be identified with a part-object [p. 301].

From this definition we see that part-objects have only partial qualities of whole persons. Likewise this is a developmental perspective so that, for example, the object of the anal-sadistic stage is feces and at that time persons are treated in the same manner as feces.

Inasmuch as Freud saw objects as tied to the instincts and their gratification, any progression and elaboration of the concept of objects should retain this essential link to the drives. The term part-object is said to have been introduced by Melanie Klein (1952) in its fullest sense, these partial objects becoming endowed with traits comparable to a person's (Laplanche and Pontalis, 1973).

The concept of part-object is easily linked to that of need-satisfying object or archaic object since they all bear the sense of an infantile form of drive gratification that should be but a step toward a more mature object relationship involving whole objects (persons) dealt with in a constant manner and not dependent on the drive state of the self.

2. *Transitional Object:*   This term was introduced by Winnicott 1953 and is defined (Laplanche and Pontalis, 1973) as designating "a material object with a special value for the suckling and young child particularly when it is on the point of falling asleep (e.g., the corner of the blanket that is sucked)" (p. 464). Reliance on such objects according to Winnicott, is a normal phenomenon that allows the child to make the transition from the first oral relationship with the mother to the "true object relationship."

At first glance there might seem to be an immediate correlation of the transitional object with the part-object (or need-satisfying object) in that both share the qualities of an infantile usage on the developmental road to appreciation of complete or true or whole objects. The link to instincts seems to be maintained, although the transitional object is seemingly tied to the oral phase. Winnicott also made much of persistent transitional objects (and phenomena) as being connected to certain forms of pathology and creativity. This concept was soon embraced, and upon close scrutiny it seemed to be popularly seen in terms of its material constituent, that is a blanket or doll or even a poem or song. This is not quite the same as Freud's clear intrapsychic usage. For him an instinctual drive cathected an intrapsychic image of an object. In fact, much of Winnicott's work on the holding environment is presented as an interpersonal theory involving the interaction of mother and child. So, too, does Winnicott's transitional object maintain a shared relationship with another so that the transitional object lies neither inside nor outside of the self. To be sure, one can posit an inner picture or image or representation of a shared transitional object (see Gedo and Goldberg, p. 59), but essentially Winnicott's work concentrates on the environment and on what the infant creates in the world outside. The transitional object is but a step into the world of relationships between the developing child and the caretakers that Winnicott explores. His is not a theory of intrapsychic vicissitudes but rather one of the nature of the facilitating environment (Winnicott, 1965). Of course, one can translate any term or idea or part of object relations theory back into intrapsychic terms and concepts. This is usually strained and unsuccessful. As Klein and Tribeck (1981) put it in regard to splitting, ". . . it is spurious to equate Freudian splitting with that of the theorists of the object-relations approach, because in the former the origin, meaning and motivation of splitting is set within a different theoretical context than the latter approach" (p. 20).

The transitional object is a part of an overall, albeit somewhat poorly articulated, theory developed by Winnicott, who was joined by others such as Guntrip and Fairbairn. It does not sit alone as a new term added to an existing theory, but rather it extends to a network of other theoretical ideas having to do with relations and joins a cluster of similar theoretical terms. If one attempts to tear it free of its own theoretical matrix then one runs the risk of minimizing its significance, reducing it, for example, to but an oral precursor of the fetish. Seen in its full sense, however, it is an essential part of a new theoretical orientation.

3. *The Selfobject:* This term does not enjoy a place in the psychoanalytic dictionary of Laplanche and Pontalis (1973). It was defined by Kohut (1971) as another person experienced as part of the self. Again, one can position the concept as belonging to that early phase of development wherein other persons are utilized or exploited for needs that do not take into account the issue of mutuality. Persons are thus not seen as whole and are only partly appreciated. The move to maturation would then allow for the gradual increase in self and object differentiation and the ultimate recognition of another person as an entity in his or her own right. In this sense, the selfobject seems to correlate with the part-object as well as the transitional object in terms of both its infantile status and its characteristic lack of clear differentiation. Of course, Kohut (1977) upset the neatness of this translation by insisting that selfobjects could be mature as well as infantile. He further strains the compatibility of the terms in his relative neglect of the drive aspect of object relations and his insistence on the structural or sustaining and supporting role of the selfobject. In this matter, he seems closer to Winnicott, but he departs from that association in his emphasis on the introspective assessment of the object. Thus,

a selfobject is not recognized in terms of any environmental or material factor but rather entirely in terms of an empathic assessment. In this respect, it is hardly equivalent to Winnicott's transitional objects save again for some sort of heroic effort to translate. For Kohut, the selfobject floats in a sea of connected concepts that see psychological data in a manner distinct from Freud and Winnicott as well as others. His theory is perhaps better articulated and therefore can be seen more clearly to be different. He attempts to incorporate much of classical psychoanalysis within his theory but more by explaining how all analysis works than by retaining its terms and ideas. He aims for a unified theory.

If single words or terms are not easily translatable, might not whole concepts instead be exchanged? Is it not possible that what Winnicott describes as the early mother-child relationship in toto is the same as that, say, of Kohut? Of course, it is possible, but a return to the fundamental ideas of these theories can easily disabuse one of the likelihood. They see things differently, but neither need be right or wrong. One concentrates on the growth of a self sustained and carried forward by selfobjects linked by empathic communicative ties. The other speaks of objects that foster independence and self-reliance. One stresses an open system that remains so; the other, a semipermeable one that must separate off. To try to make their theories as one strips them of their richness.

What of the possibility that these supposedly new theories are merely additions to or elaborations of the cluster that is the main body of psychoanalysis? If Hartmann could add to psychoanalytic psychology by way of ego psychology, could not the same be said for self psychology and the theories of Winnicott and Mahler? Are these not merely additions to the existing corpus of knowledge? The answer to this is in two parts. First, of course, a true addition to a theory is not translated or absorbed back into the theory but adds something that in no way need challenge the theory. The only translation that is needed is one to insure the continuity of ideas, and indeed this does often happen. The second, crucial point has to do with the points of linkage or addition. What appears at first to be an addition may turn out to be an incompatible concept. This, in truth, is to be hoped for because it allows one to define the limits of the previous theory and to embark on a new one. Probably Kohut's (1971) first presentation of narcissistic personality disorders was felt to fall into the realm of expanding the theory but soon thereafter was seen for the radical, and therefore untranslatable, theory that it was. Additions or elaborations of known theories either are trivial in nature or soon turn out to be unhappy guests. To quote Toulmin (1974), "The integration of theoretical concepts . . . will not consist solely in the formal running together of different propositional systems; more typically it will require the development of a whole new pattern of theoretical interpretation'' (p. 389).

We have seen that the three terms discussed seem to play significant roles in their respective theories and to occupy similar positions in the world of our psychological data. Such inviting familiarity is the natural impetus for the task of translation of terms. The failure of such an effort is due less to the inadequacy of the translator than to a mistaken idea about theories: that theories sit outside the field of investigation and are used to examine and explain the unknown. According to that idea, more powerful theories explain more and deeper, and we build on a theory to make it grow and encompass more data. To the contrary, any given part of the world seems to be capable of being understood by a variety of theories. No one theory explains everything, since theories are basically underdetermined; that is, some explain some things and some explain others, and some are better than others for some explanations (Hesse, 1978, p. 14; Gedo and Goldberg, 1973, p. 172).

Nature does not seem to care how we choose to view it, categorize it, or explain it. Whatever ''it'' may be, the world comes into being by our own vision of it, and this vision is a product of our theory. Because observations are not distinct from theory, any given chunk of the world will be seen in one way by one theory and in a somewhat different—or perhaps a radically different—way by another. In a given community of persons who share a common language and who are trained to see things in a like way, there will be a high consensus about just what is out there. The first person who discovers something new or sees something heretofore unseen asks the others to look again with the kind of gestalt switch that Kuhn (1970) describes in his pictures that yield two forms to the viewer. These gestalt switches need not change the vision of the entire world but rather of only those areas that have been viewed and agreed upon to be composed or constructed in a particular manner. The new theory must change that view, or else it is not a new theory but simply a version of the old one. Progress in science demands new theories. They need not be radical ones that shake the foundations of the old one, but they do need to be different, and different enough to force a new perception of the investigated area of the world. If a new theory can be translated back into the old one then it, by definition, is without merit. It must be untranslatable since a theory is a cluster or network of new percepts that force one to see things differently. Winnicott's (1965) transitional object would have no value to us if it were the same as the part-object. Efforts to reduce the new to the tried and true stifle scientific progress.

As Spence (1982) writes:

> If truth is contingent and if we can only understand the meaning and
> significance of an interpretation against the full set of background assump-
> tions that were operating in that particular analytic space, then we should
> not be surprised at the periodic appearance of theoretical disagreements.
> . . . these disagreements indicate . . . the less significant result of draw-
> ing conclusions from insufficient data. Supporters of one school . . . take
> into account only a certain subset of the clinical data. . . . Another school,
> arguing from another subset reaches different conclusions. Each group
> . . . [is] . . . less than completely informed [p. 277].

Unfortunately, however, Spence seems to think that this phenomenon is due to the lack of complete accessibility of all information of
the failure to naturalize our data. He suggests that until complete accessibility occurs, psychoanalysis will be grounded only in tentative
theory while the real facts remain elusive. He ignores the abundant
evidence that every science is interpretive (Hesse, 1978), that every
investigator brings a certain "privileged competence" to his observations, and thus that every theory deals only with certain subsets of
data. Psychoanalysis needs no further license to be more aesthetic than
scientific; the contingency of truth is with us everywhere (Habermas,
1978). Hard facts are a luxury that no science attains; we gather facts
from a preexisting interpretive stance.

If different theories see the world differently and if every theory
is limited and necessarily insufficient, then how can psychoanalysis
or any scientific enterprise determine what its domain of interest
should be? The subject matter of psychoanalysis cannot be defined by
the theory since it would be locked in by a community of people speaking the same language and not allowing a change in perception or
words. At times, this, sadly, seems to be encouraged by some (Moore,
1981). Kohut (1971) would have us define the field by our method,
while others would say that even that might inhibit our progress.
Whatever the resolution of that question it is certainly naive for anyone
to declare what is or is not psychoanalysis; it can be "defined" only
by social and political consensus that exists for the time being.

When and how one adopts a changed theoretical outlook is a vexing problem to scientists who may on occasion lay claim to revolutionary changes or else may find such subtle evolutionary modifications that it is difficult to pinpoint the exact point of the perceptual
switch. Not every new observation is a demand for a new theory, but
contradictory ones do beg for reconciliation. One may live with them
for variable periods of time, but, then again, as Quine (1969) has suggested, almost any theory can be modified to accommodate any

anomalous findings. An example of theory accommodation can be found in a critical review of the work of John Bowlby (Gedeman, 1982). Aside from the usual "what is good is old and what is new is bad" form of overview, the work of Bowlby is judged either on the basis of the data's being nonanalytic (since it was derived from interviews outside the consulting room) or on his positions such as those on environmental influences and object constancy, which are already shared by a host of analysts. As we have seen, the first allegation is hardly sustainable. But Bowlby is also evaluated by comparison to Mahler, whose own work was outstandingly derived from other kinds of "nonanalytic" data. The definition of that unique data base is loaded with problems for the reviewer. The other criticism suggests that analysts are not of one mind and that many of them consider the impact of the environment and the real needs of people for people outside of the mere libidinal gratification. The review implies that Bowlby was constructing straw men to attack. I shall not attend here to the merits of the particular issues, but it does seem that contradictory ideas (i.e., the environment counts vs. the environment does not count, or people attach to others for libidinal gratification vs. people attach for other supposed needs) really do exist in analysis and that Bowlby attempted to *explain* his position in a particular and different manner. Of course, one may say that it is obvious that the environment counts. However, only by theory-tinkering can one get a theory that initially says it does not count to say later that it does. Such contradictory positions in a theory may live for quite a while, and sometimes an investigator like Bowlby declares a new theory and so emphasizes the partition.

At other times we see the tinkering of theory to avoid a clash with other disciplines. For example, when Freud's ideas about psychic energy were shown by a host of investigators (Basch, 1975; Rosenblatt and Thickstun, 1977) to be incompatible with modern-day ideas about energy, the notion of psychic energy was modified: first to be unique to analysis and then gradually to denote something like psychological interest (Kohut, 1971) or even meaningfulness. For some, the evolution of the definition was palatable, but for others it could not be digested (Rosenblatt and Thickstun, 1977). Over a period of time, the accumulation of differences of opinion does permit the kinds of basic shifts that warrant a claim of incompatibility: the claim that Bowlby makes. Such seems to be the case for the several theories in psychoanalysis.

Theories in psychoanalysis are not translatable, nor should they be. Just as a given word in any language enjoys a cluster of meanings based upon its usage by the community of speakers, so too is a theory a cluster

of connected solutions to problems. Psychoanalysis seems to have at
least several such clusters. They see the world differently as indeed
they should. Some seem to work better than others, and the dedicated
and prolonged use of such theories is the single criterion of acceptability. Efforts to translate theories into one another are wasted and do
a disservice to the theoreticians. To criticize a theory as being different
or wrong is much like condemning a book for being readable: that's
what it's supposed to be.

A Unified Theory

At first glance one might look with envy at those sciences which seem
to have a minimum of controversy about the facts of the field and therefore are able to pursue a variety of research programs without argument or rancor. Certainly chemists do not openly disagree about what
a compound is, and physicists do not part company on the nature of
a simple thing like temperature. Or do they? Kuhn (1970, pp. 130–35)
tells an interesting story of how the term "compound" changed in
chemistry from the meaning attributed to it by a theory of "elective
affinity" to that explained by Dalton's new theory of atoms. The
history of the change was a reconstruction of the term "compound"
to fit Dalton's theory. The pre- and post-Dalton conceptual fabrics were
 neither incompatible with experience nor inconsistent logically. Kuhn
claims that they could not be compared using either experience or
logic. And today the meaning of the word is even different in a different way.

Even the concept of temperature cannot be said always to mean the
same thing. Philosophers may disagree about whether there even exists some unyielding phenomenon that is indeed temperature (see Putnam, 1982, for the range of arguments here). And for some it is a tac-
tile sensation, for others a point on a thermometer, and for others a
quality of molecular activity.

Given the changing meanings and evolving theories that are common to all science, one might still protest that the newest and latest
one does seem to unify or integrate everything that has gone before.
Certainly psychoanalysts are familiar with words having multiple meanings, but should we not aim for and reach a point where we can agree
on what an object or an ego is? Can we not bring together part-object
and transitional object and selfobject in a unifying theory? The answer
to these questions is a very qualified maybe, and it has to do with the
historical moment that psychoanalysis is now in.

Freud developed psychoanalytic theory to cover a particular area
of study and data. Some of his followers attempted, with mixed results,

to apply and extend the theory. Efforts, for example, to use the structural-theory of the mind to explain psychoses stretch the theory beyond its limits and result in explanations such as "ego weakness" or absence of certain structures (Arlow and Brenner, 1964). The struggle with a concept such as superego is an interesting one in which to follow the efforts of the faithful adherents of the theory to use it where it seems to have little value (Hartmann and Loewenstein, 1962). Those analysts who studied nonneurotic disorders and the psyche of the preoedipal child were hard pressed to employ all the terms or concepts of the theory and, like Winnicott, developed new terms and began to stake out a new theory. One such attempt is the theory of object relations. Klein and Tribeck's (1981) spirited condemnation of it as not being faithful to Freud is, of course, entirely misplaced, just as is Calef and Weinshel's (1979) harsh critique of Kernberg. Whether or not one agrees with him, it is to Kernberg's credit that he is different. Those voices of blame for infidelity are simply unaware of how science progresses.

As a new theory of self psychology was formulated by Kohut, a new wave of protest arose. Kohut perhaps saw more clearly that his theory was not to be integrated with classical analysis, but he chose to absorb classical analysis into self psychology. Here is a beginning attempt at unification, and it remains to be seen as to whether it will be successful. Certainly the theory of classical analysis will not remain the same if it does succeed. It does not seem that the development of unifying theories is the way of all science, and many thrive in an atmosphere of pluralism. As Toulmin (1974) wrote about James Clerk Maxwell's integration of electricity, magnetism and optics:

> . . . it remained possible after Maxwell's work as before, to distinguish between straightforwardly electrical, magnetic and optical phenomena on the empirical level; but on a more general, theoretical level such distinctions lost their earlier significance and it ceased to be necessary to keep the problems, methods and explanatory categories of the three earlier sciences separated [p. 389].

However, we cannot preserve the older or preintegrated meanings in the newer one because, as Barnes (1982) says, "Terms connect to other terms differently and they connect to nature differently" (p. 67). A new and overall theory seems to change the elements and connections so that our entire set of definitions becomes altered. The author, for example (Stevens, 1980), who urges healthy dissent without disruptive movement is confusing scientific progress with his own personal unhappiness at change since, to paraphrase Popper (1959), any change in science must, of necessity, be disruptive. But disruption should not be equated with personal animosity or discomfort. The counterclaim by others (e.g., Richards, 1981) that they seem to do well with the old theories, which therefore should be maintained in the interest of parsimony, is another mistaken personal opinion. It is an open question whether one or another theory is more parsimonious (and how would one decide that?), and it is no secret that a patient can be treated effectively under a variety of theories. The question is whether the new theory explains more to more people. Certainly a person is free to renounce the new theory—but that singular rejection would not qualify for publication in most sciences since it again confuses scientific standards with personal familiarity and comfort.

The need for psychoanalysis is not to still the voices of dissent or discordance in the name of unity or familiarity or fidelity. We do not seem to lack for our cadre of orthodoxy. We need more, not fewer, bold and imaginative theories. Psychoanalysis does not suffer from too much difference but rather from too little courage in staking out the unexplored for fear of being deposed and alienated. With a concentrated effort, we must now reject the routine connection to Freud just as we once insisted upon it.

DISCUSSION

There can probably be no correct translation of Freud. Every reader reads a different book. Each time one rereads Freud, the text means something different. There is no hard and fast rule for words to stand for certain things or for one word of one language to definitively replace another. In fact, an author often is not completely aware of his meaning until the word is written and even then it may be meant to communicate more than one idea. Interpretation is a variable thing and is brought to bear on every text and in every discourse and thus yields variable meanings. We translate in arbitrary ways and use community consensus to determine issues of truth or accuracy. One may argue that one translation of Freud is more pleasing or more reliable or more telling than another, and certainly one translation may be more popular or readily acceptable than another. But trying to define what a word really stands for or what Freud really meant is an effort to wrap truth in a package that always comes undone.

The translation of theory is a severe case of the translation of words. It is made most unlikely because we may be attending to different parts of the world; we are reading different books. Hesse (1978) says, "Theories should be more or less plausibly coherent with facts, but they can be neither conclusively refuted nor uniquely derived from statements of fact alone, and hence no theory in a given domain is uniquely acceptable" (p. 1). The underdetermination of theory is no longer controversial. It is therefore vitally important for psychoanalysis to abandon its preoccupation with translation of theory and with a search for the true or correct theory. We need embark on an effort of maximum comprehension of different ways of explaining the data of our field. We do so by a pragmatic consideration of the scope and yield of our interpretations and explanations, and not by utilizing the test of orthodox compliance. However, "pragmatic" cannot be read as indicative of "anything goes" (see Rorty, 1982b, especially p. 168, for an explication of modern day pragmatism) since every science has both a central content and peripheral expansions, and explanations should articulate with and support one another. The cluster of accepted propositions consists of mutually supported ones. They hold together both within the accumulated data of analysis and between it and other disciplines. We cannot take pragmatic as allowing the incorrect to flourish, since to be pragmatic is to have good reason for adopting one standpoint rather than another, and we do so by a process of negotiation. This new standard of pragmatism is an unhappy solution for many students trained in empiricism, as we noted in chapter 1. This standard says that we use something (as Sellars, 1963, said of philosophy) as "an attempt to see how things, in the broadest possible sense of the term, hang together, in the broadest possible sense of the term" (Rorty, 1982a, p. xiv). We hope to show in the latter part of this book that psychoanalysis can be seen as a prime example of the negotiating process that allows one to adopt the position of another and so modify one's own. Translation is a step in such negotiation, one by which we come to understand one another. But such understanding is not to be translated as convincing the other of the truth of one's position but rather as reaching a new level of comprehension.

4

The Tension Between Realism And Relativism in Psychoanalysis

Realism is a point of view that considers the world to be composed of a variety of things that we sooner or later come to know accurately as matters of fact. That is to say, we learn of the existence of a real world by way of our sense organs and scientific instruments. In its naive form, realism is the host of common sense impressions of the constituents of the world; its apples, tables, and people are exactly what we perceive. In its scientific form, we agree that a table is "really" a mass of electrons or whatever basic and more fundamental features and forms we attribute to those ordinary impressions. Scientific realism is thus the effort to determine with exactness the makeup of the world in both its past and present forms (Putnam, 1982).

Relativism is a viewpoint that considers the world as a variable thing that need have no inherent composition save as we choose to categorize it. Our sense organs and scientific instruments are devices that guide and direct all our observations and in so doing determine just what the world is capable of being to us. Immanuel Kant (1781) was most eloquent in insisting that our brains would allow only certain sorts of categorizing of the world and thus would direct a consideration of reality according to that inherent program or design. Scientific relativism studies the ways that considerations of reality change from time to time in history. In so doing, it alters the language of reality as well.

Another world view that needs definition in this context is subjectivism, which is sometimes confused with relativism. This stance is often attached as a matter of purely personal opinion, subjectivism being a view of the world that posits the subject as primary. In its exaggerated form, subjectivism can be seen to operate without constraints, and so allow one to consider a table as anything one chooses. Many hold that subjectivism may be permitted in unscientific or artistic endeavors but is suspect in scientific pursuits.

These three concepts—realism, relativism, and subjectivism—do not enjoy agreed upon definitions in philosophy, nor have philosophers arrived at a consensus on a "correct" point of view. According to Flew (1979), realism is derived from Plato and his theory of universals. "For Plato the observed world is only a reflection of the real world, consisting for Plato of the forms which are something like universals" (p. 331). It is perhaps best articulated in modern philosophy by Popper (1972) in his view of objective knowledge. Relativism is derived more from Kant, and in some sense is here allied with subjectivism. "To be a relativist is to maintain that there is no such thing as objective knowledge of realities independent of the known" (Flew, 1979, p. 261). Kant moved us away from objective knowledge. Neo-Kantians have noted that the categories of organizing the world may not be fixed. Modern statements of relativism are associated with the approach of historians such as Thomas Kuhn (1970) and sociologists such as Barry Barnes (Barnes and Bloor, 1982). The recent association of psychoanalysis with hermeneutics, or interpretive science, and its spokesmen such as Gadamer (1975) and Habermas (1971), call for a further study of realism, relativism, and subjectivism from psychoanalysis. Hermeneutics seems for some to embrace relativism readily and thus has alarmed the proponents of realism.

PSYCHOANALYSIS AND REALITY

Students of psychoanalysis have all traveled the road of the historical moments that led Freud to move from studying the parental seductions of his patients (Freud, 1925) to focusing on the fantasy of these events. As Grünbaum (1983) has so clearly stated, this movement from objective or external reality to psychic or inner reality remains within the realm of the real. "What really happened" has the same significance for the psychoanalytic investigator as for any historian, but the analyst is interested more in the subjective experience of the participant than in a particular "event" as it might be registered by, say, a video camera. Although Freud's patients were not actually seduced, the "reality" of seductions in their psychic lives remains to be reckoned with, and with an equal measure of significance: the personal effect of any given event on an individual constitutes the psychic reality with which psychoanalysis is concerned.

In this view of reality, we recognize that the subjective begins to predominate, and usually we characterize such subjectivism as the different and varied, that is, the personal interpretations of an event. At this juncture we also consider the hermeneutic approach to our data. Part and parcel of all psychoanalytic effort is interpreting whatever may seem to be merely recorded or registered by other sciences. However, as we have said, every science is hermeneutic in the sense that it ultimately subjects the registered data to some sort of theoretical scrutiny; it interprets what is perceived. Or, to put it another way, interpretation is embedded in perception.

The fact of multiple interpretations of any given event seems to unite reality, subjectivism, and hermeneutics. Psychoanalysis aims to interpret and thus to understand a real experience of a patient. Here is a clinical illustration that highlights these points:

During his first analysis, a patient recalled an event that occurred when he was about five years old. He had left school and was waiting on the steps for his father, who was to bring him home. Time passed, everyone else was gone, and father was not to be seen. The boy realized that his father had probably stopped off at a saloon before the planned meeting and had perhaps gotten drunk and had forgotten about him. Determined not to be left alone, and frightened that he did not know how to get home, the boy set out for the saloon with some dim memory of having been there before and therefore knowing where it might be. He recalled unhesitatingly making his way there, finding his drunken father, and angrily confronting him.

As an adult, he drew from this episode the conviction that his father had no particular love or concern for him, and thus that he had to make his own way through life. In a creative writing class, he had submitted an account of this episode, and the teacher had commented on the writer's remarkable success in portraying the emotional state of a lonely, frightened, and neglected child. After his analysis, the patient used this childhood story as a capsulized dramatic presentation of his early life, that is, he always had to "go it alone."

The patient underwent a second course of treatment, but the transference on this occasion allowed him to concentrate more upon the ending of the episode. He soon added a finishing touch to the tale by including the father's turning to and addressing the other drinkers and proclaiming, "That kid has a lot of moxie." The emphasis thus shifted from the forlorn child to the aggressive and proud one. Further elaboration of the story also included the fact that the school was run by nuns who lived in an adjacent convent. The boy could have knocked on the door and asked for assistance, but he was either reluctant to be perceived as needing help or else was eager for the adventure. All this material, seemingly available to the patient in the first analysis, was either ignored or minimized in the construction of the interpretations. The same point could, of course, be made of the second treatment and its emphasis on playing down the conclusions of the first.

To recapitulate: a real event occurred that could have been recorded by a video camera showing the boy and his behavior—material that is of limited significance for a psychoanalyst. Rather, from the event we explore (using our theoretical formulations) the experience of the child and interpret what it means to him. If a cerebroscope were available to view pictures of the boy's internal psychological state, we would be able to interpret those scenes. Similarly, we interpret the telling of the event in adulthood or the reemergence of some analogous event in the transference. Thus far we have joined together the issues of reality and subjectivity (psychic reality)—although "subjective" need of course not be equal to conscious awareness—and to this we add the indispensable feature of interpretation. We then might join Grünbaum (1983) in dispensing with the need for an additional term—hermeneutics—which seems to add little to the stated combination of reality, subjectivity, and interpretation.

PSYCHOANALYSIS AND RELATIVISM

The mere observation of events is usually a given, inasmuch as anyone would probably describe what had happened in the childhood scene in a fairly similar manner. A cautionary note is needed at this point, however, since the idea of a *pure* observation has been fairly well eliminated by the dissolution of the assumed dichotomy between theory and observation. This dichotomy had been used to divide the data of pure observation from the workings of theoretical ideas and assumed that everyone would agree on what, for example, was recorded by a video screen. The prevailing view, however, is quite at odds with this (Grundy, 1973). It holds that theory determines observation: until one knows what to see, one cannot make any observations. This seems clear in the need for theory to comprehend or "see" the track-ings of a Wilson cloud chamber or to "see" the parts of a cell under a microscope. We often balk at the need of theories for the commonplace, but it soon seems obvious that one must somehow know about (that is, have a theory of) apples before one can recognize an apple. Theories are but patterns of putting things together.

With this in mind, we can revisit the episode of the sad or proud little boy and notice that some viewers or listeners will observe certain things while others will concentrate on others. All will not be of one mind as to what is seen, much as different camera angles or focuses yield different impressions.

The problem soon grows and is best illustrated by an example of what is added by the observer to what is observed and the framework or perspective of observation. In Freud's (1918) famous case of the Wolf Man, a study of the psychic reality of that remarkable patient led Freud to infer that the Wolf Man had, at the age of a year or a year and a half, seen his parents engaged in intercourse, with the father approaching the mother from the rear. At no time was an actual memory of the event recovered but Freud felt fairly certain this was a reasonable conclusion (p. 37, n. 6). Although Freud at first suggests only a provisional belief in the reality of the scene (p. 39), later (p. 97) he states that whether or not the experience was real or fantasied is of no great importance. It is important to recognize, however, that even as a fantasy, the event was not recognized as such by the Wolf Man but, rather, was introduced by Freud. This conclusion is justified by Freud's statement—his theory—that such scenes are inherited endowments that may or may not be actually realized, which allowed him to "see" what no one else had theretofore seen. His explanation is undoubtedly weakest concerning the contribution of the observer. The validity of the primal scene is established not only by the sense of conviction achieved by patient and analyst but also by its necessity for coherence, or what is commonly called the best fit (Goodman, 1978), offered by this particular explanation. At another point, Freud drops the idea of the father's annoyance because the analytic material "did not react to it." He demonstrates his own rules of validity in this way (p. 80).

Throughout Freud's case histories we see opportunities for multiple interpretations, as well as the manner in which theory guides, directs, dictates—and even inserts additions to what an untutored observer would note. This has been troublesome to some, such as Niederland (1951) in his pursuit of the history of Senat-president Schreber. Here an effort was made to find out "what really happened" between Schreber and his father, and we again must recognize that this conflation of objective and psychic reality is often considered of little or no necessary value in psychoanalysis. For example, an event such as the early death of Schreber's father might have meant salvation to Schreber, whereas to another person it would have been experienced as traumatic. In that respect, one must distinguish between theories that base significance on events themselves and those that consider events in relation to the inner experience of the subjects. A later chapter in this book expands this point.

That different theories lend themselves to different observations and interpretations is the hallmark of relativism. One enters the consulting room or any arena of data gathering with the baggage of preconceptions—one's training in a community of like-minded investigators. We thus pick and choose what we see and how we organize those selections. One's adoption of a particular set of beliefs depends on the circumstances of the user (Barnes and Bloor, 1982) rather than on some fixed set of objective and external standards. This is also congenial to a further elaboration of the hermeneutic circle wherein an interpretation is formed by a continual feedback process in either a reading of a text or a dialogue between persons. And this is also a cause of much alarm among psychoanalysts who fear that this approach robs us of a foundation of true beliefs and leads to a medley of "anything goes" narratives, which satisfy only the select circle of the participants (that usually numbers but two). As Barnes and Bloor put it:

> There is no valid distinction between what is true, reasonable and explanatory and what counts as knowledge, on the one hand, and what is locally accepted as such, on the other. For the relativist there is no sense attached to the idea that some standards or beliefs are really rational as distinct from merely locally accepted as such [p. 13].

Such a stance, which is read as one of unrelieved license, is often associated with hermeneutics and warrants an investigation of that trend, which, as we have seen in one version, is highly compatible with the process of psychoanalysis or of any manner of scientific pursuit.

REALISM, RELATIVISM AND HERMENEUTICS

The recent popularity of the hermeneutic approach to psychoanalysis was probably initiated by Paul Ricoeur in his book *Freud and Philosophy* (1970). Its basic thesis stressed an internal standard of objectivity based on inner relationships that are lawlike and that themselves constitute the facts. This approach is often traced to the work of Dilthey and Schleiermacher (Ricoeur, 1981) and nowadays is associated with Gadamer and Habermas. It began in theology and soon came to be described as the art of interpreting language. For some time, as a result of Dilthey's contributions, the hermeneutic approach was felt to emphasize understanding (*Verstehen*) and was therefore associated with the human sciences, whereas explanation (*Erklaren*) was isolated as the epistemological goal of the natural sciences (Ricouer, 1981). Understanding was held to involve the grasping of a totality from within; explanation involved features seen from outside. Such a distinction is not now maintained by many who see all science as interpretive and as involving both understanding and explaining (Hesse, 1978) as noted in our previous chapter.

An incredible misunderstanding of hermeneutics has developed that seems to leave truth and reality behind and to settle for whatever is felt to be agreed upon by the participants in the interpretive act (Eagle, 1984). So too does one person's understanding of another by introspection or empathy lend itself to an unlimited range of opinion, in contrast to an appraisal determined by an unchallenged set of objective facts. The problem stems from the confusion of language: a given sentence spoken by different persons or by the same person at different times usually does not mean the same thing. One cannot objectively determine what a sentence stands for without first understanding the speaker. If we add another ingredient to this equation—the listener's own personal assessment of what he or she hears—then we are embarked on the investigation of the exchange, or dialogue, that is the focus of hermeneutics. Interpretation of the written word or of the spoken sentence involves the meaning that emerges from the completed circle of the listener (reader) grasping the total content of words of the speaker (text), which is modified by whatever particular preconceptions the listener brings to the encounter. Whether or not this is qualitatively different from the encounter with the usual objects of science will not be addressed here. Instead, we offer another clinical example to illustrate this hermeneutic exercise.

This case was presented in an analytic seminar as evidence of the folly of a hermeneutic approach to psychoanalysis. The patient, a young unmarried woman in her twenties, was having sexual problems ranging from physical dissatisfaction with the sexual act to difficulty maintaining a close relationship with a man. The analyst noted that she was seductive and flirtatious in the initial interviews, and his evaluation was constant with what a listener would call "hysterical personality." The analysis was unusual in that both patient and analyst became convinced that the patient had been involved in incestuous relations with her uncle. That event itself was not as striking as the fact that although it had occurred when the patient was around 13 years old, she had no memory of it. Efforts outside the analysis proper were initiated by the patient in concert with the analyst to determine the validity of their shared hypothesis. A letter was sent directly to the mother asking if anything had occurred between the patient and her uncle during this period. The mother's ambiguous answer did not contradict their suspicions; indeed it strengthened them. The patient, however, remained unable to recall the event.

When inability to recall occurred in the case of the Wolf Man, Freud attributed it to the failure of the 18-month-old child to comprehend what was happening rather than to a failure to lift the repression (Freud, 1918, p. 37, n. 6). In an hysteric, however, the latter is felt to be the relevant cause, and the young woman's analysis proceeded with this in mind. Despite this supposed defect in the progress of treatment (the inability to remember) the analysis proceeded to a successful conclusion, with the relief of major symptoms, and an acceptable termination. The analyst was courageous in presenting such a completed case to a group seminar inasmuch as forgotten incest in a 13-year-old seemed a questionable possibility. Yet his claim was that he had not fallen victim to a shared mythical story created by himself and the patient—they had gone outside of the treatment to verify the circumstances. And this, rather than the conduct of the case per se, was the main thesis of the presentation—that is, one cannot draw valid and true conclusions entirely from within the analytic setting, since a shared fiction is just as likely as a true account to find its place in the light of interpretations. Thus the frailty of hermeneutics: it has no checks and balances and seems no more than a conspiracy of agreement. In truth, the letter to the mother was a hermeneutic exercise in its own right.

Spence (1982) has written extensively on this problem of validation, and one cannot do justice to his ideas in a brief space. He feels that a number of different narratives can be spun from an analysis, since we are not always aware of the background data brought into an analysis. He pleads for a "naturalization" of our data to make it completely accessible to others, in order to obtain more closely or approximate the real or historical truth. He thus appears to join the argument between realism and relativism by the process of naturalization. A period of immediate scrutiny of analytic sessions by a number of competent peers appears to be the antidote to the potential conspiracy of construction of narrative accomplished in the confines of analysis.

Although somewhat belatedly, the analytic case of the young woman was "naturalized" and presented in detail to a group of analysts. That presentation could not, of course, be any gauge of Spence's suggestion, since undoubtedly he would want detailed presentations with open-ended discussion; and this did not take place. But it is of some interest to note the general reactions of the audience. One group felt that this was a perfectly sound analysis with an admittedly unusual case. Another group felt that the analyst and patient had acted out in a manner that did not allow a proper analysis to unfold, and thus the entire story of incest and its possible verification was spurious. Yet another group echoed this last point but did not feel that it mattered in terms of the value of the analysis, since the issue of whether or not a story is true is not of primary importance in an analysis. Perhaps one could also isolate a smaller group of evaluators within the last; they would claim that the reconstruction was more in the nature of a metaphor that captured a general theme of the patient's life and just happened to be cast in that particular mold without it necessarily being a matter of fact. A somewhat ill-defined response perhaps would correspond to a group that said that they would not have gotten the results or conducted the analysis in the manner presented.

Reviewing the case and the responses, we see that the latter, on the whole, seem to support the relativistic view of psychoanalysis, as well as that of multiple interpretations, observer contribution, and various forms of a narrative. The realist would opt for some grounding of the facts of the case in a truth-seeking enterprise. Although the analyst claimed a position contrary to that of hermeneutics, he behaved in a manner quite consistent with the approach that maintains that one brings a set of presumptions to an investigation and attempts to comprehend meanings through an ever-expanding set of interpretations gained by coming to understand another person. The problem that remains concerns the tension between the realist position, based on determining facts, and that of the relativist, which assumes that facts are either unnecessary or unattainable—the second state corresponding more to the view that truth shifts with changing perspectives and thus genuine truth lies beyond our grasp.

Certainly, different theoretical persuasions in analysis yield reasonably good results based on widely differing narratives. All analysts are familiar with the phenomenon of reading a case that seems totally foreign to their own mode of treatment and yet seems to result in a "cure." Of course, we give all sorts of reasons to explain away such cures, but there is no litmus test for a proper cure. In a rather sharp rejoinder to Spence's position of multiple narrative, Malcolm (1983) pointed out that such varied stories are beside the point, since the psychoanalytic transference is the only true condition that we confront in analysis. This is unfortunately an arguable point, inasmuch as Freudian and Kleinian and Kohutian transferences do not seem of one piece; yet they remain the *one true condition* of all of these quite different analyses. The foregoing case was conducted in a seemingly proper manner, and the analyst was cognizant of the central role of the transference and indeed felt this supported his fundamental stance and his unusual conclusions. Within the confines of a theory, there is usually but one true transference. Bird (1972) even claims that there are as many imputations of significance to transference as there are analysts.

A RESOLUTION OF THE DILEMMA

It seems likely that one can resolve the questions of the reasonableness of the clinical examples and the group responses by examining what is involved in these particular disagreements. This may then answer some other questions that have been raised.

1.   Does Reality Count?

Freud's statement that it matters not if incest was real or fantasied today seems in error. Accumulated evidence in child guidance clinics and in analytic practice has clearly demonstrated that the patient who has experienced incest is different from the one who has not (Gelinas, 1983). Given Freud's conviction of the universal presence of incestuous and castration fantasies, one could be forced into the untenable position that all persons would turn out the same if it were not that we *do* consider the effects of the environment in neurosogenesis. It is true, however, that we have failed to correlate the features of psychic reality with those of objective reality (see chapter 5). Because we are unable to say just what a person's subjective experience of an event will be, that experience is relative. In the case example, we would likewise have to compare the accumulated empirical evidence of incest in adolescent girls with the clinical picture of that particular patient. We would also consider the accumulated evidence that might warrant irreversible amnesia in such a case. Probably both would be found unable to support the analyst's conviction. These are examples of the gathering evidence from real events to warrant some general conclusion. They comprise our general theories of development and psychopathology, which are widely embraced by the community of analysts.

2.   What Preconditions Does the
Investigator Bring to the Study?

Inasmuch as no one approaches a case with a completely open or closed mind, we should determine just what guiding theory this analyst utilized. If he believed that incest in adolescence led to hysterical reactions with complete amnesia, then he was not quite in harmony with the community of scientists, or the way of "normal science," or the disciplinary matrix (Kuhn, 1977) in which he was operating. Although this is reasonable if one is making a discovery or offering a new idea, such moments occur at the outer boundaries of most scientific activity where challenge is expectable.

Theories of all sorts put necessary constraints on one's freedom to devise explanations for cases, and it is necessary that one indicate which one theory or several theories are under consideration. Choice of theory will be considered below, but at this point we can say that the relativism emerging with the practice of different clinicians is often a result of using theories in different ways.

3. How Can the Patient Have Been Cured if the Facts were Possibly Mistaken and/or the Theory Erroneous?

That Jungian, Freudian, and Kleinian analysts spin their own narratives in reporting the analyses of their patients is not a direct challenge to a theory of cure. The curative factor in analyses based on different theories may be the making of the story or a set of as yet unknown and unexamined points. Although several such suggestions have already been offered (Kohut, 1984), we are probably not yet at the point of determining the right theory and are thus living with a good deal of relativism about the nature of cure as discussed earlier.

4. What is the Difference Between Theories?

Hesse (1980) and Spence (1982) have noted that theories are underdetermined and thus can examine different areas of inquiry. Also, not all theories seem to work equally well. Further empirical study is needed to determine just what is being explained and how effective it may be. It is not the case that "anything goes" in an analysis inasmuch as one's commitment to any given theory is the ongoing constraint to what data are gathered and what conclusions are reached. Hermeneutics requires us to be aware of our own theoretical convictions as they contribute to our inquiry. What we bring to the field influences the dialogue with the patient, and what the patient offers us, in turn, influences us. We understand on the basis of our theories, and we interpret on the same set of theoretical patterns. The added feature of self-reflection suggested by many (e.g., Habermas, 1971) is a part of a particular theory of inquiry that seems firmly established in the tradition of psychoanalysis.

Since different analysts have somewhat different theories, quite different personalities, and even more varied degrees of self-reflection, the result of their efforts will be quite relative as well. Our conclusions from this case are that the analyst made an idiosyncratic, or at least an unusual, evaluation of the clinical evidence. His theory did not allow for the conclusions that he drew. The benefit that the patient enjoyed belongs to the wide range of unexplained or incompletely explained improvement in many such cases. The role of hermeneutics is by no means challenged from this exercise since facts are not the basis of the problem that emerges from the case; rather, the case falls outside of the constraints of the present-day theories that are utilized.

DISCUSSION

The tension between realism and relativism in psychoanalysis is a direct descendant of the philosophical struggle over the same problem. It leads to our special concerns of whether true histories can be unveiled, correct interpretations made, and rational theories formulated and followed. It raises vexing questions as to whether we manufacture fictional stories of patients' lives, and whether it matters what we say to patients or what school or discipline we seem to represent. This tension further reflects whether we are involved in a scientific enterprise regulated by a logic or sets of principles, or whether, as some insist, ours is an artistic pursuit with *ad hoc* rules and maximum appeal to creativity. Such a tension can not be resolved by merely taking a firm stand. Perhaps we can subscribe to what Williams (1977) concluded after studying the problem and deciding that no belief seemed unalterably grounded:

> [It is] a picture of human knowledge as an evolving social phenomenon. At any time, we will have a solid core of unquestioned perceptual reports, and the like, against which more marginal and less certain beliefs can be checked. But even this solid core may come in for drastic revision in the interests of deeper insight or theoretical advance. Any belief can be questioned, but not all at once. In this way, the pursuit of empirical knowledge can be seen as a rational pursuit not because empirical knowledge rests on a foundation but because . . . it is a self-correcting enterprise [p. 180].

To answer our questions in this spirit, we would say:

1.   The real events of a patient's life are significant mainly as they are experienced by the person. (See chapter 5 for an expansion of the point.) The later telling of these events is subject to constant revision according to the context of the retelling. There is no absolute truth to anyone's childhood since persons often do not "know" what happened to them: Each increment of knowledge changes the story, and

each audience or listener contributes to the tale—much in the manner Piaget details in describing the child's achievement of concrete operations (Piaget and Inhelder, 1969). Fact or fiction are relative matters constrained by coherence, continuity, and good fit, as well as by reigning theories of development that are thus true—for the time being.

2.   The interpretations we make to patients are correct not in terms of matching an external historical event to an inner experience, but in terms of the "best fit" thesis. They correspond to the requirements Freud (1918) set for furthering the analytic process, which, in turn, is constrained by the theory or theories of transference that are likewise felt to be true at a particular time in the history of our science.

3.   Our membership in a particular scientific enterprise limits and guides what we see and what we say. Whereas at one point in our science we were able to construct only one narrative with a patient, say an oedipal one, we now may enjoy a range of narratives offered by, say, Melanie Klein, Kohut, and others. These are options within the field but are not license for any and all productions, since, other theories are not currently among our acceptable notions. Acceptance occurs by way of the logic of discovery and is tested both within and outside the analytic field. For instance, if a selfobject transference discovered in analysis is posited as a part of normal development, it adds an option to our way of looking at material and is tested for endurance both within analyses and as part of developmental theories considered outside of the analytic setting. Contrast this with the counterexample that the claims of Melanie Klein do not stand up with what we know about the infant's capacity to image and reflect (i.e., fantasize) before the age of 18 months.

4.   The particular school or discipline to which we belong is important, not as a matter of allegiance, but, rather, as a way of articulating just what our theory enables us to do or to say. Thus, we have real differences and relative differences. But our awareness that knowledge is an evolving social phenomenon compels us to participate in ongoing negotiations with others of differing viewpoints. Every such negotiation can cause us to remake ourselves (Gadamer, 1975), and in this manner we thrive in the tension of reality—knowing things for sure—and relativism—knowing that things must change. More is said about negotiating later (see chapter 14).

5.   Determining whether psychoanalysis is a science of laws or an artistic effort of ad hoc rules forces a reconsideration of the puzzle of whether laws are unchangeable facts of life, such as the law of gravity, or whether they are rules created by people to meet particular situations, like the rules for playing tennis (see chapter 13). At first, a difference seems obvious, but a second look may well open up the

reality–relativism problem once again. It does seem that one gains credibility as a scientist if one discovers and follows the laws of nature rather than if one devises rules to explain problems. Psychoanalysis is caught peculiarly in this predicament and is often forced to declare itself as an art or a science by some definition visited upon it by those who know what science is or should be (Von Eckardt, 1982). The attempt to answer starts in chapter 1, but requires too much detail to be worked out here. One should at least begin, though, by determining whether the definition for scientific activity is a law of nature or a rule constructed by a society of individuals and thus is rather easily modifiable.

DISCUSSION

Many people feel that the accumulation of scientific knowledge is progressive, providing proof enough that we are embarked upon a steady advance toward knowing the truths of the real world (Popper, 1972). Others contest this view and declare that we often see an oscillation in the claims of those ultimate truths that, for instance, see the world now in one way and now in another, with no clear path of progress save that of a personal conviction (Hesse, 1980). We all, however, subscribe to a set of truths that, for the present time, dominate our lives. Occasionally, we are surprised at the findings of anthropologists who report on people who subscribe to a set of truths or world vision entirely different from ours (and we often, therefore, label these people "primitive"). A similar meeting of different worlds is a condition of psychoanalysis: usually the analyst is felt to be the bearer of reality, and the patient more often fills the role of the innocent native or perhaps the misguided and uninformed traveler. Rather than impose our truths upon patients, initially we view the world from their perspectives. This, however, is but a first step in a process designed ultimately to disabuse patients of their mistaken notions, revealed in the transference—a situation in which we assume privileged access and knowledge. Locked in as we are by our own set of convictions, our capacity to reorder the world is limited, as is that of the patients, who are similarly bound to their beliefs.

Thus, we aim to negotiate a reasonable compromise by way of interpreting what we understand to be the patient's world. This is the hermeneutic effort, and it embodies and resolves the tension between reality and relativism. Each of our realities is modified by successful participation in negotiation. Sometimes it takes years before we recognize how much these dialogues change us, just as it takes what seems an incredibly long time to confront a new scientific reality. We consider these modifications as progress, and only future generations can deliver a final and more sober judgment of the matter.

II

EMPATHY

5

Self Psychology and External Reality

Recently, rereading some of Franz Alexander's (1940) comments on Karen Horney and her work, I was struck by his insistence that Horney's emphasis on the significance of cultural factors was nowhere as original as she had claimed. Alexander felt that a thorough going discourse on cultural factors was to be found in Freud's (1916–17) delineation of the "complemental series" and his contention that neuroses were a product of constitution and experience. According to Freud, neuroses were neither exogenous nor endogenous but "if there is more of one then there is less of the other" (p. 346). These readings really jelled in my mind when I soon thereafter saw a review of a chapter (see chapter 2) I had written in a book, to which there were many contributors, in which the reviewer disdainfully called me an environmentalist. I was so pleased to see my name mentioned at all that several weeks passed before I realized that he was probably insulting me. After that wave of outrage subsided, I began to wonder if I indeed was an environmentalist. And just what is an environmentalist anyway? And is being one good or bad? My answer to these questions will have to retrace some of the ways that psychoanalytic self psychology considers the effects of the environment or the external world in the light of Freud's comments about psychopathology's being the product of both constitution and "certain detrimental (traumatic) experiences in life" (Freud, 1916–17, p. 346). It may help to bring together the questions about Horney's originality and the contributions of Kohut, who has been said to be overly committed to the role of the environment. We can then study each one's input to the problem of the complemental series, and we can fill out the issue of objective reality raised in chapter 4.

There does not seem to be agreement among schools of analytic thought about this mix of exogenous and endogenous factors. One often reads cases wherein the contributions of the real world seem of little moment, yet, in a similar manner, there is no lack of emphasis on real traumatic events to explain almost every conceivable malady. We unfortunately are not always clear about what we consider to be a real trauma save as it is evaluated retrospectively. Yet in much of general psychiatry, as opposed to psychoanalysis, there exists a whole spectrum of agreed upon stress factors ranging from physical illness to losing one's job to getting married. There is even a school of thought that assigns values to such incidents and totals a person's stress quotient. Of course, this can be seen as the extreme environmentalist position in comparison to one that focuses entirely on such issues as the intensity of the infant's drives and, so, seems to exclude the real world entirely. The problem may lie in the word "experience," which for Freud had to do with the real world's frustration of the drives for pleasure, but for those theorists who did not accept this drive-defense model, it had to do with something like the proper nutrient atmosphere for development.

Winnicott (1965) is usually cited as the analyst who most cogently brought the environment into the psychological equation. He felt that the infant and the mother were a unit, that a necessary period of holding was crucial for development or treatment, and that children had "ego needs" that transcended the instinctual ones. His acute awareness of the environmental factors in development allowed him to view reality in a way that closely approximated that of the many other analysts who considered it to be a major factor in psychopathology. It is not always clear just what Winnicott thought, since some of his writing at times tend to obscure his ideas. But it is clear that he felt "with all the good care in the world the individual child is liable to disturbances associated with conflict arising out of the instinctual life" (p. 67). He felt that what he called "personal difficulties" *had* to be resolved within the child and could not be prevented even by good management. He credited environmental issues as being the cause of psychotic or schizophrenic disorders but not for the psychoneuroses. He modified this position somewhat by stating that the environment is relatively less significant than instinctual conflicts at the later stages of growth. But he is wed to the instinct theory, he sees growth as leading inevitably to independence, and he draws the usual psychoanalytic distinction between what is inside and what is outside of the child. As we have seen, his transitional objects are an effort to bridge this conceptual quandary, one that I hope to show is handled differently by self psychology.

Experience either is or is not traumatic according to one's theory of a normative program for growth, and here is where I think self psychology has something different to say about the effects of external reality. To pursue this point, I must first outline some basic ground rules that the self psychologist subscribes to and considers fundamental.

BASIC CONCEPTS

The position of self psychology rests on a premise that is fundamental to and in accord with Freud's idea of psychic reality. It restricts its data to the observations of vicarious introspection and thus speaks only for the experience of the patient and the reconstructed experiences of the child. Thus, self psychology seems to have absolutely nothing whatsoever to say about external events per se. Whereas a sociologist or psychiatrist might collect a large sample of cases of patients who lived through something like a divorce as children and then might offer a host of generalizations about the effect of divorce on the children, only the prolonged empathic stance for a self psychologist will yield any information about the effect of that divorce on that child. Therefore, in its own radical way, self psychology is a totally intrapsychic study. Any mention of reality or experience or environment is read as having individual meaning and import; that is, it is translated back to personal experience. This is not quite so radical a position as it may appear to be. Most psychoanalysts would subscribe to a central focus on psychic reality, but they usually add the need to adapt to external reality to the mix. Self psychology suspends all evaluation of the real world to concentrate on what it means to the patient.

In apparently sharp opposition to this posture, the self psychologist is simultaneously acutely tuned in to relationships. Repeatedly the self psychologist concerns himself with such events as separation and disruption and empathic breaks. This preoccupation has led many naive observers either to consider self psychology to be a "two-body" psychology or else to equate it with various kinds of interpersonal theory. But this is because those observers tend to embrace what one psychologist called an integumentive theory of the self—you end where your skin does (Goldberg, 1983). Compare this definition to that of William James (1950), who saw the self as "the sum total of all that he can call his, not only his body and psychic powers but his clothes and his house, his wife and children, his ancestors and friends, his reputation and work, his hands and horses, and yacht and bank account." I (1983) have suggested that we use metaphors other than inside and outside to conceptualize the self. We need especially to incorporate the sense of relationships into our self psychology concept. Self psychology considers those "other persons" of relationships to fulfill roles as selfobjects or persons experienced as part of the self. We have expanded the vision of the self to a functional system that is composed of sets of relations, that is, self-selfobject relations. Disruptions or separations thereby remain within this view of the psyche and not at all in the area of activity between people; once again, as intrapsychic and not social. Words like intersubjective and interpersonal betray a mistaken notion of the area of study as lying between two persons. To be sure, the observer is a person striving to gain access to the inner world of the patient, but this is to misplace the problem, which must remain patient-centered or self-centered. When we achieve some level of understanding of another person, we become a part of that person's self-system. Self psychology redefines understanding as a communicative link that thereupon participates in the structure of the self. In what may seem to be a play on words, we do not subscribe to the view that two persons seek common agreement, but rather that one person shares in the world view of the other. Such sharing allows us to see the existence of a selfobject relationship as that which functionally expands and so structuralizes the self.

In a recent review of current thinking about depression, one psychiatrist was quoted as saying that there was no evidence for the existence of endogenous depression. For him the real world and its events always were necessary precipitants of depression. And for that essentially exteroceptive stance there is probably little argument: something always happens out there. For the introspective stance, there are only endogenous depressions, since the events that happen have no weight save in their bearing on the internal world. Most assuredly something always happens but . . . it is not out there. Whatever happens, happens *to* the patient and so *within* the patient.

The other basic tenets of self psychology have to do with laying out the pattern of the self. One needs to fashion some image to picture the complex sets of self relationships. Since all the data for this task must, of necessity, come from the psychoanalytic setting, the suggested forms of the self derive from the observed self-selfobject transferences. Kohut (1971) has listed three such narcissistic transferences and has further described how they can interact with each other. These are the mirror transference, based on a responsive selfobject; the idealized parental transference, based on an admired selfobject; and the alter-ego transference, based on an identical selfobject.

I cannot do more than mention them here, but my feeling is that they are observable developmental progressions and regressions that become reactivated in all analytic experiences. The unfolding selfobject transference is thereby read as the self pattern that is reflective of this particular patient. The temporal sequence of its emergence in the analysis is likewise reflective of the similar events in the patient's growth albeit in the reverse direction; that is, patients retrace their self-development in analysis in a backwards direction: what is first seen is what was last accomplished. For the self psychologist, the presentation of familial transferences is considered significant mainly in terms of selfobject functions, since we are studying the pattern of self-development, and we see it as built up from empathic bonds with parents and later with therapists.

These transference configurations are self-patterns; and as these are followed through time, they allow us to say that the self is an enduring temporal and spatial system. (This will be elaborated in chapter 10.) It emerges at a moment in the developmental unfolding when the selfobject relationships create a feeling of cohesion and consolidation. It moves along axes determined by innate programs and available selfobjects. It thrives in an atmosphere of sustaining selfobjects, and it suffers from the absence of these nurturing others. Thus is the door opened to our examining just what external reality means to the concept of an intact self.

External Reality

A friendly critic of self psychology said that it really only differs from other outlooks in where it draws the line. He meant the boundary line between inner and outer, subject and object, or merely the I and the you. The self psychologist does not feel that he is an external observer or a partner in a dialogue or even a separate object of transference. Rather, he is part of the system and remains so by virtue of his therapeutic presence and activity. The changes that occur during treatment are not so much due to the presence of the observer, who necessarily contaminates the field of observation (which we all now know from Heisenberg to be a universal phenomenon) but rather, for the self psychologist, the observer completes the field of study. Thus the breaks and disruptions that we see are true disorganizers, and the self psychologist's concern with fragmentation bears witness to the concept of a literal breaking-up of the self that follows the absence of the sustaining selfobject.

If we grant this freedom to draw the boundary line where we wish, then we probably can revisit the problem of external reality with certain provisos. The first is that the field of external reality will often be one that the objective observer describes as exogenous, or outside the person, whereas this may not correspond to the experience of the patient. The second is that we may still be able to formulate certain principles of reality that do correspond to meaningful issues in the patient's inner world. These, of course, will not be gross events, such as divorce, parent loss, or school graduation. Instead, they will be based on those features of our self theory that allow us to create a construct or concept of the self. They will derive from the forms of the self that we have fashioned from the observed selfobject transferences, and they will be literal, even concrete expressions of those transference configurations. Thus we should conceive of a self that positions external and internal in a new way (Goldberg, 1983), and we will likewise see that persons can be both selfobjects and "real" objects, since "person" derives from a social sense. To illustrate this, let me turn to a clinical example of a patient who seemingly organized his life around a real, traumatic external event.

CLINICAL ILLUSTRATION

This patient came to analysis because of difficulty in managing his sexual life. He was a homosexual who wished not so much to change his orientation as to gain some control over it. He had had a number of affairs, scores of one-night stands, and at times engaged in a variety of sexual activity that frightened him by its intensity and frequency. As the analysis progressed, the dominant feature of his childhood seemed to have been his parents' divorce when he was a child. One could easily see this as an organizing principle of his life, and the transference seemed to confirm his considering it as the major trauma that determined his later pathology. The question that we must address is, What exactly was it about the divorce that was so devastating? Was it really the divorce or the pathology of the parents before and after the divorce, or the inability of an immature psyche to master the event, or all of these things, or none of them? I shall concentrate on an analytic event to see if we can dissect out just what this profound external event meant to this patient.

The analysis was characterized by the patient's experience of it as protective, supportive, and important. Most of it could be considered a father transference, and much of it connected to memories of his father and their aborted relationship. Mother was an interloper and an interference. The patient's homosexuality began in his teens and dominated his life, although it remained a secret from most of his colleagues at work. As the analysis proceeded, the sexual behavior diminished, and soon the patient began to feel that he could alter his life to become heterosexual. His sexual escapades had been connected in the analysis to separations and absences, and as he developed a sense of mastery as a result of this insight, he found that he had less interest in sexual acting out. He usually idealized his analyst, who he felt to be head and shoulders above what he had heard about other analysts. Disappointments in the analyst were keenly felt and responded to, and, indeed, much of the interpretive work was done around the issue of disappointment. Here is one such example that leads to an answer about the nature of the environmental problem:

The analysis was askew. I had had to change several appointment because of a teaching schedule and had also announced my vacation plans. Although there were no missed appointments and the patient easily accommodated the changes, he made no secret of his displeasure at this irregularity. This complaining was actually an accomplishment of his treatment, since he had previously endured change in a most compliant way. On the very last day of the changes, the patient phoned and left a message to be called back. I returned his call, but missed him. A series of misconnections followed until the time of his appointment, when he called to announce that he was at home since he had assumed his appointment was much later that afternoon. I asked why he had not, during one of the many calls that he had made, simply asked that I leave a message about his appointment time. He said he had not thought of that.

The hour after the missed appointment came after the weekend, and he reported an aborted sexual encounter: He had picked up someone at a bar, brought him home, handcuffed him, and urinated in his mouth but was too angry to get any sexual pleasure from this and soon sent his companion home. He also reported that he had not masturbated all weekend. This was as rare as was his feeling of anger. His weekends for some time had been more like sexual frenzies, with no clear feeling and with little discrimination of partner. But during analysis this had markedly changed to long periods of abstinence.

One of the dreams reported by the patient following his return was as follows: "Some people are watching a movie, and I am bouncing a ball against the wall. Each bounce of the ball jars and disrupts the movie. The movie is also about me. I see myself turn into a monster in the movie, but when I turn to the audience they see only my normal face." He associated the dream and the movie to the analysis and its interruptions. He seemed to feel some culpability about missing the appointment, much as I had suggested over the phone. He associated to the visits of his father after his parents were divorced when he was about six. He had always reported these visits as erratic, and now he wondered if he perhaps had not wished to see his father. He knew his mother was openly critical of these visits. He remembered his father saying that he had stopped by the school to pick him up but had missed him. Maybe his father had been lying. He seemed unable to locate himself between mother and father in terms of wanting or not wanting to be with his father. But he did remember the sense of excitement at seeing his father's car. He would get in and either at that moment or after a short drive, his father would put his arm around him. The following hour he continued to associate to these memories and soon remembered a long forgotten incident: It was at school, and a girl told him that his father had stopped by, but had missed him. Father was angry at being stood up, just as the patient was when he missed his appointment. The monster of the dream was his rage at the disappointment, which he usually kept hidden. He recalled the times he had given up doing things in order to see his dad, who then did not show up. He was terribly lonely at times, and if his father did not visit he would go home to an empty house, his mother being at work. He was between two fears: of disappointment and of loneliness. His father was just an unreliable and undependable man who declined over the years. That is what worried him about his analyst, that is, that he would "go off."

As this material was presented and discussed by the patient, he also reported that he had had his longest period of "celibacy" in his life. He said that he had been masturbating or having sexual relations daily or several times weekly for the past twenty years. He felt very good, now that he seemingly had that under control. He next talked of his sexual behavior during those lonely periods without his father. He would go home, undress, parade in front of a mirror, wrap himself in a sheet, and arouse himself. He reported a dream of telling a woman that she was hysterical because of her father. He was that woman but was not quite so agitated and hysterical. He felt he now had self control. (This case is elaborated in chapter 15.)

The thesis suggested here has less to do with the unearthing of unconscious or repressed memories and fantasies than with the relationship between self and selfobject. This relationship is examined under the general term of structure and is seen to depend on qualities or features that describe such linkages. There is a host of words to describe these qualities, but the ones notable here—perhaps generalizable to all problems of self control—are predictability, dependability, and reliability. It is suggested that the child's relationship to the idealized other is posited on these qualities. The child must be able to anticipate the parent and so develop a feeling of a predictable world. The child must feel that the parent can be counted on, is dependable. And the parent must evidence the posture of stability and so insure reliability. No doubt these words are easily interchangeable, but the kind of linkage that guards against disappointment and loneliness is one of such predictability and reliability.

The patient just discussed did not have that bond with his father and therefore suffered a structural defect that led to a lack of self-control and a diminution of those self-functions that allow for mastery of the self. His sexual urges were not impulses that could not be controlled but rather were reactions to the selfobject that could not be controlled. With the attainment of a dependable analytic linkage, he achieved the sort of stability that might make it appear that his impulses were being mastered but in reality did not call on impulses to safeguard the self. He relived and reenacted in the transference a relationship to an idealized other who was capable of a traumatic withdrawal, which was essentially the same as the missing qualities of predictability and reliability and dependability. A long analytic experience with those qualities allows for the mastery of the problem in the analysis. The patient gains self-control as the selfobject evidences the necessary qualities. The paradoxical disappearance of those qualities in the clinical vignette was probably a dramatic re-enactment that had happened countless times before in the treatment without our awareness, but now became more fully capable of being understood and reconstructed.

The selfobject, seen as providing certain functions to the self, may suffer in our studies from a disregard of its own particular qualities. We speak of the idealized selfobject as omnipotent and omniscient, but only in our detailed clinical accounts do we describe what it—the parent—was like. So, too, do we note the disappointments and empathic breaks in the self-selfobject linkage, but this generalization is primarily detailed in the reports of the working through of the transference and seldom in the report of the qualities of the parent. There is a tendency to speak of failures of the selfobject without subjecting these failures to some sort of categorization that would allow us to form generalizations that lie between the good and the bad selfobject. This is not dissimilar to reports of the oedipal struggle, which is so global as to be meaningless, until a particular case is discussed, which is usually so local as to be of only limited scope. If we wish to attend less to the particulars of the unconscious fantasy and more to the meeting ground between the fantasy and its fate—to the impact of the environment on the child's development—then we need to develop some categories about just what is optimal for development.

In a sense, our developmental psychologists have failed us because we lack good ways of categorizing good versus bad parents except in the reports of individual cases. The qualities of optimal parenting are taken for granted or else are included under the rubric of "appropriate empathy" or "optimal frustration" or some other totally appropriate but empty term. A beginning suggestion is that one can correlate the problem of self-control with parental qualities of predictability, reliability and dependability. These attributes are related to some sort of regulating activity of the nascent self more than (say) such a quality as affection or, perhaps, power. Deficiencies in the parent's ability to be seen as someone who can be predicted to perform in a certain way, who can be relied on to be consistent in a certain set of characteristics, and who can be counted on to relate in a certain manner may transmit themselves, by way of the developmental process, in the manifest defect of self-control and self-restraint in the child and later the adult patient.

DISCUSSION

The external event of reality for Freud was whatever caused the frustration of drive gratification. His theory of drives and their vicissitudes led him to read the environment as helpful or traumatic to the degree that it aided in reasonable drive discharge and the ensuing pleasure. Most other psychoanalytic theories are of this same general thrust, since the placing of the drives at the center of human psychological function necessarily treats trauma and pathology as dependent on this central focus. All nonanalytic discussions of the effect of reality on the psyche lack meaningful content unless they can explain just what it is about any given event that is deleterious. To say that divorce is a shattering experience for a six-year-old boy is a description that floats in the air without any substantial explanation. Stress is often translated into physiological terms to lend support to its deleterious effect, but its counterpart in psychology is vague unless we can offer something more than an appeal to the fragility of the infantile psyche. Self psychology does have a different explanation. It posits the reality of others as being the structure of the self. The traumas of such external reality are thus essentially breakups of the self-structure, and the ensuing pathology is seen as self-disintegration or fragmentation. Much other pathology can be seen as efforts to forestall the breakup, as in the sexual behavior of the aforementioned patient. In this theory of the effect of environmental failure or trauma, drives are relegated to a secondary place. Expressions of drive discharge are likewise secondary phenomena and thus play a minor role in our consideration of external trauma.

But self psychology can derive principles concerning external reality, and there are ones that reflect the nature of the theory. To the degree that others function as selfobjects in one or another form of the self, we can designate and evaluate their significance. External objects to the impartial observer are internally meaningful if they function as phase specific mirroring or idealizing or twinning selfobjects. At each level of development certain essential qualities are needed for such functioning, and at each level there must exist specific forms of failures in these functions. It is the job of future generations to detail just what mirroring and idealizing, for example, consist of for a three year old versus a 13 year old. Only then can we make meaningful causal connections between events and psychopathology. The case described here is a beginning effort to unpack the general items of external trauma to yield the specific needs of the developing child in relation to the sustaining selfobject.

AND INDEPENDENCE

Before ending this chapter, I would like to say a few words about dependence and independence in the light of self psychology. It is common in most of psychoanalysis to posit a line of development toward increasing independence, certainly Winnicott felt strongly about this idea. Now, it is not always clear what analytic theorists mean about such independence, because they do not equate it with isolation from others or with a form of self-sufficiency that eliminates others from the equation of psychological health. When I ask the Mahlerians what they mean by their insistence on the individuation of the child, they have little argument with the notion that the child still needs people, but they usually claim that there is a quantitative difference. External reality becomes something that one can reckon with without undue anxiety or depression, according to the ideal definition of independence. Sometimes the problem is solved by introducing the concept of healthy dependence, which often adds up to one's being dependent on people who are not mean or sadistic or exploitative. It is not always easy to pinpoint exactly what the healthy endpoint of independence lays claim to, but seldom is it ever abandoned.

I think it is a legitimate counterposition to say that self psychology believes in the everlasting need for selfobjects. They do not simply emerge as one becomes anxious or distraught or during periods of regression. Rather they compose the self. Thus, one never becomes independent of one's selfobjects; that is a contradiction in terms since one cannot be free of oneself save in certain mystical experiences.

Wallerstein (1980) once wrote that the idea of lifelong selfobjects was not a tenable one, but that was in an essay that stressed the integration of self psychology with classical psychoanalysis. In truth, Kohut (1977) insisted that selfobjects are so vital to us that the experience of death is best understood over this very point of abandonment; and I have seen striking examples of effective psychotherapy of the dying by utilizing the principle of the reliability of the selfobject.

It still remains a proper task for self psychology to delineate what independence means to it. We say that the selfobjects change from archaic to mature and that this change is characterized by diminished urgency and greater flexibility in our deployment and use of selfobjects. But they are always there, listening to us, applauding us, ignoring us or just being with us. I think this presence adds a powerful dimension to the concept of the ameliorative effect of the very presence of the therapist. It also adds a clear dissent from the western world's picture of health as independence. It stresses interconnectedness and elevates dependence to a universal goal of well-being. Thus, independence is no more than our ability to deal with our selfobjects. In systems parlance, it is the number of options that our connections give to us, and thus it offers a more complex or variegated self-system. The freedom that we attribute to independence is this range of options so that we are not rigidly bound to only one sustaining selfobject. Loss can be managed by reinvestment rather than disintegration. But freedom can never mean being free of others. Self psychology believes that our very structure throughout life consists of our relationships. Our external reality is always an internally experienced organization, and the expansion and contraction of the self allow us to draw the ever changing boundary of the self.

SUMMARY

Heinz Kohut liked to think that he was in the mainstream of psychoanalysis. Alas, he was not always welcomed into the orthodoxy, the single claim to such a place being accorded to those faithful to Freud. Just as Alexander (1940) claimed that Horney had nothing new to say, so too do we hear the same of Kohut with the added stipulation that anything new is wrong anyway. It can be terribly hurtful to wish to make a contribution to psychoanalysis and to be rebuffed and rejected by the very group from whom one needs recognition and approval. So many of our great contributors to psychoanalysis have been castigated as dissidents that one must wonder about the root cause of such regularized exclusion. I like to think that self psychology offers us the best explanation for why we suffer so when our peers reject us: we see them as selfobjects who fail our mirroring needs. Self psychology also helps to explain why it is so painful for others to hear of our wanting to reassess Freud: that in itself is potentially damaging to an ideal that has held us together for so long and so well. But not the least of explanations that self psychology offers is that of the twin-ship transference, or selfobject: the one who makes us feel that we are among people who are essentially like us, who share a sameness that lends comfort and support to us. In that sense, external reality is alien territory and needs to be made part of an expanded self.

6

Compassion, Empathy, and Understanding

After several weeks' absence from the house, an adolescent girl's mother returns from the hospital, where she has been treated for her first schizophrenic episode. The girl, Debbie, visited her mother periodically during this hospitalization, but says that her mother was "out of it" for much of that time. Only shortly before the discharge was it possible to have even minimal conversations with her mother. When the mother returns home, the girl is away at a nearby school, where she lives during the week. Later that day she hurries back to see her mother, who was accompanied home by her sister, the patient's aunt. Instead of finding an occupied house, Debbie finds only a note, which reads, "Debbie, please have your room straightened up by the time we get back." She reads this and is instantly enraged. She immediately writes a long response to her mother, accusing her of being unfeeling and unappreciative. She was eager to see her mother after her terrible ordeal in a psychiatric hospital; she faithfully visited her even when these visits were upsetting. She was a buffer for the strain and tension between her mother and father, and for all of this she has received only this curt and nasty note. After her extended literary effort, Debbie returns to school to wait for an apology from her mother, whom she has summed up as being essentially unempathic. Later that

COMPASSION, EMPATHY AND UNDERSTANDING

evening, she receives a phone call from her father, who is now the calm arbitrator, but who confronts Debbie with *her* lack of compassion for a vulnerable and not fully recovered woman who needs things to be as calm and settled as possible. The father cannot see that he readily embraces this particular role in order to escape his usual openly depreciating and belittling attitude toward his wife. He is totally out of tune with his own participation in the family's unhappiness. Debbie reports all this to her psychotherapist and wants some understanding and clarification about who was in the right.

Debbie is not a particularly troubled girl, but for some time before beginning treatment she had anxiety attacks. After seeing a series of therapists, she found one who she felt was able to understand her. Her treatment focused initially on her ability to confront her own feelings despite efforts to placate and be liked by others.

Her therapist at this particular point in the treatment had a variety of reactions and responses. A host of options seemed to race through his head. He seemed to know how everyone must have felt: Debbie, hurt and angry and fearful of her mother's weakness; the mother, confused and embarrassed and pleading for some stability in the time to come; the father, relieved and frightened that his wife was no longer crazy and demanding a divorce, but worried that she might collapse again if pushed too severely and secretly wanting his daughter to help him preserve things as they were. The therapist also knew his particular role vis-à-vis his patient, who valued direct confrontation and longed for someone who had the answers.

This is an exercise: its intention is to clarify the substance of such qualities as compassion, empathy, and understanding, not to determine appropriate and correct definitions. It is an attempt to determine just what methods and tools therapists employ, and more properly, what they do or should do. We are all familiar with the mixture of the aforementioned qualities in a person, and we hear of the virtues of therapists who are in possession of them. All too often, a therapist is selected or rejected on the basis of these qualities, but it is not clear whether they indeed are essential to the practice of psychotherapy, nor whether they are proper concerns when teaching treatment methods to others. There does seem to be a need for clarifying and comprehending what is inborn, what is capable of being taught and learned, and what is an integral part of treatment procedures.

To begin with, the question is one of differentiating between compassion, empathy, and understanding. Debbie's therapist felt he had all three for everyone. That is, he felt he was able to feel sorry for everyone, to identify with all, and even to see how they had all gotten to where they were. Though not overwhelmed with sympathy, he could see the predicament they all were in, and he could envision his own plan to extricate his patient from her particular plight.

Compassion and sympathy are often confused or given parity with empathy and understanding. Especially in dealing with depressed or severely traumatized patients, these particular emotions are given a predominant significance. Sometimes we handle feelings of revulsion by having opposing ones of pity, and sometimes we resort to mechanisms of disavowal and preoccupation to avoid the pain of feeling sorry for others. It *is* painful at times to pity others, and usually we conceptualize the phenomenon as involving identification with the sufferer and the possible benefactor. Welfare patients notoriously evoke a multitude of responses clustering around the poles of indifference and overidentification. Workers and therapists are continuously urged to listen to their clients and to avoid being cold and mechanical, but not, on the other hand, to allow themselves to become one with them. Some therapists are uniquely comfortable with needy patients who evoke pity, and they insist that keeping one's distance is an essential ingredient in assisting the unfortunate. No treatment is ever free of demands for sympathy or of realistic entreaties for it, and these demands often take the form of asking to "be understood." An understanding therapist becomes one who is appropriately in agreement with the patient's own feeling of misfortune.

Let me illustrate with an unusual example one dilemma concerning sympathy for a patient or client. The following vignette demonstrates the trouble that results from helping without listening. It comes from a class given by a social worker to students and was designed to teach them how to appreciate the transference.

> Many years ago I met a social worker who had had her throat cut from ear to ear by a client but who survived to tell the story. She had worked for a welfare department where a man applied for help. He had a large family and was a low-wage earner, and she had a great deal of sympathy for his needs. Therefore, she did more for him than duty required of her and gave him the maximum grant possible. The one day when she refused an excessive request, he took out a knife and cut her throat. Later she could only explain his action by saying that the man was insane. Yet during several years of contact she had never thought he was.

The author of this vignette cites this case as being one of the worker failing to consider the re-creation of the infantile expectations in this client. She says that in order to recognize such feelings, one must develop an ability to listen and help a client obtain an emotional reeducation. This advice is oversimplified, to be sure, but it does point out that an awareness of transference and its reasonable interpretation can be effective. It does not, however, give advice about assessing the psychological state of the client or about technically handling the problem.

Other than praying that such naive advice is confined to only a few select social work training centers, one cannot but wonder if the author is suggesting that anyone to whom we are nice or overly kind might yet cut our throat if we fail to listen and to reeducate the person. I cite this illustration because of the subtle and peculiar harshness of its author, who shifted the problem to the worker. She may have been errant in giving too much, but she hardly needed a critique of *her* performance. The problem she faced was not an inability to listen, but not knowing what to do with what she heard. This leads us to the issue of empathy and the unreasonable position it has come to assume for some therapists.

Just as the therapist's sympathy for Debbie and her family was not enough to do the job of treatment, and just as the social worker's kindness for her client led her astray, so is empathy alone insufficient for a proper therapeutic mix—although it is often evoked as the crucial ingredient. Indeed, empathy has become the new key for excellence in the science of psychological assistance, and no greater blow can be given to a therapist than the accusation of being unempathic.

Empathy can be defined as vicarious introspection. As the often abused phenomenon of self-observation hosted a psychology based on its particular findings, so too does vicarious looking inward become the new tool of our analytic psychology. From the inception of the give-and-take in the mother-child relationship, developmental psychologists have been able to trace the growth, nurturance, and deviance of this particular tool of human communication[1]. It has involved a partial identification of one with another, a transient merger of self and object, or

---

[1] The concept of a developmental line of empathy can be seen to be gathering credibility, although some writers avoid seeing this mode of communication in this manner. Stern (1985) prefers to speak of attuning behavior, which is likened to a matching of feeling; the affect rather than the behavior is matched. He also notes states of unauthentic attunement and overattunement. However, he differentiates the state of attunement from empathy, which has a sequence of emotional resonance. This knowledge is subsequently integrated into an empathic response, and there then ensues a transient role identification (p. 145). Cognitive processes are involved in empathy. Attunement, for Stern, need not proceed toward empathic knowledge in response.

Basch (1983), as well, differentiates affective communication from empathy, with the latter demanding a separation from feeling and an awareness of the significance. He feels that empthy is the *process* of coming to know and can be unconscious. He later says that a line of affective development ends in empathic understanding, and thus he leans in the direction of a developmental line for empathy.

perhaps even an externalization of a model of another person. Many mechanisms have been suggested, and there is some truth in them all. Some people are unbelievably empathic; some are quite unable to participate in this activity. There is no doubt that to some degree it can be taught and developed. We can hope that one day it will be more commonly accepted as a tool in other scientific endeavors. But just as Bettelheim (1982) cautioned about love, empathy is not enough.

To return to our original example, Debbie's psychotherapist felt that he could be empathic with her. He had the clear conviction that she was angry at being unappreciated, and that she had temporarily suspended her realistic assessment of her mother's condition because of her narcissistic rage. Such bursts of anger were not unusual for Debbie, but often they became diverted to something other than overt aggression. To complicate (or perhaps to simplify) the picture, it seemed clear as well that most of this anger was directed at the therapist himself, who was about to leave for a vacation. He could imagine how it feels to go from being the center of attention and concern to being abandoned and neglected. He was able to move back and forth between sensing how Debbie must feel and how *he* felt as a partial instigator of Debbie's upset. He also found himself quite critical of what Debbie had done and somehow felt that he had to take some sort of a position in regard to her behavior. Perhaps, he thought, he was too much identified with the mother.

The social worker was not in as enviable a position as this therapist. She did not have much difficulty feeling empathy with her clients, but she rarely sensed their rage at their own depreciated position. The problem was less that this client has been infantilized to an oral dependent stance than that he felt persistently and unflaggingly humiliated. No one can long maintain self-esteem when one depends on an outstretched hand, and we are all familiar with the paradox that small doses of gratification or minor avenues of hope serve primarily to increase rather than diminish violence. Of course, one cannot say in retrospect if a more sensitive and attuned worker could have prevented this man's psychotic outburst. Perhaps she could have explained to him that she knew how he must feel. My own suspicion is that the entire structure of institutional giving is unempathic or insensitive, and one should be wary of blaming those who participate in the machinery. It is better to train people to recognize severe psychopathology than to foster in them the hope that by comprehending transference, they will be able to help lifelong traumatic personalities. I tend to agree with the social worker that the client was insane; I would caution the author that we seldom drive people to insanity by way of kindness.

But here my empathy is with the worker, and in Debbie's case the psychiatrist's was with the mother. The psychiatrist's quandary highlights a problem of empathy, because often it is plentiful and we are not sure of what to do with it. That is to say, we must move from a viewpoint that concentrates on experience to one that has more scientific credibility, as was discussed in chapter 1. Of course this is what psychology and, more particularly, psychoanalysis has always sought. To develop this point, I must digress to a debate that has gone on in psychoanalytic circles for many years: whether psychoanalysis is a psychology of understanding or of explanation. It must be noted that a psychology of understanding fell into disrepute historically because it was felt to be basically unscientific. Hartmann, in his famous article entitled "Understanding and Explanation" (1927) traced the origins of understanding psychology from its early advocate, Dilthey, who emphasized a primarily descriptive psychology, to Jaspers, who added the crucial ingredient of empathy. Hartmann feels that understanding must be rejected as *the* method of psychology because it is fraught with errors and because it fails to recognize that psychoanalysis is a natural science with a body of laws and regularities. Understanding, in this context, is more or less equated with seeing the connections between meanings. It is not restricted to conscious or expressed meaning but does encompass all the conditions of the psychoanalytic situation. Jaspers would say that understanding psychology could never lead to the formation of theories. Hartmann would say that an explanatory psychology must do just that. For Hartmann and others who followed him, psychoanalysis is an explanatory psychology that empirically tests hypotheses and validates theories. He pointed out, for example, that many psychoanalytic concepts do not point at all to understandable connections as in the elements of the psychoanalytic theory of dynamics and energetics (Hartmann, 1927).

It is unnecessary to trace the probable basis for this psychoanalytic dilemma or to list the various proponents of one or the other position. Some understood and others explained, and each event usually took place in a different conference or case presentation. What was a division in the delineation of the proper boundaries of psychoanalysis became a division in the practice of analytic therapy. One choice was involved in empathic understanding, which, according to Jaspers, "leads us right into the mental connections themselves." However, people were so suspicious of errors of self-judgment that they insisted that the scientific goal of understanding laws and predictable patterns of occurrences was the only worthwhile endeavor. Sometimes we would witness heroic efforts of reconciliation by the proponents of a purely scientific attitude in which we heard that a patient's ego would beseech his superego to neutralize his aggressive energy, rather than that someone would simply be telling himself to calm down. On other occasions, we would be captured by the wizardry of the intuitive therapist, who could only smile secretly when asked to explain just what had transpired in the latest miracle cure. No one trained in social work, psychology, or psychiatry seemed to escape the dilemma of the two worlds of theory and practice.

It is no secret that a more satisfactory solution was offered by Kohut (1973), who suggested that psychoanalysis should both understand and explain:

> While scientific methodology in the field of psychology formerly could be applied to comparatively simple data concerning the behavioral surface, psychoanalysis undertakes the scientific exploration of the complex and significant dimensions of human life in depth. It has found the bridge between the two opposing approaches—understanding and explaining to the inner life of man. It has achieved the first valid integration of, on the one hand, the observer's ability to understand the endless variety of psychological experiences through introspection and empathy with, on the other hand, the theorist's ability to conceptualize these data at higher levels of abstraction and to formulate their interrelatedness within a system of experience-distant explanations. Mystical introspection may understand but it does not explain; and pre-analytic scientific psychology explains, but it does not understand. Psychoanalysis, by contrast, explains what it has understood [p.14].

Kohut's stance in allowing introspection to take its place in a scientific discipline has implications for the practice of psychotherapy. It defines our primary tool, data gathering, but it simultaneously insists that we formulate valid generalizations about the observations we make. Empathy becomes modified, or it may develop into cognitive empathy. Those images, ideas, and concepts we gather by vicarious introspection must be examined, clarified, and scrutinized to see how they fit the theories derived from or postulated about such observations. This is merely an elaborate way of saying that we urge everyone to examine carefully how he feels and what he thinks about patients. Ultimately these things must make sense and be communicable. Kohut differentiates levels of generalization in terms of experience-near phenomena and experience-distant abstractions or theories. (See chapter 7 for an examination of these terms.) Others would argue that theories often move between such levels and that any generalization is but a description of regularity. Further, the argument states that we had best steer clear of abstractions such as energy concepts, which primarily lead one to think one knows more than one does. No matter that the controversy may be about the nature of a theory of treatment, we cannot entirely dispense with theory, and we must always return to it to coordinate and validate our empathic and intuitive reactions and hunches. Such an endeavor allows us to reexamine the opening clinical example, in order to determine whether the use of theory, or of the explanation part of analytic inquiry, may be of help.

Debbie's therapist felt that her reaction had merit but that she was tactless in its execution. A variety of explanatory concepts were entertained, ranging from the way Debbie usually behaved when angry, to the fact that the anger seemed displaced from the therapist to the mother, as well as to the particulars of the transference relationship to the therapist, which was the meaning that he had for this patient. It was clear that Debbie's reaction was one of narcissistic injury and likewise that the therapist had been functioning as a narcissistic object, possibly an ideal parent, for her. At that point, the therapist realized that Debbie feared for her own sanity. He recognized that her need for the therapist, coupled with the anticipation of his absence, terrified her. He understood that she doubted her own capacity to carry on without him. Such a fear was immeasurably intensified by the craziness of the person with whom she had been identified and who represented to her, her own destiny and fate. Debbie's plea to the mother was that she be realistic, stop being crazy, listen to her daughter's needs. All these messages were directed to her own amalgam of mother-therapist-daughter.

No doubt this insight was available to many who first heard of this episode. Unfortunately, explanations always sound more labored than they actually may be in the immediacy of comprehending a complex situation. The steps that go into building up a complex configuration are not necessarily those that are consciously communicated, and no doubt the therapist had a good deal of preconscious awareness (if we can use that word) of Debbie's predicament. The conscious elaboration of the conclusion involves avoiding closure until all the pieces fit together. Our empathic understanding is a process of matching complexities, a process eased by our similarities to each other and one that is inherently imperfect and incomplete. At various points, however, the elements fall into place, and a fit is attempted and made. Hence the plea for a pragmatic approach that aims for the best fit. The demands on the therapist are to tolerate the anxiety of forestalling closure and to exercise all options in order to accomplish a matching configuration. One test of a successful comprehension of another person's feelings is that more information becomes available. Understanding means connecting meanings so that one can achieve a greater grasp of a situation, which should lead to its clarification. One result of the therapist's awareness of Debbie's fearful picture of herself was, later, an explanation of why she had seen so many therapists before finding one who seemed to please her. She was not a fickle girl, nor was she someone who had a notion of an ideal therapist. Rather, Debbie was trying to see how and what these therapists thought about her. In the broadest sense, one could say she was wary of acceptance or rejection, but in truth, she wanted to know whether they thought she was crazy. Earlier, one excellent therapist was dropped immediately because, Debbie later confessed, he seemed so worried and concerned, like Debbie.

The last part of the therapeutic exercise is really the easiest: it concerns telling the patient what you know. Some literature on tact (Poland, 1975) has attempted to separate it as the efferent or motor part of the arc of empathy. Such a separation, however, may be artificial or unnecessary, since one can seldom exercise but one branch of this continuum. Debbie's therapist told her that he felt she had acted incorrectly in the note to her mother and that she knew this. She immediately agreed. He then said that she was upset about his upcoming vacation because she was still unsure of herself and probably was very scared that one day she would be like her mother. Debbie very much doubted that she was that dependent on her therapist. but she had little argument with the rest. She was relieved that her anger was not a central issue.

Essentially, Debbie's therapist told her all that he knew or was fairly sure of. He said nothing about his own feelings, since he felt she had enough to worry about herself. He made no interpretations about her childhood or infancy because those would, at this time, be conjecture. The overall aim of this transmission of information to the patient was to help her to see herself differently, to gain a new self-concept. Debbie saw her frightened and crazy part and her independent and self-sufficient aspect, and she continued to build up a coherent image or picture of just what she consisted of.

In a sense, all therapy is devoted to enabling patients learn more about, and build up new concepts of, themselves. At times we say that our aim is that patients become empathic with themselves, to understand themselves, and ultimately to take over for themselves the task of therapist. Indeed, this process of introspection and empathy, followed by the ability to explain things to oneself, is the essence of how we progress in treatment; it is also the goal of treatment. We strive for patients to see themselves differently, just as normal growth and development are stepwise achievements toward greater self-comprehension.

Compassion or sympathy in psychotherapy is like politeness: it is a natural part of interpersonal harmony, but probably has nothing whatever to do with psychotherapy. Unfortunately, it has addictive properties and can become an indulgence for many people. Also unfortunately, it can become a substitute for treatment. The antidote for it is not, however, the cold and impersonal posture of pure interpretation. Psychoanalysis can be caricatured in the image of the surgeon whose scalpel is a cutting interpretation. Too often a sadistic attack is rationalized by calling it straightforward and truthful. Neither overkindness nor cruelty qualifies for the therapist's armamentarium; rather, we must educate ourselves and others to developing empathy. Empathy is a tool, a way of amassing data and transmitting information. It is hardly a virtue, and its drawback is that it sometimes hides a deficiency of cognitive comprehension. Understanding is so confusing and all-encompassing a word that it carries no argument. Everyone wants to understand, and everyone wants to be understood. But for us, the proper use of that idea must be in tandem with explanation. We must reach for cognitive modes of grasping the meaning of things, and we must be able to tell others what sense we have made of them.

Ultimately psychotherapists deal with ideas or concepts and not with chemicals or energy transfer, or even microscopic entities. Therefore, our efforts should result in changes in these ideas or in conceptual shifts in our patients. Our work is neither that of laboratory science nor of mystical transformations. That we are human and subject to human reactions is both a boon to our efforts and a possible pitfall, but it is no license to be lax in our attempts to chart the methods of our work. It is no secret that psychoanalysis and analytic psychotherapy are seen as struggling to establish themselves as scientific enterprises. For this reason they sometimes emphasize a variety of activities peculiar to so-called natural science and speak of mental structures and energies and processes with clearcut causal connections, so that they seem to be as respectable as organic chemistry. When people stop arguing over whether there really is such an entity as the ego or superego, they sometimes retreat to vague or global prescientific or nonscientific ideas, such as being in touch or in tune. This is but a short step toward convictions like the crucial ingredient in psychotherapy is kindness, or openness, or some other apparent virtue. The most difficult task is to bridge what seem to be opposing issues, in order to move toward a scientific goal of psychotherapy. We must be able to explain what we understand without resorting to neurological reasons for specific behavior or falling back on intuitive, inexplicable wizardry. As far as wizardry is concerned, as Ludwig Wittgenstein (1922) said, ''Whereof we cannot speak, thereof we must be silent.''

7

Experience: Near, Distant, and Absent

In *The Mind in Conflict*, Brenner (1982) presents a very brief clinical vignette of a young man in analysis who, as he lay on the couch, picked at a sore on his hands or face, rubbed a shoulder injured some years earlier, or gave some other indication of pain or injury. His attention was directed to this behavior, and the fact that these gestures were unconsciously designed to gain sympathy was made apparent. The further elaboration of this behavior had to do with guilt over actions that would be disapproved of by the analyst, and later it was seen as a transference of a pattern of behavior involving self injury following a fantasied violent conflict between the patient and an opponent. The patient's competitive strivings were directed against an older brother and were inhibited and dealt with by self-punishment. All this was confirmed and filled out by a host of other clinical evidence.

In this case we may begin with the statement that the patient's gestures are signs or a form of communication that we, in turn, read. This is the field of semiotics, or the science of reading, interpreting, and decoding the messages or meanings contained in signs and symbols and language. Not everyone would attach significance to the patient's picking at a sore, and certainly not everyone would see it in the same way as did Brenner. He was, however, clearly intent on determining the meaning of this form of behavior, and he began with a series of suppositions and assumptions. Some might question whether he was involved in an introspective or subjective assessment of the patient, but the ensuing material does seem to confirm that his aim was to determine just what these signs meant to the patient. His orientation was to enter the patient's inner world, and a comparison to an evaluation of someone picking at a sore by a dermatologist should dispel any notion that this was anything but a depth psychological approach.

One simple assumption (or prejudice) that depth psychologists bring to bear on clinical material is that the patient is, at some level, telling the truth; others would say that the patient is always, in one way or another, dissembling. Allowing for all sorts of compromises in these two positions (i.e., the lie covers the truth, they sometimes lie and sometimes are truthful, etc.), one remains with the conclusion that these are quite different approaches. Even if one feels that one position is more salutary than the other, it remains a value-laden approach that is at the same level of significance as its opposite. Essentially these are two different theoretical stances or what some would call "experience-distant generalizations" that have no intrinsic worth save their utility in the task of allowing us to better pursue our decoding of the patient's signs. The one that insists that the patient is indicating that he is suffering is by no means equivalent to the one that says he is basically fending off his aggressive urges. They may or may not come together at some deeper level, but at first reading they remain quite disparate. In all likelihood every succeeding step of inquiry is guided by powerful suppositions or prejudgments. Our experience-distant concepts thereby determine what we see.

As Brenner's account proceeds, he introduces the concepts of sympathy and guilt. The first is said to be the motive of the patients vis-à-vis the analyst, and the second is a complex affective state that the patient is experiencing. Each word is a carrier of introspectively oriented frameworks, and it is said that each idea is abundantly confirmed by succeeding clinical evidence. One must be oriented to the feeling state of the patient to reach these conclusions, and yet they also seem quite dependent on the assumptions made (and confirmed) about how the patient got where he is: assumptions about competition with an opponent and the like. That is to say, one cannot simply "read off" a state of guilt without a host of orienting and guiding notions about human behavior and dynamics. The data are carried along by the theory.

Without much difficulty, an alternative set of assumptions and conclusions could be reached. One could say that the patient's behavior is that of a mistreated person who feels victimized and abused by a powerful opponent. It seems plausible, if not reasonable and convincing, that the patient is demonstrating the state of the analysis and the transference. He takes his analyst's comments and interpretations as attacks and subsequently feels injured and wounded. His sores are evidence of his hurts, and his rage is but a response to this series of attacks. Thus, the patient correctly perceives an aspect of the transference that re-creates the history of his childhood. It was not so much his competitive strivings that led to guilt, but his rage at mistreatment that caused his anguish. He was not so much the perpetrator as the victim. He is, indeed, locked in combat with a superior opponent. His older brother may well have been the tormentor of his early life, just as his analyst is in his adulthood. The image of self-injury following a violent conflict between himself and an opponent is an accurate portrayal of the transference and, hence, an accurate portrayal of his childhood experience.

Any experienced clinician can weave a variety of tales around patient productions, and it is futile to argue the value of one tale over another. Psychoanalysis has long struggled with the problems of alternative explanations and has a series of devices to allow one to select one over another. This exercise is not designed to prove the worth of one over another but rather to question the reasons that honest, empathic observers manage to reach such diverse conclusions. If it is plausible to see the different results, then it is equally plausible to ask how this could happen.

THE CATEGORIES OF THEORIZING

There is at least some uncertainty within the field of psychoanalysis about the exact meanings of such phrases as experience-near, experience-distant, experiential, subjective, objective, as well as "knowledge by acquaintance" and "knowledge by description." At the extreme, there is a sharp difference of opinion about the sources and form of psychoanalytic knowledge or data, with one school embracing phenomena that can be experienced while another insists on facts that exist outside the mind or can be objectified and so minimizes the experiential. Some of the difficulty lies in attempts to bypass philosophical discussions about these issues, some derives from the sort of scientific training analysts have in their background, and some comes from a certain casualness in the use of words and phrases. The problem has recently resurfaced with the popularity of self psychology and its emphasis on empathy alongside a series of discussions about the hermeneutic status of analysis. It has led to a concern with the primacy of subjective, or personal, truths in psychoanalysis as well as, or perhaps versus, an equal emphasis on replicable and verifiable data that are felt to be more impersonal, that is, objective. The major point of contention seems to be the weight and significance given to the word "experience" and its definition. Psychoanalysts argued over it when Alexander (1940) opted for a corrective emotional experience, shied away from it when phenomenology claimed it as the lynchpin for their psychiatric approach, and embraced it when considering it as the basis of psychic organization (Atwood and Stolorow, 1984).

There is some unanimity that in the selection of a therapist for a patient the two people should be able to share experiences. We hear of trying to fit a patient with a therapist in terms of a similarity in lives. If one is referring a patient who has suffered a particular vicissitude in life, such as a loss or a unique sort of challenge, we often hear of efforts to find a therapist who has gone through a similar ordeal and so will understand the patient. There is a conscious effort made to match the patient with a therapist who has mastered the painful issues of living and so can, if not advise or tutor, at least comprehend what the patient is going through. I remember one of my very first patients in practice, the father of a self-destructive and alienated adolescent, asking me if I had any children. I took refuge behind the anonymity screen, but privately I insisted that I could certainly understand parenting without being a parent. Alas, only being a parent could convince me of the folly of that posture. But I could never be sure if that conviction was a narcissistic accretion of being more worldly or if there indeed was a genuine distinction, between knowledge by acquaintance and knowledge by description—between knowing a lemon by its taste or just hearing about it from others. Though this is folklore, the underlying belief is that one needs to have some sort of similar experience to know someone else. My parenting is not equal to that of others but enables us to approximate some mutual know-how. Just how we do this seems to go beyond our having the same experience.

The puzzle of how we know what we know is not one that a psychoanalyst can solve. The philosophers have themselves hardly reached consensus in even defining what knowledge is. But perhaps analysts can agree, or at least not disagree, on some definitions and distinctions between what we do (or seem to do) and what we definitely do not do.

SOME DEFINITIONS AND DISTINCTIONS

An experience is something that has been lived through. Some authors elaborate that definition by the addition of "or observed." The usual features that fill out the definition have to do with some aspect of feeling, and here we seem to agree that some affective component is needed to qualify an event as an experience. Freud (1913) asked his patients to report their associations as if watching the landscape on a passing train, and it can be argued that such mere reporting or observing may diminish the acting-out component of behavior; that is, we talk about rather than do. But observing does seem to allow emotionality to qualify as an experience, albeit in regulated or manageable form, as any theatregoer can testify. The "willing suspension of disbelief" allows us to participate vicariously in the events on stage and thus to *have* an experience, even if we call it a diluted and controlled and manageable one.

Analytic observation seems to be of a piece with this particular idea of experience. The analyst listens and observes but is still in a state of feeling, even though involved in "even-hovering attention." But the writers who divide knowing by experience from knowing by description say that only the former is telling, and thus only the analyst who has had the experience or its equivalent can really know. Being in love is wholly different from reading about being in love. Of course, that distinction rests on a logical error. Both activities involve experience, but they differ not in the matter of love but in the matter of doing versus reading. I can understand a patient in love if I have been in love, and I can understand one who reads about it if I have done that. All knowing for the analyst, however, ultimately involves doing. We observe by analogous or similar or identical experiences, and in this manner we "know" what we may but see. Thus, mere "knowledge by description" seems lacking in experience and gives rise to the question of whether we can truly know the taste of a lemon without tasting it. We can approach it but can never completely capture it because of the missing experience. If, then, the crucial item is experience, just what should we make of that? And is it possible that knowing without experiencing is sufficient? Our tentative conclusion seems to be that some experience is necessary for knowing, but they are not yet equivalent. Something seems to be added to experience to produce knowledge, but we first must review the ideas of those who argued that experience was quite enough.

EXPERIENCE: NEAR, FAR AND RELEVANT

Edmund Husserl was the philosopher who founded phenomenology, the school that places the experiential at the center of investigation and concern. For Husserl (see Bubner, 1981) the concern with the subject, a concentration that Descartes initially offered in order to arrive at reality by way of doubt, was carried still further to a concern with the center of all knowing. Husserl asked that we suspend our focus on the world as such in favor of an investigation of what consciousness itself is. By a series of maneuvers called "bracketing," he urged grasping the essential nature of consciousness, that is, the capture of pure consciousness irrespective of the world. All phenomena in the world are thus secondary to one's intentions toward them. And all other persons come together by a joining of subjective states, through intersubjectivity. In a somewhat contradictory manner, Husserl developed phenomenology as the fundamental science of knowing (Barratt, 1984) by assuming a match between the world and our phenomenological investigations of it. In the words of phenomenologist Merleau-Ponty (1962), "Everything that I know of the world, even through science, I know on the basis of a view which is my own, or an experience of the world without which the symbols of science would be meaningless" (p. 17).

An exercise suggested by phenomenology is that of looking at a cube. You may see only two or three sides of the cube but imagination carries you into a six-sided visualization of the figure. If the cube is colored, then you likewise attribute to the entire form the same color that you see. In this way we actively participate in creating what we see, since the portion that is visually accessible is but the entry to a full comprehension, that is, an experience of the cube. This approach echoes that of Gibson (1966), for whom perception is an active participation in the surround rather than a passive registration. Most students of perception now see the image as a construction of the mind instead of a replication of an unalterable object. This idea seems to lend more weight to the experiential component to observation and to underscore that an active "being in the world" is the sole route to knowing the world.

Thus, experiencing, in this frame of reference, is clearly a part of—or for some the sum and substance of—knowing. This is validated in Piaget's (Piaget and Inhelder, 1969) study of the growth of cognition, wherein the early sensorimotor behavior of the child becomes the basis for all further learning. The later stages of cognition can be seen as growing out of or succeeding or layering over the sensorimotor schema, but the earliest action patterns are reactivated in all later stages.

If we agree that the access to knowledge is experience, then it is an easy task to differentiate experience-near from experience-distant and nonexperiential. This last term fits areas where there is no clear relevance to experience. That immediately raises the question of just what these areas are, since there are many studies in neurophysiology that have to do with functions involved in knowing and learning; and we may quickly return to the conundrum about defining the boundaries of fields. Relevance to experience, of which we shall say more later, has no easy indication for limiting an arena of inquiry, but it certainly is not the same as utilization of experience, which seems true of all knowing. Thus, nonexperiential is a wastebasket term for areas that seem outside of our range of interest for the time being.

The term experience-near was popularized by Kohut (1959) in his studies of the methodology of psychoanalysis. It has been taken up by others, like Stern (1985) in infant observation, and, not surprisingly, is a value-laden term. In contrast to experience-distant, it is felt to be a desirable way of data gathering. Experience-distant was meant by Kohut to encompass concepts that were generalizations, such as ego and superego, and so covered wide areas of facts and observations. These ideas were distanced from the immediacy of perceiving or knowing and were employed in the service of a convenience of description. A host of observations could be swept up in a single word, much as all science aims for generalizations or abstractions that can apply over diverse fields of examination.

Such generalizations, of course, have a proper and necessary place in science. The unfortunate negative valuation that may be associated with them is often a result of a misplaced usage; that is, seeing an ego in a patient can be a way of avoiding seeing something more easily described in terms of immediacy and common parlance. This misplaced usage leads to the logical conclusion that one is unable to take an experience-near stance, either because one is defending against the experience or because one wishes to make a statement that has a wider applicability than to a single case. The former is familiar to every psychoanalyst. The latter merits further study.

Before pursuing the role of generalization in observation, we should reaffirm that the picture of phenomenological investigation is challengeable not because of its emphasis on experience but because of its exclusive concern with subjectivity. Subjectivity is usually defined as the study of conscious states, and here we divide phenomenology into the conscious states that compose it. One is concerned with one's own consciousness as well as with the consciousness of others. A psychoanalytic concern with subjectivity would be an examination of self-consciousness as well as of another's consciousness, accomplished by what is usually called intersubjectivity. The criticism of such a form of inquiry lies in its restriction to consciousness, which naturally lops off what seems to be the main area of psychoanalytic concern, the unconscious. One could posit an extension of subjectivity to encompass the dynamic unconscious, but this seems to run contrary to the usual considerations of subjective states, which are considered as owned by the self or by part of the self or as capable of being reflected upon by the self. This extension, in any case, calls for a revision of the concepts of subjectivity and intersubjectivity, since the use of introspective data to see oneself or vicarious introspection to perceive another would make psychoanalysis little more than ordinary conversation.

Kohut (1959) solved the problem by stating that the preconscious and unconscious, as concepts, are approached with "introspective intention" and are considered within a framework of introspected or potentially introspected experience. For him, introspection and empathy were essential to psychological observation. Thus, we can probably make a case for a subjectivity that is potentially graspable by introspection and empathy. To do so would seem to demand a set of concepts that, according to Kohut, are "further from the observed facts" and are those abstractions and generalizations that are more or less directly related to the observable phenomena. It seems to follow logically that this is what Kohut meant by experience-distant, that is, those concepts or devices that he described as the framework of introspected or potentially introspected experience. Experience-distant, then, refers to the theories or generalizations that we use to allow us to approach and ultimately "observe" experience-near facts or phenomena. To recapitulate: Experience-distant is the means by which we gain experience-near data. Experience-absent is what we choose to consider to be beyond our realm of inquiry.

THE ROLE OF LANGUAGE

The limits of our language are the limits of our world. So said Wittgenstein (1953) and so insists the study of language. One of the arguments leveled against a pure phenomenology that aims to reflect pure experience involves the role of language or any form of semiotic communication. On one hand, phenomenology is said to exist without a concern for the object or the thing out there and to concentrate instead only on the experiencing subject. It thus can dispense with a need to categorize the objects of the world. To be sure, it needs to be able to articulate the subjective meanings, but that can be seen as putting language in a secondary place. But how can one begin even to categorize a subjective feeling or choose one feeling over another or decide that one is possessed of a feeling without a language? How can experience become more than a vague sort of physiologic unrest until it is shaped by language. Just as Goethe insisted that everything factual is already theoretical, so too must one say that every subjective experience is already framed by a theory expressible in language. These frames, or structures, are what Heidegger (see Bubner, 1981) referred to as "the forestructures" of understanding and what Kohut called the frameworks of introspection. They make up the guides or maps or theories that compose the preunderstanding that data fits into. They are the indispensable givens that are the background for all accumulation of information. One cannot see a cube or feel sympathy in oneself or perceive guilt in another without a precommitment to cubes, sympathy, and guilt. These are not givens, and they do not exist outside of language, because our language determines the dimensions of our world.

The world is never directly revealed to us; it is mediated or represented. We make no direct observation; we only form images based on expectations or preconceptions. As we grow, our view of the world is mediated by a system of representations that reside mainly in language. Language sits between us and whatever is out there and soon is a powerful determinant in shaping our work.

If one agrees to the preexistence of language, need one necessarily be committed to a complex set of ideas such as a theory? The argument can be raised that there are a multitude of words that are commonly used and have agreed upon definitions that can live free of intricate concepts. We know that the child's beginning use of single words is really a miniaturized sentence; that is, "bear" means "I want the bear." So, too, are most words embedded in sentences and thereby gain their meaning in context. No single word can stand alone outside of a dictionary; it is only in the intent of the usage of the word that we are able to say what it means.

When Waelder (1962) proposed his thesis about our ordering of data, he suggested that we observe single facts, which then become arranged in patterns in ascending order up to our generalizations, theories, values, and even our view of the world. His axiom, that one builds from simple facts outward to more and more complex configurations, is a product of logical positivism (a scientific set of principles) that held that facts could be validated or disproved. We now know that every fact, every perception, is directed and defined by a guiding theory. Therefore Waelder's ideas are essentially topsy-turvy. We begin with our values, and no bit of observed data is ever free of these issues, such as wanting to do good, wanting to make money, and so forth. We move on to our theories, our clinical generalizations, and finally to an observed incident that is thoroughly theory impregnated. Thus, our single and isolated bits of clinical data are part of a complex, preexisting network of values and theories.

The question next arises, Why do certain experienced clinicians in psychoanalysis claim that they rarely use or think of any theoretical concepts or terms; that they have effectively dispensed with theory? One study (H. Paul, personal communication, 1986) showed that clinicians used and spoke of theory more when first starting to practice but did so less and less as time went on and their experience grew. Paul suggested that what occurs is a gradual absorption of theoretical ideas into everyday practice until there exists no clear demarcation between what is felt to be theoretical and what is felt to be obvious or natural or apparent on the surface. Thus, when experienced clinicians claim that they can dispense with theory, most likely their theories are no longer distinguishable from a general approach to the patient. A novice coming across the same patient will experience a disparity between theory and observation, since there is an attempt to fashion a proper fit. But the same process occurs more easily and naturally with time and usage. Here the experience of a situation blurs the theory and the fact, so that they appear as one. Thus, for a novice, a selfobject is an experience-distant term that needs some familiarity to effect a happy union, whereas someone who has lived with the term for a long time will see it as experience-near. But this is a personal assessment that robs the term of its place as a concept. Terms like selfobject and the ego's integrative function are generalizations that wait to be filled by particulars. Thus we can say that a concept or idea that needs to be filled in is experience-distant; once filled, it is experience-near. *All* experience-near phenomena, then, are already carried by a host of values and generalizations that are implicit except for the period of adjustment to their use that requires that they be explicit. But ultimately all concepts or experience-distant terms can be freed of the singular facts that they embrace.

Language can manage a remarkable economy of effort since a whole set of concepts can be encompassed in a single word. The problem occurs when one attempts to articulate the various levels, such as those Waelder (1982) suggested, and communicate them to others. Such an effort lends itself to the claim that one is working without theory or values when, in truth, they more likely have been lost to discourse. Too often it is said that "higher-order theories limit our vision and cannot be relied upon" (Tolpin, 1986). It is more accurate to say that one is not able to articulate clearly just what theories are being employed, since they are so embedded in the "lower order" ones that are said to be utilized. The fact remains that the theory impregnation of facts does not allow for any such entity as a "lower-order theory" that sits freely by itself. Rather higher-order theories too are part of the inverted pyramid of values and theories that guide any sort of percept or observation. The attempt to "order" theories according to levels is really an effort (albeit necessary) to impose one's personal theory and values on observations. There is no inherent level or order to anything except as it fits into the theory brought to the field. The sore that the patient picked at can be everything to the dermatologist and hardly anything to the analyst. But *anything* can limit our vision, and we should not blame the theory instead of ourselves.

EXPERIENCE AND ITS REALM

Psychoanalysis both experiences and studies experience. Its method of gaining access to another's feelings is also its area of concern and inquiry. When Kohut (1959) defined the boundaries of psychoanalysis as determined by its method of vicarious introspection, he made a claim that seemed to ignore the accumulated facts and data of the field. For him, prolonged empathic immersion was to determine the borders of all depth psychologies. The arguments about this idea ranged from the insistence that avenues of inquiry other than empathy were available to psychoanalysts, all the way to the claim that psychoanalysis was at times (mistakenly) concerned with issues outside of experience. The first was answered by gathering up whatever was gained from extraception into those frameworks of introspectively derived data. The second seemed to suggest that one could determine the field of study that was relevant to psychoanalysis by ascertaining if it either was accessible by way of the experiencing subject or was tuned to the experience of the studied object.

There are wide areas of the world that lie outside the realm of the study of experience. Kohut certainly did not mean these to be the experience-distant issues discussed earlier. He did seem to be saying that we could ignore the study of biochemistry and neurophysiology as long as they were not accessible to empathy. No doubt many people believe that is a hasty conclusion, since we cannot now tell how relevant such studies will be. On the other hand, it also remains unclear whether neurophysiology has a ready relevance to the process of empathy, and so one must reserve judgment here as well. More important restricting the field to the method is only half the story. Empathy must be guided by the experience-distant theories that allow access to the data of observation. Method and theory must go together. Empathic people without analytic theory are not analysts, just as theoreticians without empathy cannot practice.

DISCUSSION

Our field encompasses experience in the *what* that we study and is almost equivalent to experience in the *way* that we study. However, to equate psychoanalysis with the realm of experience is an unwarranted shorthand. All of our knowing is a product of a complex network of guiding and constraining principles, theories that become complete by way of the lived experience. The concepts or principles are distant from experience but become alive by way of the immediacy of experience. But experience per se has no life apart from the network. Regardless of one's awareness or capacity to describe the ideas or concepts by which one lives, they are a necessary part of the very process of the lived experience. Together they form the unit of experience that for psychoanalysis must go beyond consciousness and intersubjectivity, in the sense of the phenomenologists, to a depth that is unique to the field that studies the unconscious. For psychoanalysis, our experience-distant structures demand that we see phenomena differently than do people who do not carry the same concepts as we do. Our empathy is determined by our theories, which require the use of such concepts as transference, repression, and the like. These experience-distant concepts essentially carry us to different realms of data, and so we can never say that theory does not matter or that it gets in the way. It is the only way. Nor can we say that we empathically understand another by a joining of subjectivities. That would make ours a work of conscious agreement and make our essential concept of seeing the unconscious unnecessary. Our theory cannot work without the principles of unconscious psychic contents, and every communication of the patient is read with that in mind. Thus, we can conclude that our field is relevant to all studies that relate to experience; that our field is composed of a network of essential experience-distant theories and concepts; and that this network allows us to make alive the experience-near data that occupy our lives in our practice.

8

On the Scientific
Status of Empathy

A cursory review of the literature on empathy, and especially on the role of empathy in psychoanalysis, sees it divided into two camps. One holds that, as desirable as empathy may be in the diagnosis and treatment of patients in analysis, it is a relatively rare phenomenon. It is unusual for one person to be truly empathic with another. Furthermore, empathy is unreliable, fraught with the dangers of error due to deception and countertransference; and the achievement of true and reliable empathic connections is realized only after sustained effort and repeated failures. This camp also contrasts empathy with an equally controversial and misunderstood word, inference. It states that inferences are unempathic conclusions based on or derived from either observations of overt behavior or preconceived formulations. When one cannot be empathic, then one relies on inference. However, it is certainly not the case that all those who adjure empathy are as enthusiastic about the use of what is attributed to inference, for some may also ally empathy with inference (Buie, 1981) and thereupon denigrate empathy even further, since they say that inference is not the same as direct observation and thus is unreliable. Thus, both empathy and inference are considered, together or apart; and the one or the other is surely a problem.

The other camp of interest and involvement in empathy takes the equally severe but contrasting position that empathy is a universal mode of communication between people. Just as direct observation allows us to understand others by drawing conclusions from overt behavior, so too does vicarious introspection allow an equal gathering of data and the reaching of conclusions. So, too, do *both* direct observation and empathy run the risk of mistaken conclusions as a result of deception by what is observed or by the observer. This view says that there are two ways of knowing: direct, outward, public observation (extraception); and inward, private observation (introspection). The combination of introspection and putting oneself in another's place is empathy.

Before sharpening up the contrast between these positions, it may be necessary to say once again that the accuracy of direct observation depends on a theory of observation; that is one does not see anything unless one already knows what to look for. And usually we infer beyond what is immediately sensed. Some say that noninferential observation does exist, especially when we see the familiar. But to infer, as we shall describe later, means only to think logically; and it hardly seems necessary to divide observation into that which is real or true and visible and that which is but merely inferred and thus less likely. Students who look into microscopes for the first time usually see nothing until they are given a theory *and* a set of logical steps to follow. Recall also that the data of sensation are not of themselves equivalent to perception; the latter demands some conceptual equipment to construct something of the sensory data. Tables are not presented to the mind. The retina and the brain make tables from sensory impressions. The work on visual illusions seems to substantiate this position (Brown, 1977). Thus, all direct observation is theory laden and logically dictated. A word is necessary here about the concept of "a theory." Ever since Quine (Quine and Ullean, 1978), scientists have recognized that no theory stands in isolation. Rather theories are connected one with the other in a network of beliefs, and a change in one necessitates modification everywhere. Quine also felt that this adjustment was readily accomplished in any theory by alterations that allow one to maintain one's theory and insist on its rightness, even in the face of new findings.

Further study of mental and physical observation has led most philosophers of science to conclude that there is also no inherent advantage of one over the other but rather that they are two different kinds of observation (Sellars, 1963). This is not to say that physical and mental sciences are necessarily the same in terms of other forms of scientific investigation such as the determining of evidence and questions of validity and predictability. Rather we seek only to disabuse the reader of the notion that the special status of mental phenomena or introspective data is unscientific because they are private. It seems to be the task of psychoanalysts to determine how they secure the private data of the mind and to determine if they differentiate this data from the more public, observable behavior of the person. The question thereupon to be answered is, If empathy is rare, how do we *ever* learn about someone else, and if empathy is ubiquitous what makes it such an achievement for psychoanalysts?

This chapter will not attempt a review of the literature on the role of empathy in psychoanalysis but rather will direct its effort to delineating the position that it can be defined and can enjoy a scientific place in the field.

EMPATHY AND PERSONAL MEANING

It is a longstanding and perhaps also a permanently unsolvable problem whether one person can know just how another one feels. Philosophers have called this "the question of other minds," and they usually come to a halt around the problem of whether one can ever reliably say that the sight of redness or the taste of a lemon is the same for you as it is for me. Psychoanalysts live and work with the very clear conviction that they are able to penetrate and know another person's mind, yet they often bear the burden of the philosophical conclusion that one never really knows. They can only make a guess based on analogy, and there is certainly no way to prove one is right. The problem of this penetration becomes more complex when we confront the fact that while others may tell us how they feel, we can never be sure of their sincerity. There are groups of people with whom we must depend on avenues of information that are outside of verbal language; foreigners and infants, for instance, are, for all practical purposes, mute.

One of the earliest writers to tackle the problem that ultimately confronts all psychologists who wish to understand another person was Wilhelm Dilthey (see Hartmann, 1927), who proposed that the act of *verstehen*, a sympathetic insight into another person, allowed one to build up a picture of that person's life and thus to understand the other person's experience. Dilthey often stands as the model of the dilemma of psychoanalytic data. His stand was strongly opposed by those who felt it was unscientific. Philosophers, psychologists, and sociologists have long debated the process of such understanding. Empathy is considered the basis of all human communication, yet some say it has no place in a scientific enterprise because it never can claim the status of certainty. But, as Wittgenstein (1950) has said, "Perfect certainty is only a matter of attitude."

It should be clear at the outset that the whole problem of comprehending another person's mental life commits one to a position of "mentalism," or the belief that there are, indeed, personal or subjective states of mind that are ascertainable. This is in sharp contrast to the opposing stand of the behaviorists, who would deny any scientific status to such inner and thus unobservable sources of data. The *form* of the inner life remains open, but the posture of commitment is a primary one.

It follows that concentration of these inner, or personal, or subjective experiences is necessarily subsumed under the broad category of introspection which means, simply, examining the private or inner or personal (the subjective) experiences of an individual. Unfortunately, such an introspective posture becomes confused with another use of the word "subjective," which means biased or swayed by personal feelings. Introspection stands primarily in opposition to extraspection, which is a perception of the external world. As such, introspection must be "objective," or free from bias, as well as concerned with nonexternal phenomena. It is in no way subordinate to or at odds with any form of scientific study. It is a matter of direction. Mental phenomena observable by way of introspection into one's own mind are equally obtainable by way of vicarious introspection into another's mind. The "data" of one's mind are just as available as the data of the physical world.

But we may often feel on shaky grounds about knowing exactly how someone else feels. Gathering up all the cues given by one person to another, plus the information told to us by the other person, allows a shared meaning to be formed. Such a sharing is a union of meaning. It is certainly true that most explanations of such empathic communication are based on some form of a merger experience, but it is certainly not true that merger is an illusion (Buie, 1981). Mergers are not the physical melting of one body into another but rather are the characteristic state of minds that share meanings. The infant is merged with the mother when they participate in a shared experience, and the teacher is merged with the student in an equally intense but significantly more mature form of this relationship. One cognitively knows the boundaries of one's physical body without confusing that knowledge with one's mental boundaries, which may remain open. Indeed, all open-system thinking commits one to erasing the idea of sharp and closed boundaries to permit a free exchange of information. A boundary is drawn by the lack of such exchange and not by one's skin.

Kohut's (1971) felicitous combination of introspection with vicarious or substitute experience allowed him to establish a working definition for empathy that is no more than a method for finding out about another person's inner life. It must of necessity include all the safeguards of any scientific investigation; it must be as nonsubjective (in the biased sense) as possible, and it must be considered as a form of data as much in need of verifiability or falsification as any other piece of evidence. There is no greater contribution from empathic observation than from so-called objective descriptions, which are equally laden with the contributions of the observer. It seems likely, therefore, that questions about empathy as a valid source of information about another person's mental life are often confused or ill founded. Unless one believes in pure behavioral manifestations (including a variety of physiological responses) as the sole source of knowledge of another's mind, one is forced to examine both introspective reports of the person and one's assessment of the person's mental states by way of substitute introspection.

Psychoanalysts differ over whether to use the data of self-reports (Ricoeur, 1977), or of empathy (Kohut, 1971). We are, however, all introspectionists (Brenner, 1968, 1980). I suspect that the self-report versus empathy division is also not a real one. Any patient who reports that he feels angry is naturally looked upon as presenting a statement that is only a pointer. We always attempt to determine just what is behind that report as well as what it is a part of, or essentially what is the meaning of such a report. The variety of observable external phenomena such as voice tone, facial configuration, preceding and subsequent comments, and so on are all collected into a total complexity that is taken in via empathy. That the empathy may be missing, defective, misplaced, or excessive is not the question addressed here. *Any* kind of perception is subjected to those problems and thus demands constant scrutiny to maintain objectivity.

The next problem to consider—one that is a source of confusion about the form of our data—contrasts empathy with inference or, worse, opposes it to theory. The first comparison, that with inference, is the easiest to clarify since all thinking involves inferences, which are no more than probable deductions from observable, that is, introspective *or* extraceptive, facts. When we cannot directly perceive something, we make an inference. On a hot day, we assume that people tend to go swimming; and a sad face suggests a misfortune. These are both inferences, though one can be checked by looking and the other by asking. Since we cannot see everything, we, of necessity, infer many things. Some inferences apply to vicarious introspection and some to extraspection. But inferences, patterns, and theories are indispensable to all forms of thinking and hardly need to be considered as being in opposition to any. It is the use of a theory without the data that is to be avoided.

The fact is that most of science is based on inference because there are very few things that can be directly perceived. The path of an electron or any subatomic particle is inferred from the tiny markings produced in high energy acceleration. Chemical reactions that result in new compounds are derived by a process of inference. The demand for verifiability by direct observation enjoyed only a brief heyday in the philosophy of science before it was seen that this was not only an unreasonable, but an unnecessary requirement. To be sure, some sciences, anatomy for example, lend themselves to concrete examination; others, like physics employ abstract concepts such as force and energy, which can never be "perceived." Especially in the historical sciences do we lean heavily on inference and implication. However, logical inference should not be grouped with erroneous conclusions that do not fit the data. Inference is not the same as presumption. It is a result of reasoning and not an alternative to observation, as some have suggested (Buie, 1981).

If a patient is silent, we are faced with the dilemma of either attaining an empathic position by other than verbal means or else relying on a theory without sufficient data. Again we do not *infer* the meaning of the silence, because we lack the data to proceed. We may guess at the meaning of the silence by way of one or another theory, but our job is to gather correct data and only then to make inferences.

EMPATHY AND THEORY

It is sometimes difficult to realize even so simple a fact that a child who recognizes a toy is operating within a theory of observation. It may be easier for us to think of this supposed theory as a series of conjectures or hunches that become confirmed or discarded on the basis of trial and error. Children around one year of age, who begin exercising their new capacity to recognize, may call all four-legged animals "dogs." As they learn more about more animals and their particular differences, they modify their "all animals are dogs" *theory* to engage and consider a wider variety of domestic and wild beasts. Such growth and elaboration of observational theories are the foundation of all knowledge, a position that was best detailed as the "conjectures or refutations" of Popper (1963). His point (though it hardly began with him) was that the theory *precedes* the observation and is verified or changed as observations proceeds.

The central position of empathy in psychoanalysis in no way deviates from this process. Empathy is first and foremost a method of observation and thus is guided by a theory that directs it. There can be little doubt that sophisticated and easy-to-articulate theories are not readily available to most people, who nevertheless may be quite capable of empathic contact. That may be why one is tempted to think that a pure observation precedes the construction of a theory. Perhaps a change to the use of the words "conjecture" or "hunch" or even "guess" might facilitate the idea that the earliest forms of empathic observation depend on primitive feeling states that one builds upon and then modifies as one grows. The impetus for a merger of mother and child in order to achieve a unity *presupposes* some glimmer of an idea of such unity.

To contrast "assessment made from psychodynamic formulation with empathic assessment" (Buie, 1981) is to compare an assessment made from a theory that is not filled in by data to one in which the data are not supported by a theory. Each comparison is in error. Let me illustrate by a dynamic formulation of depression based on loss and the concomitant grief reaction. If we use this theory in an assessment of a patient, then we fill it in with our empathic observation of the patient. Is the patient sad? Does he or she speak about the loss? Express ambivalent feelings about the lost object? The theory guides but does not determine our perceptions, which are fundamentally empathic, introspective ones. Even the observations of motoric behavior, speech patterns, vegetative signs are part and parcel of the building up of this inner, or personal, picture of the depressed and possibly suicidal person. And to reach a conclusion on the theory alone is bad science because it is an example of a form of premature closure.

On the other hand, let us see if careful empathic assessment sans theory is more fruitful. We should seek a sensitive and completely uncommitted observer to assess the depressions of our sample patient. Realizing the impossibility of finding a person free of all preconceptions, we might agree that our observer should have a minimum of bias. Such an experiment need not even be attempted; psychoanalytic history shows us that before Freud the existence of ambivalence in grief was simply not seen as such. Uninformed observers do not know what to look for no matter how "empathic" they are. Of course, here we have an example of naive empathy, which can take its place with the naive realism of direct observation. Those who say that tables are tables and not swarms of electrons are right but naive. Those who say that this depressed person is just sad at the loss is also correct but lacking in the theoretical underpinnings that flesh out our observations. No assessment of another person is full without the combination of data gathering guided by theoretical preconceptions aided by inference. To pit these aspects of science against one another is unfair, unwise, and untrue.

As more elaborate and complex mental states emerge, one's empathy, or capacity to think oneself into the mind of another, evolves from an even more elaborate and complex set of conjectures. This growth of the guiding theory is fundamental to all our contacts with the world, which require the continual modification of or refutation of those things we may "take for granted." That is why an analyst who is empathic may be forced to change a theory that sees others only as separate objects into one that includes using others as selfobjects. The gap between the observation and the articulation of the theory employed in the observation may, of course, be a matter of years. The implicit knowledge of such use is there long before it is "known." It arrives through trial and error, is used and found useful, and then can be told to others.

If everyone is capable of both extraspection and introspection, we can readily see that these forms of observation are both trainable and communicable. One cannot tell someone to go out and observe without telling him what to look for; nor can one instruct someone else to be empathic without a similar sort of a guide. Thus, when we say that an analyst must be a good listener and must be empathic, we do little more than outline the basic equipment needed. It takes a lot more than a microscope to make a histologist. The mere capacity for empathy is simply not equal to the special kind of listening and introspection that psychoanalysis requires.

The argument against the universal deployment of empathy would restrict it to those rare moments of mutual resonance that only a few gifted individuals achieve in the course of life and then usually in a psychoanalytic setting. It seems crass to think that the ordinary transactions of life involve this special ability, but it also seems hard to think otherwise. It appears likely that all communication between people is an effort to achieve shared meanings. Some of this involves direct observables, and some involves elements of sensitivity to another's inner states and feelings. Although some people no doubt tend to be extraordinarily restrictive in allowing themselves to be caught up in empathic assessment, it is hard to get through a day without it. The bulk of human interactions—from buying a newspaper from an irritable vendor to enjoying lunch with a colleague describing his pleasant vacation to hearing from your child about his school successes—all depend on your inner, subjective sense of knowing what someone else means by sharing it with them, however momentary, with or without self-reflection, and however comfortable or uncomfortable. This is what a psychology based on mentalism as opposed to behaviorism is all about. We do not feel the vendor is irritable *only* because of his behavior; angry gestures in strange cultures or people who act angry but are not are obvious refutations of this position. Our delight in our colleague's vacation and our pride in our child's exploits are part and parcel of normal mental life, and our experience based on such communication is an empathic one.

Of course, we can be dead wrong in our empathy. Our friend may have had a lousy vacation and is covering it up, and our child may be embarrassed to shine. It is equally true that some customers, friends, and parents could be much better attuned to the inner life of vendor, friend, and child. But, just as good and accurate direct observation requires both theory and training, so does accurate empathic observation. Though one is probably never in absolute perfect harmony with another after the first few weeks of life, nevertheless there is an aysymptotic curve toward such an achievement.

It is sometimes suggested that the "true empathic method" requires the suspension of all preconceptions and formulae in order to enable an immersion in a patient's experience, which is totally unique to that individual. Such an approach requires resisting all inclinations to prejudge or suggest anything to the patient or to direct or influence the patient. It is, of course, difficult to know just what the analyst *could* say, under these conditions, other than repeating the words of the patient; but, more than that, this approach confuses the logic of discovery with the logic of investigation. If none of your theories seems to make sense of the data and you correctly resist forcing the data to fit, then you are embarked on a creative effort to discover something new. This happens but once or twice in 100 years, and the field of psychoanalysis is an excellent proof of the rarity of such an event. Just how a creative act or a new discovery is accomplished is, of course, a question that merits a separate research of its own; it is appropriately called the logic of discovery. But the vast majority of scientific work consists of applying theories that are known and accepted to advance or rediscover the known. Psychoanalysis, especially, rediscovers its truths in each patient, no matter how much individual variability we may see in our patients. If each patient were unique, then our profession would be not only more art than science but without the essential ingredients of communicability to future generations of analysts. Though we must remain open to the logic and possibility of discovery, we must not confuse it with the ordinary practice of psychoanalysis.

One other factor must be added to the psychoanalyst's capacity to use a theory to determine the personal meanings of another person. That is the ability to sustain empathy. The vast majority of day-to-day interactions between persons rely on a minimum of empathic contact in order to gather enough data to react. Most of our relationships are posited on organizing a response of one form or another, and we are geared less to immersing ourselves in another's psyche than to action of some sort.

One clinical example of this phenomenon occurred after a diagnostic case conference at which a psychiatric resident presented the initial interview of a schizophrenic girl. The conference was geared to examining the moment-to-moment emotional state of the patient, who was frightened, suspicious, unsure of her boundaries, and wary of the therapist's intrusion. It was a fairly successful teaching exercise, but one student seemed relieved when it was over. When asked about this response, she said that it was all so "intense." In truth, this was probably an unusual experience for a beginning psychiatrist, who was just learning to *stay with* another person's inner feelings for prolonged periods. The tendency we all share is to break away from such mutuality of experience as soon as practicable for deciding our own reaction.

Another clinical illustration has to do with a patient who had recently returned from her sister's funeral and was describing the events to her therapist, who listened carefully and followed the material fairly well. At one point the patient told of someone who had behaved in an especially kind and thoughtful manner. Both at the time and in the recounting the patient experienced profound sadness and tearfulness. The therapist found himself struggling against a full participation in his mourning patient's feeling state, which seemed to signal to him an equally intense episode of tears. He then realized that his listening was essentially "from the outside"; in other words, it was an example of the use of theory either without the data or with a minimum of data. Had he allowed himself to sustain his empathy, he would have awakened similar painful feelings in himself; and he had naturally resisted this posture. Rather he had allowed only momentary incursions into the other person's mind—just enough to maintain contact but not so much as to upset. These are the points in treatment where we usually turn to an examination of the analyst's countertransference or his inability to be empathic. In all likelihood, it is a natural resistance to sustaining one's empathy and a natural inclination to employ the theory as a shortcut.

To restrict empathy to the perfect union is to flirt with the mystical. Better theories will enable the most sensitive person to see even more. Better training will help the uninitiated to focus on the inner life. Efforts to lift transference and countertransference distortions will assist both the sensitive and the naive. The misuse of theory will lead to premature closure without enough data, and the supposed accumulation of data without theory leads to the lack of a selective capacity. The latter is always the prevailing state of affairs until someone like Freud shows us just what we have been seeing and hearing. People were exquisitely empathic long before psychoanalysis came on the scene, but they were not psychoanalysts until they knew how to order their data.

One never limits psychoanalysis to empathy in spite of the fact that Kohut (1971) and others have said that it defines the field. The method needs a guiding theory to allow one to glean the significant parts from the massive amount of material offered by a patient. Sustained empathy may or may not be peculiar to psychoanalysis, but our inquiry also must somehow be directed to salient features; that is, we must know what to look and listen for in order to complete the marriage of method and theory. Together they define the field for that period of scientific history during which the theory holds sway. Since theories are fated to be replaced by better ones, we may say that the method defines the field but never encompasses it, since the facts of our field of study grow out of the mutuality of method and theory.

AN ANALYTIC EXERCISE

Psychoanalysts are said to listen for intentions, goals, and purposes. They look for unarticulated, disavowed, ambiguous, or hidden meanings. They do so with a variety of implicit assumptions and formulas. One illustration of the kinds of listening they do is presented here to demonstrate the observation-theory interaction. The reader is cautioned not to assume that this is an illustration of technique, which is not the relevant issue here.

> A patient enters the analytic hour and notices the Kleenex tissue on the pillow and announces laughingly that he thinks it is the same one he used for yesterday's hour.

At this point, a psychoanalyst parts company with almost every other form of investigator when he asks himself what that means. As we shall see later, the simple clarification of whether or not it is indeed the same tissue or a simple pursuit of the truth or reality of the situation is *not* a psychoanalytic activity.

> As the patient talks about his feelings of using a supposedly soiled tissue, he presents himself as struggling with a feeling of being taken advantage of by the analyst.

It is this total state of mind that engages the analyst in his determination of the meaning behind the used tissue. He identifies with and recognizes the most general form of configuration of the patient's presentation.

> The patient has many associations to others' being used and abused, but soon this narrows to a concentration on people who are relatively unmoved by adversity. A special connection is made to his mother, who remained stoical under a barrage of angry vituperation from both himself and his father when he was a child. She suffered abuse silently.

The analyst listens to determine if the patient is identifying with the aggressor or the victim. He listens and is guided by a theory that hopes to extend and thereby to elaborate what this means to the patient. Of course, this need not be explicit.

> The patient talks of his own need *not* to be thrown or upset by others' abuse of him. The analyst has himself associated now to a planned missed session. He asks the patient about this. The patient is somewhat responsive but soon reveals that it is more than just that one session.

The analyst shifts his scrutiny to the particulars of the transference and the nuances of the relationship with the patient.

> The patient next associates to feeling sad and upset at what the analyst said a few days ago about the patient's wondering about an extra, or fifth, analytic hour. The analyst said this would not necessarily speed up the analysis. The patient subsequently felt hurt and devastated. He accused the analyst of earlier encouraging an interest in another hour and now discouraging it. He [the analyst] probably had the free time when he encouraged it and now he had filled his hour with someone else. This selfish sort of an attitude was so typical of him and so typical as well of his father. The important thing was not to reveal how much this feeling of wanting the extra hour meant to him.

The analyst's empathy shifts from that of the abused victim to personal recollections having to do with the passive, submissive position that this patient evokes. He recalls Freud's warning that the bedrock of some analyses is the inability of a man to assume a passive stance in relation to another man. He recalls Kohut's (1977) modification of this in relation to a developing idealizing transference. He chooses to respond empathically on the basis of all the data gathered, processed, and formulated under the general aegis of what it means. The sequence is, of course, a personal one, but the overall process is a general one.

By "responding empathically," we define empathy in its natural oscillating state between patient and analyst and do not divide it into afferent, or receptive, and efferent, or motor, branches. The empathic response maintains and sustains one's connection with the patient and affords one the liberty of joining, listening, and responding in the single word. To suggest that we listen empathically and respond tactfully may be an artificial division of a reciprocal feedback process.

The exercise is intended to sketch the thesis that psychoanalysis employs empathy and a guiding theory in order to determine personal meanings. It is this pursuit of the significance of what may seem to be a solitary event—such as a soiled tissue—that launches the analyst on his journey to those elaborate psychological configurations that make up a meaning. Unfortunately, meaning does not spring full grown from individuals, and psychoanalysis must first study its development. It has a long and involved growth that necessarily includes cognitive and affective components and that needs multiple perspectives in order to grasp its totality.

It is impossible as well to situate accurately just where and how we will examine meanings because our penetration into the mind of another person carries so much baggage with it in the form of our theories and our inferences. The question of whether the meaning is ours or the patient's or is a mutual construction of the two of us remains to be considered as well. No matter what the resolution of that question may be, it is one that demands the attention of every scientist who cares to consider whether there are really objects (i.e., people and things) in the world to be examined or whether all such objects exist primarily in relation to the perceiver rather than autonomously. The coming together of a theory, a method of observation, and the clinical inferences that we choose to make results in the knowledge or the meaning that we attribute to another person.

EMPATHY AND ITS FORMS

The literature on empathy suggests a classification of the phenomenon, and a brief note is in order here. Efforts to categorize and classify empathy from primitive to mature or from "self referential to imaginative to resonant" (Buie, 1981) are based on a sort of telephonic model of communication. They are concerned with the delivery of facts or feelings from one source to another. They involve codes, systems of delivery, and translations and are necessarily and understandably limited by a closed body system of thinking. In contrast, efforts to categorize empathy in terms of open systems of exchange involve such issues as shared meanings, intersubjectivity, and free exchange. Thus every fact is constantly being modified by input from other parts of the system. In textual analysis, the difference is of a reader's reading a book in a fixed rendering of its contents versus reading as an almost different person as he or she changes from day to day. The first is a closed system, and the second is open. It is important for psychoanalysts to realize that there are different approaches to the scientific study of empathic communication, that one is not necessarily better than the other but that the yield from each will be different. All this is fundamental to the scientific study of empathy and an effort to reach conclusions about its scientific status. It is essential that one approach these tasks with a clear understanding of the problems inherent in evaluating something as complex as a method of gathering the data of depth psychology.

If, for example, a contrast is made between the classification of introspection and the classification of direct perception or extraspection, we find that an ordering of data in terms of the observer's feelings, preconceptions, or resonance is usually of minimal significance. One does not classify apples on the basis of personal hunger or memories of this fruit, but rather on issues derived from botanical science. This is not to say that observer error is not always to be checked and considered, but rather that there are more overriding issues in perceptual categorization. Two major divisions of direct perception are empiricism and phenomenology. We learn more about objects of perception by a careful attention to sensory data aided by our guiding theories. What is needed for psychoanalysis as for any imaginative science are bold and innovative theories used by empathic observers. Only these will allow us to see more, and only these will enable a valid classification of our means of data gathering.

Therefore, a future and desired classification of empathy might follow the sort of fundamental distinctions that psychoanalysis often employs, for example, a developmental model based on the sharing of experiences ranging from mother-infant to student-teacher communications. One cannot study empathy in isolation. We are always empathic "to" or "with," and the object of our study determines our stance as much as does our own competence and posture.

A second, but by no means secondary, reason for a clearer and more definitive classification of empathy is the need to explain the beneficial effects of one person's being understood by another. As we move from thinking of individuals as isolated systems to viewing their participation in open and contiguous systems, we recognize that becoming a part of a larger system changes one's very makeup. So too does a position of empathic understanding have marked therapeutic effects on its object. This is best seen in a developmental scheme wherein the mother-infant unit is held together by a communicative feedback that is essential to the infant's well-being. The most promising field for a future classification of empathy seems to be its consideration along developmental lines, which would most cogently account for the therapeutic benefit of its employment.

In conclusion, one can say that the scientific status of empathy is both reasonable and justified as long as scientists treat it as they do any means of data gathering. That is to say that we are objective, are able to use a variety of theories to guide us, and remain alert to the effects of our own observations. The many colloquial uses of the term seem to have joined with equally vulgar employments of words such as inference to bring about the temporary abandonment of our scientific stance. To recapture the role of empathy in psychoanalysis is but to define it as our method of observation.

DISCUSSION

This chapter is an attempt to clarify the scientific status of empathy in psychoanalysis. It defines empathy as a method of observation that gathers data which are dictated by a guiding theory. It also clarifies the role of inference as the set of logical deductions that follow from the theory. Inasmuch as empathy seems to have a therapeutic effect when sustained, a future classification of empathy that considers relations in an open system and that follows the maturation of empathy in terms of a shared experience is suggested.

9

The Unempathic
Child

Empathy is an endangered word. The threat comes not from the scarcity of its presence but from the plundering of its meaning. There is the risk that soon a learned article will be published announcing that the word has become so overused and abused that we must all immediately cease relying on it to account for anything. But until that event, this chapter will indulge in the assumption that the range and extent of its definition is not yet harmful. Given that some would insist that any one man's version of empathy is simply not up to what the standards required, perhaps we can say that we all have a general idea of what it is. Pressed for a definition, I would pick the most modest one: that it is a means of gathering data about a person's inner mental life (Goldberg, 1984). The qualifications of good and bad empathy, primitive and mature empathy, therapeutic or hurtful empathy and brief or sustained empathy are all relevant but need not affect the basic definition. But this is an essay that focuses not on its presence but on its absence, and perhaps that will be less cause for arguments.

SOME PRELIMINARY HYPOTHESES

The child lacking in empathy no doubt grows to be the adult with the same deficiency, and we assume that all such adults derive from that

111

sort of child. Such children may be thought of as cruel, sadistic, self-centered, or simply insensitive, but they often stand out at a fairly early age in sharp contrast to the child who seems able to show interest, concern, and care for others. Professionals as well as lay people tend to link this insensitive child to some sort of psychopathology, and more often than not the unempathic child is visited both with scorn and varied diagnoses. Yet we can fairly easily disengage the linkage as soon as we reflect on the fact that some fairly disturbed schizophrenics show amazing sensitivity, many extremely narcissistic persons are quite adept at divining the feelings of others, and, indeed, no particular diagnosis seems peculiarly connected to a lack of empathy.

The simplest explanation for the failure of children to achieve an ability to be and stay empathic with others is that they suffered such a reciprocal failure from their caretakers. Thus, nonempathic parents produce offspring who carry the problem on for yet another generation. But once again common sense shows us that this is simply not true. Although some such identification may occur, we certainly see quite sensitive individuals who come from rather severely insensitive families, and we also see some strikingly nonempathic individuals born of a fairly empathic milieu. The primary caution to be observed is that we should not equate mental illness with deficiencies of empathy. Exquisitely empathic and severely narcissistic mothers may have very unempathic children; relatively insensitive but nonneurotic mothers may have sensitive, normal children. The unempathic child is a developmental puzzle that is not yet solved.

That the issue is developmental is highlighted by a host of data that describe the necessary empathic connectedness between mother and infant from birth on (see, for example, Kohut, 1971; Provence, 1983; Stern, 1985). The feedback of affective communication that exists in the mother-infant dyad is felt to be vital for the very survival of the baby. Such early levels of connectedness are felt to mature into ever more sophisticated means of being "in tune" and so to reach later levels of empathic understanding or generative empathy or mature empathy—a plethora of terms to denote a desirable endpoint of achievement. It is to the failures in such progress that we must address ourselves, since they seem implicated in their own way to psychopathology. Even though we say that a one-to-one correlation is not to be found, we also hear it said (Kohut, 1971) that empathic failures of the caretaker lead to pathology of all sorts. The parents are nonempathic, and the child suffers; the therapist is empathic, and the patient benefits. But how empathy comes about differs from what it is said to do. It does seem likely that the child needs to be in tune with the parent and that equal attention should be paid to that part of the equation as well. Thus, a preliminary task should be to suggest some hypotheses about what may be responsible for the emergence of the child without empathy.

COGNITIVE DEVELOPMENT AND THE UNEMPATHIC CHILD

The first psychoanalytic report of the vicissitudes of the child's intellectual endowments to promote or make unlikely the assimilation of information was that of the Wolf Man (Freud, 1918). In the case, Freud (p. 37) doubted that a child of a year and a half could have assimilated the contents of the perception of this parents having intercourse. Freud used the analysis to prove the correctness of his surmise by noting "the reactions" that were brought about. Later (p. 80) he suggested an additional fact of the child's father manifesting annoyance and this being dismissed because "the analysis did not react to it." Freud postulated that at about four years of age the intellectual endowment of the Wolf Man had advanced to the point where the child was able to grasp the event that had occurred earlier, and thus it "operated not only like a fresh event, but like a new trauma" (p. 109). Whether or not one accepts the likelihood of this sequence, it is of some historical interest that Freud felt that "some sort of hardly definable knowledge works in a child to produce neurosis" (p. 87). He also connected this to a quality of compassion (which some erroneously feel to be related to empathy; see chapter 6) that arose in the Wolf Man in relation to an incident with a water-carrier when he was three-and-a-quarter and that later manifested itself in regard to the father (p. 87). For Freud, sympathy was a symptom tied in with the Wolf Man's castration complex. One cannot, of course, make a judgment about the Wolf Man's empathy or lack of it.

For the most part there is no clear distinction in psychoanalytic writing about the change in empathy that occurs with development, inasmuch as the range of approach to the subject goes from a rather naive one, which compares empathy to some sort of affective resonance and holds it in contrast to cognition (Buie, 1981), to a more sophisticated one that carefully plots it along Piagetian stages and sees it as an endpoint involving the highest achievement of formal operations (Basch, 1983). Some writers have noted that children with learning disabilities are notoriously unempathic (Shane, 1984) and that such children have as much trouble reading people as they do reading books. Others, such as Stern (1985) feel that there is an affective core that is a necessary but not sufficient condition for empathy. There is some consensus that empathy changes over time, that children of different ages manifest behavior that lends itself to a consideration of the development of empathy and that the opposition of empathy and cognition is totally unwarranted (Bruner, 1986).

Basch (1983) has suggested a line of development of affective communication that has its culmination in the person who is able to separate himself sufficiently from his feelings and emotions so that instead of reacting to them he can establish their genesis and the significance they have in the context in which they are experienced. He called this later stage that of empathic understanding and contrasted it to earlier stages of attunement, feeling, and emotion, which more or less correspond to Piagetian stages of sensorimotor activity, pre-operational thought, and concrete operations. Such a viewpoint stresses the internal program of the child unfolding vis à vis the environment and is in contrast to one espoused by Vigotsky (cited in Furth, 1981), who held the environment to be the dominant factor in the child's development. Of course, neither the internal program nor the environment as dominant is an absolutist position, but since empathy is a two-way issue, we do need to study the intermediate area that, for example, occurs when the infant somehow manages to be in harmony with the mother (Brazelton, Kowlowski, and Main, 1974).

The contrasting position to the one that holds empathy to correspond to an end stage of formal operations considers all communication to be based on empathy and considers it to have its own line of development, which need not correspond at all to Piagetian stages. Kaye (1982) describes his observations of mother-child behavior in terms of an interaction that begins at birth but that has infants only gradually becoming partners in the process. They move from creatures of innate rhythms to social beings over time. He speaks of the built-in rhythms of the child determining the mother's role of fitting in and producing a dialogue for which she alone is primarily responsible. His research followed mothers and infants from birth to the third year and examined the feeding situation, face-to-face contact, and verbal exchanges. Essentially, he feels that the mother imagines all sorts of infant behavior as part of a conversation and early on treats the infant as a partner in a dialogue that is really nonexistent. The particulars of his research will not be reviewed here, but it seems fairly certain that infants up to a year old simply do not participate in such a dialogue. Rather the mother fits the infant's innate reactions. The parental attitude toward the child over time does allow him what Kaye terms an apprenticeship to the family system, and if the baby's innate cycles are organized and smooth, then his caretakers will fit in more easily. Infants who do not arouse easily tend to reject parents, but that is a unintentional happenstance. Once the child can speak, the turn-taking goes much more smoothly since the signals are more clear, but studies show that even at this point adults create and maintain the social discourse. Only when the child engages in symbolic discourse governed by rules of mutually recognized obligation of behavior are we able to speak of that quality of taking another perspective of the world into account. The oft-repeated statement that the mother and baby develop a harmonious interaction seems in error. Children do not fit into the mother's pattern, and the two do not adjust to one another. Rather, the mother (and father) are always ahead of the child while they imagine an equal partnership. Some children manage to attain this partnership and some do not. Although Stern (1985) may make a claim for early child participation in the dialogue, let us follow Kaye for a bit.

Kaye describes four stages in the child-mother interaction. The first is shared rhythms: from birth to 5 or 6 months there is no true system of mother-infant. The mother does the matching. The parents are indispensable for the child's survival, but there is no mutual anticipation or a joint effort of achievement. Each partner does not play a role and expect the other to play a role. The second stage is shared intentions. After six months the infant is an apprentice, and at least some of the time the parent-infant interaction takes on the character of a single system with the parent providing most of the planning, guidance, and memory. There are then some expectations on both sides about the roles to be played. But the infant is not fully a system member until those roles demand the reciprocal use of equivalent signs. Intersubjectivity begins when the infant and parent compose a system (p. 152).

The third stage is one of shared meanings. As parents complete or facilitate the infant's intentional system toward them and toward the world, the gestures become conventionalized signals within their shared experience. Gradually, the parents introduce the appropriate conventional symbols of the linguistic community. As we enter the fourth stage of shared language (duration), the signals the infant learns to provide are those that he comprehends when they are produced by others. Use of such symbols entails anticipation of how they will be interpreted. According to Kaye, "Only then is the infant communicating" (p. 150).

These studies are not cited to minimize the significance of the mother-infant exchange but rather to underscore the fact that infants do implicitly train parents to respond but in a fairly limited range. Infants and toddlers evoke parental fantasies, and flexible parents carry the child into the realm of meaningful conversation and dialogue. Children can, of course, fail parents at any moment because of their very limited repertoire. They must ultimately learn how to behave in order to evoke certain responses, but this is a long and sometimes delayed and not always successful process. Sonnenschein (1984) has shown that kindergartners can watch people exchange messages and learn by observing in the listener whether or not the particular message was an adequate one. But the children require specific and explicit feedback about ambiguous messages in order to learn to decipher such messages by themselves. Sonnenschein confirms Bruner's (1986) claim that children are egocentric only to the degree that they are cognitively confused. Thus, until at least five years of age there are normal cognitive problems in the area of correctly reading others and responding to them. Children need a great deal of parental activity and instruction to find their way into the parents' world. The learning disabled child is greatly handicapped in this effort, and premature expectations by the parent may add to the burden. Although children may be able to imitate parents in a wide range of behavior, even to the point of looking concerned and caring, they cannot conceptualize these phenomena and satisfy the criteria of empathic understanding until a certain level of self-consciousness has been attained. For the most part, the fantasies of the parent seem to socialize the child and to train the child to behave in a manner that will communicate to the parent that the parent is understood: thus the child's empathy. This is not too dissimilar from the therapist whose theory allows him to understand the patient, who in turn must "catch up" to the therapist in order to reciprocate this understanding.

An overview of cognitive development seems to indicate that aside from the initial, almost biologically determined attunements of infant and mother, there is an ever present series of tasks imposed on the participants to comprehend one another. For some time the child is limited in the ability to modify behavior in order to influence or adapt to the caretaker. No doubt a major cognitive achievement is that of decentering, but the need to learn what others mean continues through childhood and into adolescence.

Whether we use the word empathy or affective communication or attunement, it is clear that its developmental path is a long one. We can break it up according to levels of cognitive achievement or emotional substages based on psychoanalytic principles or descriptive ones posited on expectable social interaction. For some, its presence is a given and its absence is striking: especially in a child who is expected to have accomplished the job of effectively communicating with others.

ANXIETY AND THE UNEMPATHIC CHILD

The second factor to be considered in the assessment of the child who is relatively incapable of a correct perception of another person is anxiety. Given a baseline of development that would enable some accurate perception of others, we see that it is often a tenuous accomplishment easily upset by a variety of disturbances. For the most part, we find that the noxious effect of the anxiety is due to the particular vulnerability of the child at various stages of growth. Mild anxiety need not be an impediment to empathic assessment of others, and some feel it even aids learning. Rather it seems to be that a state of severe anxiety or potential self-fragmentation goes along with the shift to stilted or cruel or insensitive behavior. Naturally, a relatively unstable self will more frequently experience such severe threats and may, almost chronically, exhibit this sort of world misperception. We tend to see this distortion more in adolescence or latency children who, not uncommonly, are seen as being particularly unfeeling of the emotional states of others.

It is rare to hear or read reports of young children who are nonempathic or insensitive to parents or other children without the children's being described as disturbed. Infants who respond slowly or fail to smile readily are felt to be lethargic or deviant; toddlers who do or say inappropriate things are considered troubled; and somewhat older children who are insensitive or cruel are felt to be manifesting mental illness. Dahl (1983) reported the treatment of a 27-month-old boy who greeted him in the waiting room by exclaiming "Fuck!" The therapist quickly translated this message into some other meaning. She described the subsequent treatment of the child as decoding the meanings of his speech and behavior. The treatment was fairly successful and supported the therapist's position that she needed to "make sense" of the child's productions. What would be labeled a totally inappropriate comment in any other setting is seen as symptomatic by an empathic therapist.

The child who is not understandable may or may not be similar to the one who does not, in turn, understand. Another example of the former can be seen in the case of a 23-month-old child reported by Pruett (1983). This boy was disturbed enough to be hospitalized to control his destructive impulses. The treatment of the boy was directed to changing the parents' perception of the child. For example, the child's ripping up his father's sandwich was understood as wanting to feed the tuna fish sandwich to the cat, instead of wanting to destroy the father's lunch. The parents accepted the therapist's acting as "spokesman" for the child and began to change their view of him and experience him as less malicious though not entirely likeable. Once the child was taken into treatment, his language development, which had been delayed, underwent rapid progress. His anxiety, especially with the therapist, seemed to diminish; and he was able to hug the therapist spontaneously. The other part of the equation now was in evidence, and the reader of this case cannot help but see how the less anxious child could now evoke positive responsiveness in others. The explanation for the change was given in terms of the therapists particular theoretical orientation, but the message was also one of a child who treated people in a more reasonable manner. He had traversed the path to evoking what he needed in others.

Learning of proper ways of living with others remains fragile and easily lost because of changing requirements and persistent needs for what can only be thought of as feedback maintenance. No doubt certain children learn how to be charming or ingratiating and utilize that demeanor to manage in life. But the contrived behavior is always subject to failure because of its limited range and lack of flexibility. The greatest threat to the maintenance of attunement, besides the failure to read the subtleties of the surround, is the sudden threat to one's self-cohesion.

An example of a sudden transition in an adolescent was given by a parent who described a family outing to a restaurant in a racially tense neighborhood. The mother was anxious about the trip and sharply criticized the dress of her teenage daughter as they entered the restaurant. This girl was a vulnerable and poorly organized person who nevertheless was in fairly good control for most of the trip . . . until the criticism. Once inside the restaurant, she asked if she could sit with her younger brother at a different table from her parents. She was refused and reluctantly took a seat. She began speaking to her brother in a loud and rapid voice. She compared black people with whites in a derogatory way, and her parents repeatedly had to subdue her. She seemed almost oblivious of the people nearby who might hear her. She was impatient for her food and began telling a near-paranoid story about certain kinds of meat. Her parents were distraught, ended the meal quickly, and exited rapidly. The girl remained in this "out-of-it" manner until she got home and changed her clothes. Later, when she looked back on this episode, she focused entirely on the mother's insult and could say little about her conduct in the restaurant. It seems that the narcissistic injury inflicted by the mother led rapidly to the form of regressed self that treats others with a quality that is readily described as unempathic. Again one could perhaps posit a spokesman for the girl who could explain what she said and felt to her parents, who might then have understood and been able to diminish her anxiety. In this sense, empathy is always social, always judged in context, and always in need of feedback.

THE FAILURE TO LEARN EMPATHY

A seemingly irreverent question that should be answered is why anyone learns to be empathic at all. The "Why empathy?" issue is a teleological one and directs us to the fact that empathy is learned and develops to handle a particular set of needs: those of discordance. It develops out of the states of attunement. The matched infant and mother, or the child who enjoys a caretaker who manages to tune in, needs no capacity to handle discordance. It grows out of sets of breaks or disruptions that the child must learn to handle, ideally at a phase-specific and untraumatic moment. (See chapter 16 for a discussion of this point.) But perhaps even more desirable is the state of harmony that is not a product of union following disunion, but rather is based on an attunement that is more of a given. Of course, this is a fantasied ideal, but it permits a smoothly running relationship versus one that is made to run smoothly by mutual (or one-sided) understanding. We seem to need to develop empathy to the degree that we must manage the inevitable mismatches of life. Normal mental functioning is a product either of there being no need to achieve understanding (i.e. it works fine without effort) or of an ability to manage this achievement. Thus, two kinds of normality: the nonempathic but nonpathological and the "psychologically minded" developed to forestall pathology. One must initially separate the intellectual effort from the psychopathological result to properly ascertain the relative importance of these issues. Failures of empathy are thus revealing of circumscribed arenas of hoped-for or expectable human interaction that does not take place. It is to those encounters that are characterized by negotiation of misunderstanding or of potential misunderstanding that the word applies.

It is not uncommon in the evaluation of adult patients to find either gross or fairly well segmented areas of failed empathy. We sometimes consider such patients to lack "psychological mindedness" and wonder how treatable they may be. We assume that one cannot be empathic with people from markedly different or foreign backgrounds, and limitations in any one person's empathy are taken for granted. Yet we are sometimes struck by markedly aberrant deficiencies in empathy that seem to go beyond such natural limitations. At times in psychoanalysis we may be able to reconstruct the origins of such failures.

To illustrate: A forty-year-old professional man came into his second analysis because of a reemergence of perverse sexual activity. During the course of this analysis he told of this problems with a business associate with whom he felt at odds over a number of issues. It turned out that this was not the first man with whom he had trouble, nor was it the first business association that had floundered. As he spoke of the dealings with this associate, it was clear that he had a remarkable lack of understanding of this man and indeed of most men. He never seemed to be able to figure out any of his previous partners, and although he remained friendly and cordial to them, he was usually at a loss about their motives or feelings. He had a stiff and formal way of dealing with other men, and he relied on social correctness to navigate his way among them. In talking of his first analysis he repeated some rote dynamic formulas learned from his first analyst but had relatively little to say about the analyst save that he had once ridiculed the patient. He did not, however, harbor any resentment toward the analyst. Nor did he seem to have much curiosity either. This patient did not seem flat or cold or schizoid; rather, a knowledge of the inner life of men in general eluded him.

Not surprisingly, a narcissistic transference developed in this second analysis, and it was characterized by a variety of struggles over maintaining a connection to the analyst. In the reconstruction of the childhood of this patient, the relationship to the father seemed paramount. The father was a busy doctor who rarely had much time for his son, who was alone for long periods. He worked well with his hands, and, on rare occasions, worked alongside father in repairing or making things. For the most part, he waited endlessly to be with father. One poignant memory was listening for father's car to pull into the driveway, running out to see him, and quickly scanning his face to see if father would or would not respond to him. As we reconstructed that event, we learned (or rather the patient verified) that the father had been a barbiturate addict who was often in a drugged state of lassitude and withdrawal. The son could not connect to him except during sporadic and brief moments. He remained bewildered, feeling like an outsider, wondering just what was going on inside his father. There were furtive attempts at homosexual behavior in high school, repeated depressions in college, some unsuccessful ventures with working for very charismatic men in his professional life, and finally an analysis that seemed only marginally satisfying. In his return to analysis he began work on the mystery surrounding his father.

The suggested hypothesis for this and similar failures in learning empathy is that the parent cannot readily expose himself or herself to the child or is simply absent. Kohut (1971) has noted the deleterious effect of what he characterized as the hidden psychosis on the developing self of the child. It seems equally true that any absence or apparent absence of the parent can inhibit the development of reciprocal empathy of the child. Even though infants are said to be able to respond to the affective state of the mother, this is probably only true for that period of time when the mother-infant unit is rather rigidly constrained by the innate patterns of infantile rhythms. As more subtle and symbolic gestures and language come into play, the participants in the dialogue can be more adept at hiding their feelings. The deficiency that is being highlighted here is not the failure in parental empathy that may lead to depression or other forms of pathology. Rather it is the lack of opportunity for the child to learn how to read and respond to others. The real parent eludes the child. This failure is of the same order as that suffered by someone from a different culture whom we cannot comprehend. There are parents who remain a mystery to their children and thus create a chronic inability to decipher the inner life of others. The particular struggles that children endure to breach this barrier may lead not necessarily to forms of psychopathology but occasionally to certain forms of creativity. These creative efforts, then, are unusual efforts to devise alternative modes of relating and communicating, the uncanny results of lacking ordinary methods of communication.

Often we are able to carve out areas of mutual understanding and comprehension and thus apparently confirm that we can learn empathy. The ingredients that produce this kind of learning are yet to be determined. Demos (1987) has listed the possible types of caretaker responses that aid or hamper the child's development and become characteristic of the infant-mother system. The flip side of her list of caretaker responsiveness to or misperception of the child must alert us to the developing child's perception of the caretaker. The first requirement for this somewhat skewed dialogue is access to the parent. The unempathic child remains puzzled about what remains hidden and may spend much of life trying to solve the puzzle.

SELF-EMPATHY

Upon the return of his analyst from a long weekend that necessitated cancelling an hour, a patient reported being quite upset at not having wished the analyst well upon his leaving at the end of the previous hour. He wondered for some time if this failure reflected his anger at the analyst's going off or some other inner, unknown feeling of his. He had gone to a party over the weekend and was able to be gracious and cordial to everyone while avoiding entanglements. He is ordinarily very alert to "all the moves" that people put on one another and terribly disdainful of them. He related a dream of the night before the hour: He was performing oral sex first on a man and then on a woman. He was attuned to their pleasure and was very curious about the anatomy of the recipients of his action but had no particular pleasure himself.

The patient's associations to the dream circled around his perpetually having to consider and care for others. As a child he had learned to read his parents quite accurately in terms of just how much of him they could tolerate. He always felt that he was intruding on them, and they made little pretense that he was not. He had learned to be a good boy and often brought little gifts to his mother, who filled out the role of a burdened woman. In the transference there seemed to be an erosion of his hypersensitivity to others and an emergence of a tuning-in to his own needs. The dream seemed an effort to paper over this breakthrough of self-centeredness, and the change from a man to a woman was felt to stand for the change in the schedule and the change in the patient.

This patient would be categorized by many as very sensitive and empathic to others. He would agree with this assessment, but add his own rather severe opaqueness to himself. Classification of such deficiency in self-comprehension are varied and range from a neurological defect with a diagnosis of anhedonia, to an early lack of appropriate language to name feelings, to obsessive-compulsive neurosis with isolation of affect. McDougall (1982) characterized the problem of alexithymia in the sexual perversions as an inability to name, recognize, contain, or work through affective states because of radical defenses that guard against psychotic fears of fragmentation. Alexithymia cures the self by severing affective links and leading to anhedonia or lack of emotional pleasure. It is a defense against inner liveliness. The aforementioned patient was found by some diagnosticians to fit in each of these different categories and had appropriate treatment for the particular diagnoses considered.

Without attempting extensive review of the literature or speculating about this particular man's malady, we can perhaps make some broad generalizations about his lack of empathy with himself gleaned from the specifics of the analytic transference. There is no doubt that his position may be seen in terms of the disavowed or split off or never experienced aspects of personal experience. To borrow a recommended metaphor (Goldberg, 1983), the concept of ownership can be used to mark the progression of assuming a wish and feeling as belonging to oneself. Initially the patient has a flat and unemotional stance that sees need only in others. Then follows a frightening and nearly explosive experience of overstimulation and overexcitement. The analyst serves as a merged selfobject to help contain and modulate the agitation. Over time the patient begins to test the personal ownership of particular feelings, and this testing is associated with intense feelings of shame. This patient felt that he was annoying and a pest to others, who could barely tolerate him. At that juncture, the analyst became the estranged selfobject, who competed with the patient for dominance of the center stage.

If one can manage to be empathic with this feeling of estrangement, then the patient once again can tolerate personal feelings of specialness and wonder that are vulnerable to rapid and traumatic breakdown. The particular selfobject needs are those of very early mirroring, which permit a gradual movement to one's claim of individuality and its associated affects. The required shift is from the intense fitting in with the demands of the caretaker's selfobject to utilizing another as a proper functioning selfobject. This takes place along the entire lifecycle. One discovers one's own feelings and need in an atmosphere that allows the experience to emerge and be tolerated. Each achievement of the developing child needs a confirmation that can be claimed, communicated, and shared. Self-empathy develops over a long period of phase-specific states that are allowed to exist without feelings of loss and fragmentation. The narcissistic mother does not allow such states in the child since they threaten her own cohesion.

Caution, however, is indicated lest we equate self-empathy with psychological health. The child who can have a listening and responsive parent for some moments of development will necessarily be different from the child who is without such a parent. But the need for such selfobjects is variable, and so the need for later self-study and self-contemplation is equally subject to change as we grow away from responsive parents. As is true of consciousness in general, the activity of reflecting on something is called forth only when that something is awry. One thinks about how one feels, what something means, and what to do at points of uncertainty and problems. Self-empathy is called forth for trouble spots and so enables one to establish psychological equilibrium. But its absence may reflect a relatively trouble-free developmental course as well as one filled with psychological trauma. We shall focus more closely upon this in chapter 10.

DISCUSSION

In any discussion of the reciprocal nature of mother-infant or parent-child dialogue, the final fault is usually found with the parent. Much is made of the parents' "use" of the child as a selfobject or of their efforts to expand their own narcissism to feelings of well-being. But every parent uses the child as a selfobject, just as every mother needs the baby's responsiveness to continue the feeding, the cooing, and the dialogue. Spitz (1964) said "the mutual exchanges between mother and baby consist in a give and take of action and reaction between the two partners, which requires from each of them both active and passive responses. . . . I designated these seriated response exchanges as "the precursor of dialogue," as a primal dialogue (p. 774)''. A dialogue requires two, and the supposed partnership of infant development is really a journey to true intersubjectivity preceded by a long series of negotiated steps. Children somehow fool parents into seeing them as equal partners in working out the patterns of give and take, but we are essentially always dealing with parental fantasies about children until the child can disabuse the parents of their image of the child. The child of a depressed mother can manage to understand her and treat her accordingly—and perhaps one day even become a therapist. Such children are empathic by way of successfully negotiating what is necessary to remain in continual contact or in a reciprocal relationship with the mother. That child may or may not be himself depressed or disturbed, but that is fundamentally a different issue. One may feel that it is unfair for a parent to so mold a child wittingly, or otherwise, but the nature of the developing process is unfair and accords preferential status to the parent. In like fashion, the child of a mother who masks her depression may not have access to those qualities of the inner life that allow empathy to develop. This child will be different by way of a failure to maintain a communicative contact and will have thereby negotiated a different form of relationship. Again, one cannot make any judgment about the child's mental health from this scenario.

Psychoanalysis and psychotherapy parallel this development of the growth of empathy. The two participants are engaged in a dialogue that is essentially unequal no matter how much one or the other professes otherwise. The analyst entertains a series of fantasies about the patient in terms of explaining the origin and conditions of his present mental state. He, by definition, knows more and is ahead of the patient. The patient attempts to gain access to the analyst's imaginings (or theory) and, in a sense, to fulfill the expectations of the therapist. The procedure involves language and gesture but digs deeply into the earliest form of rhythms and turn-taking. The negotiation that takes place on these different levels ideally changes both partners, who become more in touch with one another and thus achieve something that more closely approaches reciprocity. This process should result in enhanced empathy for both participants and is much like successful parenthood in this regard.

SUMMARY

The lack of empathy in a child derives from at least three sources: (1) the basic equipment of cognitive development; (2) the presence or absence of disruptive anxiety, and (3) access or barriers to a parent who allows for empathy to be learned. The deficiency of selected areas of empathy is not to be equated with psychopathology. In the most general way we might say that children develop empathy via a long developmental interaction with parents, and that process may or may not result in mental illness. There is no simple transfer of empathy from parent to child. If mentally ill, a child may be said at times to be lacking in empathy for others, but this too is not always the case since other factors bring about such empathic failures. The mentally ill child is said to need empathic responses from others for cure to take place, but that simple prescription is likewise inadequate. As Kohut (1984) notes, empathy is but one factor in treatment, and empathy with oneself is not the same as empathy with others.

If empathy is on a different track from mental health, we certainly need to know why such a brief is made for its helpful and therapeutic powers. The answer may lie in its selective application, in its sustained use, or in some not yet fully explained and detailed developmental line of empathy. As of now, all one can say is that the unempathic child makes others feel isolated and distraught and that an empathic environment certainly makes one feel better. The long process of ascertaining how this transforms to self-empathy and how this, in turn, leads to psychological well-being merits much further analytic scrutiny.

III

CHARACTER

10

The Structure of
the Self

The man who is considered the founder of French semantics and a forerunner of the philosophy of stucturalism, Ferdinand de Saussure (1916), offered an illustration of the concept of "structure" in his telling of the planned stop of the 8:05 train from Paris to Geneva. This particular train arrived regularly at approximately 8:05 and is thus distinguished from the 7:05 and the 10:05. It is composed of an engine and a number of cars, but these are not necessarily the same from one day to the next: one day the new cars and the next day the old. Neither the composition nor the elements nor the particulars of the train need be constant in order for it to be the 8:05. Rather its position in the general pattern of train arrivals and departures and its relations to other trains' comings and goings becomes the single issue in considering it as the 8:05. "Structuralism", then, directs our attention to the forms and patterns by which the composite elements connect and relate to one another, while it also lessens our attention to the particular composition of those elements. To be sure, we often identify the unique element as essentially embodying the structure—a favorite seat on a favorite train might lead one to feel he is riding the "old 8:05" as it wends its way to a different destination at a different time. It may seem to be folly to try to distinguish and separate form from content or pattern from composition since they remain an inextricable unit. However, a great deal of work in fields allied to psychoanalysis, for example, linguistics, and especially the work of Noam Chomsky, has prospered under just such a division. For language, it may simply be separating syntax, or formal structure, from semantics or meaning.

For psychoanalysis a similar project may offer a fruitful road of inquiry. The task for a psychoanalytic division of labor between pattern and elements would be to decide a proper object of study, e.g., the ego, for the pattern or organization, and to then determine if it and its stability would override issues of composition, which would then become secondary (the 8:05 may use the cars with the seats of red upholstery as well as those of yellow leather). The implications of this investigation may or may not be far ranging but certainly might over time modify our concepts of health and disease. We might be able thereupon to classify disorders as primary and secondary: those that had to do with a basic organization would be more or less the primary determinant of psychopathology, whereas secondary elements would only lend color and substance to fill out the basic program.

There exists a host of mental phenomena that exhibit structure whether we define it as innate constraints or capacity to act or enduring function. Visual perception, for example, is a mental process that is limited by the quality of the light rays that can stimulate it or arouse a response. It is evoked in a learned manner that can, for example, be investigated by raising kittens in the dark or by ablating certain neuronal pathways. It has adapted in special ways in certain cultures— such as the Eskimos with snow—so that certain things are perceived in very particular, learned ways. All mental processes naturally may become involved in a psychoanalytic investigation, but only some will be relevant to the analytic situation and a readiness for change with analytic intervention. Thus the task becomes narrowed.

If, following Kohut (1971), we choose to select the self rather than the ego as the basic form or organization that we will study, then a number of principles as well as questions will present themselves. This particular form will be a stable configuration at certain periods of life and will undergo modification during growth and development that will follow some sets of rules and regulations. Any other organization that we choose to study, inside or outside of the realm of human psychology or biology, likewise preserves some fixed aspects that allow it to be considered the same over periods of time, even though it may undergo extensive modifications and even dramatic recastings. Thus the fixed form of the self is a phenomenon of varied manifestations throughout a person's life. Any particular method of studying this form, such as psychoanalysis, will reveal certain crucial or dominant types of this configuration and will allow us to consider the form in its plural sense; that, we seem to show different selves at different times. A transformation of such a fixed and relatively stable form means not only that the configuration is seen to look different, that is, not only to operate in a manner different from the usual, but also that a different set of rules governs the operation of the system. Thus when see a particular person or self-system engaged in a creative pursuit, we can say that the self is in a transformed state and is functioning according to a different program or set of plans. To be sure, this sort of conclusion is only valid according to the method of inquiry that is being employed and the kind of data that one is able to gather. And it follows that psychoanalytic observation of creative persons may or may not reveal whatever is crucial to the unique operations of a creative self.

When we say that a form is operating under certain rules, we should remember that these range from the constraints imposed by the physical limits of the system—for example, the retina is not responsive to certain wavelengths of light—to the limits imposed by the particular environment one lives in—certain sorts of behavior are more acceptable than others and certain kinds are strictly forbidden. Unfortunately, psychoanalysis does not always have a neat set of rules for observing the proper or healthy operations of the phenomena that we study, and we likewise are uncertain about the rules that we follow in our therapeutic encounters. But we need to know that, either explicitly or implicitly, we can apply a sort of normative program to developmental lines as well as to the process of analytic treatment. Such rules are evidence of proper functioning of the observed system, and in a somewhat circular fashion we say that our evaluation of structure is based on unchanging or slowly changing function. Our rules of governance of a system or organization are a complex amalgam of cultural values, personal prejudices, and empirically tested and validated prescriptions of behavior. Examples of rules, which need much further elaboration (see chapter 13), range from the capacity to free associate to Freud's goals of maturity being the ability to love and to work. Examples of not following the rules would be some sort of acting-out behavior or an inability to form or sustain a workable transference. Rules become a measure of, or guideline to, intact or healthy structure.

The elements of a structure call for an important point of differentiation. If a given organization is operating smoothly under certain agreed upon rules and procedures, then the particular aspects of one or another part of the pattern are of secondary importance, becoming part of the background. Just as the 8:05 is considered as doing its job on one day or another if it arrives, departs, and delivers its passengers according to schedule, so too does a self function well if it follows its own set of plans. But the makeup of the train, although of interest, is not of primary relevance, nor is the makeup of the ego or the self-organization. Following Kohut (1971), we would say that mirroring, for example, is a function that can be carried out by a variety of selfobjects without attention being paid to their individual makeup. If we grant this assumption, then we might go so far as to say that the particular meanings attributed to any given form of ideation or behavior by a person are *delivered* by the self-system but perhaps also are essentially of secondary significance. Now, meaning per se is a very loaded and hotly debated point within and outside of psychology. What something or someone means is often felt to be the hallmark of a depth psychology and in case conferences is often delivered in a somber tone loaded with profound significance. Without in any way taking away from the profundity of that moment, we would offer the idea that meaning is subsumed under the smooth functioning of the self. The structure delivers the meaning. It is the framework within which meaning and its associated term understanding, are able to operate and to be articulated. Just as rules and regulations demand a more elaborate description, so too does this complex notion of meaning. For now, we note that our attention to particular moments of meaning may detract from our comprehension of the underlying framework or matrix within which it lies and can be expressed.

A true structural psychology can be outlined that places structural considerations at the bottom or as the basis of our study of individuals. A given bit of behavior may mean something that can be decoded, much as Freud and his successors in psychoanalysis have done with symptoms, parapraxis, and jokes. Hence, there is a story of sorts told within each such unpacking of one or another mental complex. But it is also the case that the delivery of the symptom or joke reflects a basic underlying structure that is revealed along with the phenomenon that is being scrutinized. Some stories are decipherable only if this structure is intact, and whether or not the story is demonstrated in one or another manner becomes of secondary importance. There is no doubt that much of modern psychoanalysis has assumed some sort of structural integrity as a given and thereupon has devoted itself wholly to the intriguing task of investigating the varied forms of meaning that an intact structure would deliver. Here we see the myriad ways that the oedipal conflict is lived out. But perhaps a case can be made for this being essentially a misplaced emphasis since it is the system that merits our attention. To pursue our analogy, the train tracks must be intact. What emerges from the system is understanding (Goldberg, 1983).

A therapist tells of a patient seen some years ago in a long analysis. He describes her retrospectively, using the idiolect of modern psychoanalysis, while noting that his ideas of that time were not abreast of the knowledge of today. Thus he would say that when first seen the patient fit the criteria of a borderline personality, and her treatment followed the trials and tribulations of the work with such a category of disorder. After a period of time she seemed to settle down and improve and, in today's parlance, assumed all of the appearance and behavior of a narcissistic personality disorder. We assume that the experience and knowledge of this analytic practitioner led him to these categories only by a correlated appearance of the appropriate transference manifestations. He continued his analysis of the patient, and over time she showed what he described as classical oedipal problems with their concomitant display of jealousy, rivalry, and intensely competitive issues. The analysis was terminated apparently successfully after the supposed resolution of these belatedly revealed conflicts. After termination, the patient continued to correspond with the analyst, and, to his dismay, a reverse regression seemed to ensue. She wrote irregularly, but often enough for him to see the gradual deterioration of her condition to the point where he was considering her to be once again a typical borderline personality with episodes of near paranoia, addictive propensities, and a fairly isolated condition. He attributes much of this to the loss of some important real figures in her life, but he remains puzzled as to why the treatment seemed not to hold. One may say that the patient seemed to demonstrate a structural regression, but it is not quite so clear that her improvement is equally a structural progression. If we concentrate on what are essentially the secondary phenomena of a personality organization, we may indeed see that patients do essentially tell different stories at different times of their (and our) lives. But the stories need not correlate or exist parallel with the state of structural integrity. Schizophrenic patients often have vivid oedipal conflicts. This patient *may* have utilized her therapist to insure her self-integrity but without its becoming the central focus of the interpretive work of her treatment, it soon evaporated under the stress of her life.

The question that naturally arises is, how does one pay attention to these issues of pattern or organization that we consider evidence of structural integrity or structural defect? Are our accustomed investigations of meanings not an appropriate avenue to determine levels of psychopathology, and are we indeed listening to the words instead of the music? And, perhaps equally important, mightn't all our attention to the nuances and particulars of our patients narratives really be besides the point? Might we not be listening to a set of meanings that are at a different level than those which reveal the state of integrity of the system?

To answer the question of how one determines and then attends to the level of communication that reflects a state or condition of underlying structure rather than addressing the secondary characteristics of the presentation, we must separate a category of data that is appropriate to our posed problem. That requires, first, a clarification of the nature of the connections or links that make up the organized whole. We ask how aspects of the self come together; this mechanism reveals itself in the manner of any self-selfobject linkage. It is in the communicative process that we find how parts of the self system join up, and it is in the process of understanding that we unravel the complex matrix of meaning. People connect to one another by a series of affective exchanges that run the gamut of gestures and verbal exchanges from infancy to adulthood, and this intricate web of connections comprises the structure of the self-organization. The messages exchanged between persons travel along a system that must allow for the delivery of particular meanings. This may sound more mysterious than it is meant to be: it merely separates the conditions for understanding, such as a mutual possession of a common language, from the actual message that is sent and received. In the psychoanalytic situation, the task is to see the transference as a medium that allows communication between patient and analyst rather than as something that is primarily about the mother or about the father.

As a contrasting illustration of this view of the self as an organization, let us examine one that considers it as composed of units that operate and predominate at different times (Eisnitz, 1980). The situation is likened to a gestalt, with one unit being more highly cathected than others at anyone time. This dominant unit exerts an organizing influence on the remainder of the self-representations, which become less highly operational. Thus, at any given time, the person operates in one mode, say in his or her occupation, while others, such as one's family life, are subsidiary. Since there are many ways to slice a pie, our earlier analogy can perhaps be extended to suggest an alternative view. Railroads do many things: they deliver goods and people, are a part of the local and national economy, are objects of aesthetic enjoyment for some people and phobic objects for others. These various functions are, however, not units of the railroad, as are the parts that make up the depot, the barns, and the trains. Rather they are simultaneously operating functions that evoke different, selective, and quantitatively varied attention. One must take care in choosing whether the units of the self have to do with varied emergent functions or with other sorts of constituent elements. What "makes up" the self has to do with its underlying structure. To say that it consists of units that connect with objects, past and present, unconscious wishes, superego and ego goals, and the necessary ego faculties seems to conflate the underlying organization and its many operative capacities (Eisnitz,

1980). So too can we say that the self does many things simultaneously and that the same self shows different aspects at different times. Complex wholes certainly do allow one aspect to dominate at one time or another, but these aspects are not units anymore than the place of the railroad in the country's overall transportation system is a unit. A puzzle thus presents itself as to where and whether one can effectively delineate the basic structure from the more simple and more complex phenomena that are perceived.

We are faced with the problem of exactly what a self is made of when we try to differentiate its basic components, say arms and legs, from basic representations, such as fathers and workers. In the same way, we may attempt to separate off a basic configuration of any system.

It is tempting to see the self as composed of units and to follow its growth as one builds a whole from these units. This may not be possible and may defeat the idea that the self is a whole or a set as it comes into being and so is *not made up* of smaller parts. Thus there may be a vagueness in our determination of the elements of the self, which as a whole thus far can be defined only as the relationship (i.e., the connections) that makes for understanding. One patient, for instance, tells of making several appointments with friends over a weekend in order to stabilize and regulate himself and prevent a sort of regressive disorganization that occurs when he is left to his own devices. One of his appointments was abruptly cancelled by a friend, and subsequently the patient did experience the expected state of disorganization. Although the patient insisted that the missed meeting was merely a nodal point or a precipitant in his feeling out of sorts, the therapist could not let it rest at that, since he wondered if there were not accompanying feelings of hurt and anger at what was essentially a rejection. Was this an example of fragile structure held intact by a schedule with fairly replaceable others, or was this a case where one needed to examine the particular nature of the relationship that was a dimension of concern that goes beyond the basic organization? The railroad could be said to be made up of tracks and trestles or nuts and bolts, but this could defeat the point of having a definable unit as a basic structure. We choose such a unit on the basis of its special place in the overall form: for the railroad it may be the Paris-Geneva connection rather than a car or a depot; for the person it is a meaningful relation rather than a body or a body part.

The determination of a meaningful overall form of the self should therefore be the fundamental goal for our study. It, in turn, will be composed of relationships or connections. It has a multitude of manifestations or representations and therefore is the object of our study because it displays a variety of messages or meanings. But we look beyond these phenomena to what is underlying: the structure. This structure, then, is composed of a set of relations, has rather fixed forms, and delivers many meanings as it is represented. Similarly, a railroad consists of trains and tracks that spread out into a regular schedule and serves many functions for the community and environment in which it operates. Thus three levels: the nuts and bolts, the basic structure or organization, and the multitude of observable activities or representations.

A CLOSER LOOK AT THE LEVELS

Since any word or concept or object can be seen to have many meanings, one can never be certain of the single or main meaning assigned. A patient's upset over the cancellation of an hour may be due to a fantasy about what would have been done in the missing time or a specific reaction to the manner in which it was handled or to the mere introduction of an irregularity into an accustomed sequence. Much as we take comfort in our assumption that the real meaning will arise in the associations, we have learned that this may be false reassurance. The patient's associations do deliver meanings, but we do not always hear them, or the problem may not be articulated in the statements that emerge. It is in the first of our three levels, the underlying elements of the structure, that this is often the case.

Evidence of problems that occur on the level of the building blocks of the structure is seen in just those cases whose stability depends on the apparent contentless aspects of treatment. Patients who seem to pull themselves together or reintegrate when they are hospitalized or put under a strict schedule are said to use the environment as structure, but just what the structure is, is often hazy. Likewise, adolescents who thrive under various forms of external controls or limit setting have their improvement explained in a similar manner. Analytic patients who seem primarily interested in the rules and regulations of the analytic setting and whose stable transferences seem to dissolve under small changes in the setting are also members of this group. Indeed, no one seems totally immune to a potential state of agitation that demands some period of settling down (see Gedo and Goldberg, 1973, for an extensive discussion of pacification). The major factor in this consideration of such tension regulation is that it seems relatively free of psychological content (or meaning) and does not yet qualify for inclusion in one or another particular form of transference. The range of pathology goes from the narcissistically vulnerable person, for whom an average day is a series of horrible rebuffs, injuries, and disruptions, to the well-adjusted person, whose move to a new home or office requires a long period of getting things in their place and getting oneself in a proper alignment with everything. Such conditions lend themselves nicely to metaphors of construction—psychological glue, the nuts and bolts of everyday life, the holding environment, etc. Using a communication metaphor, we probably would say that all the wiring is in place; in a social service agency we might feel that the support network is intact.

The category that we seek to delineate by the introduction of the building blocks for stability is to be separated from the kinds of messages that are carried by the intact wires. These messages have to do with our consideration of the concept of understanding whereas the intactness of the aforementioned structure is a prerequisite and thus is more properly considered as preunderstanding. No doubt everyone can claim a sense of ownership to those structures that constitute the building blocks of the self, but, more often than not, they are exchangeable, interchangeable and easily adapted.

The distinction of the second level is that it is a specific form of organization. It is shaped by and composed of the kinds of selfobject transferences that Kohut (1971) described, and thus it serves particular functions, primarily in the regulation and maintenance of self-esteem. The connecting links between self and selfobject that constitute this form, that is, a stable configuration over time, are themselves composed of affective exchanges that fall under the broad rubric of understanding. We relate or communicate with one another by virtue of empathic exchanges that are the medium by which we say that we understand one another. Certainly much of human exchange may take place without the ingredient of empathy, and there seems little doubt that our baseline for communication probably should be misunderstanding. That is to say that we usually start with some sort of misunderstanding and then struggle to achieve understanding. There probably is no clearcut answer to the question of whether infants and mothers are naturally attuned at birth and become periodically disrupted, or whether attunement is an achievement of mutual effort (see chapter 16 on Mirroring). Nevertheless, it does seem clear that attunement becomes a variable state between infant and caretakers as well as between the developing child and adolescent of later life. The sine qua non for effective analytic therapy is to understand the patient. This is said to be ameliorative, if not curative, and necessary, if not sufficient, for any longlasting effect of treatment. In Kohut's (1971) concept of treatment, the process is characterized by a series of empathic connections or states of understanding followed by empathic breaks, which are then repaired by interpretation. This leads to his term for structure building: transmuting internalization. Thus, the meanings that are focused are those that have to do with the affective state or charge that accompanies feeling understood, feeling a break in being understood, and the subsequent reestablishment of a merger, which Kohut considers equivalent to a state of mutual understanding. This state is not merely that of the glue or holding previously discussed; the particulars of these transferences demand specific sorts of messages. So, too, the interpretations that are designed to heal the disruptions require the explanatory material that have to do with the individual and unique exchanges between patient and analyst. Yet the basic ingredient of this approach is a singular emphasis on interpretations that refer to empathic breaks, and, in a parallel way, reconstructions that deal with similar failures in attaining and maintaining empathic understanding between patient and child.

The implications of Kohut's thesis are far reaching since it is essentially a reduction of all psychopathology to a dysfunctioning self that comes about from empathic breaks. The nature of the disorganization, the fragmentation, is a secondary phenomenon that is also of secondary importance because it is readily, albeit not easily, eliminated once empathy can be restored. For the moment, we can put aside the developmental progress that follows in an empathic environment as we concentrate on the pathological issues. If all psychopathology is the result of a less than intact system, we can assume that the system can, once intact, serve a variety of other functions that need not reflect any psychopathology per se. This says no more than that many kinds of communication can travel over the self-organization or between self and selfobject, that functions which are not related to self-regulation are not relevant to this state of disorganization, and that many meanings are exchanged that are not a part of mental illness. This sounds like a computer model that demonstrates that intact hardware can be used by a variety of software. But this is the least significant comment to be made about a self structure, since there is no easy separation between structure and function. In our view, the different functions will come to be seen later, in the third level.

The third level of concern has to do with the many sorts of representations that this structure may manifest. If the train and its tracks and stations and equipment are connected and running, then the system can deliver people or cattle or grain, all of which are secondary to the railroad system. These particulars, as opposed to the elements of construction that we took as the first level, or building blocks, are of primary significance to many concerns about the railroad but not to its operation or functioning per se. Nor are they the same as the operating capacity of the system. That exists, as noted earlier, as an overall form that sits between the elements and the representations. The meaning of specific representations not only occurs within, and is hence shaped by, an overall form, but must also be gauged with respect to the resulting understandability of the form itself. Thus we build upon the state of understanding that we introduced with the self-selfobject linkage. Under pain of overstretching our analogy, we can imagine states where the train is late to arrive because of schedule problems, too many cars trying to use too few sets of tracks, or a variety of other problems that are akin to the dynamics of the situation. These phenomena may show what appears to be a conflict, but the appearance of conflict is not a result of any structural problem; rather it has more to do with the ability of the system to manage the demands placed upon it. Just as a conflict can be resolved by a reordering and redistribution of relative demands and capacities, we can say that an intact self can survive many conflicts without any sign of pathology, that is, of structural breakdowns. Thus, the third level of meanings that are exchanged have to do with the many stores or narratives that are created during treatment. How it is that so many different theories of treatment are seemingly effective is answered by recognizing that these stories are more like epiphenomena than directly related to the formation of a dissolution of psychopathology.

Most of what transpires in psychotherapy and psychoanalysis has to do with just those stores that come alive in the process. Although understanding of a patient is essential, it is neither sufficient nor an answer for everything, Kohut (1984) felt that the explanations that follow such understanding enabled a higher level of empathy. This proposition may do a disservice to the significance of the exchange of meanings, the explanations that go on. Kohut probably wanted to emphasize the underlying structural component while minimizing explanations in his concept of cure. But the third level of meanings, the narrative exchange, does comprise the major activity of most treatment, and it adds to the cure by allowing the achievement of a mechanism of self-reflection that may be likened to a mechanism of self-maintenance. The ability to think about and reflect upon one's relationships to others is essentially the ability to explain to oneself what has been understood and thus insures the continuity and later development of the self. The stories are important. The meanings that are delivered are significant. Though perhaps secondary in the psychopathology, they are primary in the development and maintenance of the relations to the sustaining selfobjects. It remains our task to distinguish these levels and to search for empirical support for what makes for psychopathology and what is needed for its treatment. The story may, in turn, tell about the very need to maintain connection and so doubly insure the needed form of help.

ILLUSTRATION

Level 1—The Basic Connections

A female patient in analysis for several years showed a repeated problem that occurs whenever she or the analyst take a vacation. She found herself apprehensive before the separation, but regardless of the particular pleasure or pain of the time apart she was always temporarily "out of synch" for several hours after her return. No matter if she had a fantasy of what happened when she or the analyst was gone, she remained in a state close to disorientation until some time, often several days, had elapsed. She felt quite strongly that she could not be hurried into resuming the normal work of analysis nor could the analyst say or do anything to facilitate the reentry. He could, however, make it worse. It became worse, for example, when he gave her hours to other patients while she was away in order not to charge her for the missed times. This was quite unnerving to her because she needed to feel that the hours remained hers, that they were in place for her whether or not she was able to utilize them. Thus, when she had to leave the analysis for a brief period, she was much relieved to feel that her analytic hours would remain hers and not be even temporarily offered to other patients. No amount of scrutiny of her reaction to separation revealed any particular psychological content to this problem or to the solution of keeping the patient's hours open for her.

Here we have an example of a vulnerable person for whom the regularity of the analysis shored up the fragility of the self. Such regularity is akin to the rhythms of exchange between mother and child but is inevitably more than that since it is a part of almost every form of human relationships. Usually it is taken for granted. Most people have enough such basic connections to allow it to remain in the background, but it is essential to the further development and elaboration of the complex organization that is the self. Further development of the self is, however, something effected by action rather than insight, and so is not easily approached by a pure psychological intervention.

Level 2—The Self-Structure as a Basic Form

This patient over time developed a selfobject transference to the analyst that dealt with the emergence of an original, creative, and self-sufficient individual. Overcoming great resistances having to do with a multitude of somatic symptoms, she revealed a talent for writing that was quite stimulating to her but in perpetual need of a buffering response. This mirroring relationship was seen to have been only temporarily emergent in childhood because the birth of a very sickly brother had caused her parents to turn from her while asking that she be of no trouble and concern so that they could tend to the brother. The transference enabled her to have the nascent exhibitionistic feelings understood. It was likewise seen to effect a transformation into a highly creative person who during periods of creativity could operate in an expansive and daring manner but who at other times was indecisive and uncertain.

This thumbnail sketch of one form of the self is reflective of the mainstay of the work on narcissistic disorders. This self has one form and one transformation and illustrates how the basic connections coalesce to the complexity of a self-configuration.

Level 3—The Meanings

The patient was a poet who composed intricate and moving pieces that could be decoded to reveal the story of a lonely and neglected girl whose parents had little time for her. Some of the analysis had to do with filling in the story of her childhood; some of it had to do with the dreams that related to her wish for recognition of her talent; and some had to do with the construction of the product of her efforts, her poetry. Her history, her dreams, and her poetry were at one time or another all representations of the form of her self. If the patient felt understood, then the explanations that followed filled in her life's story, made sense of her dreams, and better constructed her poetry. Some of the explanations were about being able to be understood, following Kohut's basic premise that the disruptions of analysis are the groundwork for interpretations. But meanings are much more complex than this single line, no matter if everything ultimately is reduced to it, and some lines of her poetry were so rich in meaning that it would be a disservice to reduce them to this singular intent. The act of making poetry became the vehicle for self-reflection that allowed the patient to become free of the transference that had sustained her. The creation and exchange of meanings allows us to understand ourselves and of others.

This overview of the structure to which we attend is designed as a paradigm for all therapeutic evaluations and interventions. It opens the door to the possibility that psychopathology that responds to analytic treatment pertains to the integrity of the basic organization.

If the components of this organization are missing or feeble, then the treatment will have to do with issues of rules and regularity. If the self is defective, then the treatment will have to do with increasing the avenues of understanding. Then the decoding of the many representations or manifestations of the self will enable the self-reflection that is essential to the maintenance of a vigorous and adaptive self.

11

On the Nature of
the "Misfit"

This chapter describes and explains a particular form of character that has not heretofore received attention in the psychoanalytic literature: the misfit. Fenichel (1945) defined character as "the ego's habitual modes of adjustment to the external world, the id, and the superego, and the characteristic type of combining these modes with one another" (p. 467). Kernberg's (1970) addition to the accepted knowledge of character pathology was based on a consideration of "structural and genetic-dynamic [factors] in addition to purely descriptive ones" (p. 820). This paper will offer a developmental perspective, describing the misfit as a person in transition from one developmental stage to another, unable to either forge ahead or adapt successfully through retreat. Being a misfit has a certain universality since everyone has at some time had the experience of being in a situation and feeling he or she simply did not belong. Some individuals, however, have a chronic and pervasive subjective feeling of not being able to fit in; thus, we can examine this as a particular form of character pathology.

In discussing the manifestations of a person's character in analytic treatment, I would echo Freud's (1916) statement that "peculiarities . . . which [the patient] seemed to possess only to a modest degree are often brought to life in surprisingly increased intensity, or attitudes reveal themselves . . . which had not been betrayed in other relations of life" (p. 311). This emphasizes the fact that a psychoanalytic definition of character is less concerned with overt behavior or a phenom-enological nosology and more with the analytic method for develop-ing such a classification. Our focus is thus on the patient's subjective sense—the patient's feeling about himself or herself as it becomes revealed in the transference. One of the problems of character classification is that it attempts to bridge intrapsychic and interper-sonal considerations and thus may blur what should remain a primari-ly psychoanalytic method of organizing clinical material. Just as depres-sion is a diagnosis that concentrates on the subjective sense of sadness rather than merely the objective listing of depressive features, so too the psychoanalytic definition of the misfit conforms to this focus on the subjective.

DEFINITION OF MISFIT

When Hartmann (1939) discussed adaptation as an individual's rela-tion to "a typical average environment" (p. 16), he was emphasizing the coming together of ego and external world; and he underscored this as the basis of the concept of "health." To isolate the misfit as a person with a particular form of character pathology, it is necessary at the outset to define the term primarily in its *subjective* sense as a feeling of not belonging, of not fitting in. Of course, this feeling need bear no relationship to how successfully a person adapts to the en-vironment in reality. Misfits are people who *feel* themselves alien to those around them and who, for a variety of reasons, fail to attain that comforting harmony that Harmann felt was so essential for a designa-tion of health. Their actual success in functioning is therefore subor-dinate to their lack of a sense of union and connectedness.

Misfits are defined in terms of their individual relationship to the larger group. As such they merit comparison with another charactero-logical subgroup of Freud's, the "exceptions" (Freud, 1916). These are people who claim privilege over others because of suffering they experienced early in childhood, suffering they regard as an unjust disad-vantage. Freud used the deformity of Richard III to exemplify how one such person had converted an early narcissistic injury into a privileged position and thus into exemption from "life's impor-tunities." He likewise noted that women in general regard themselves as having been damaged in infancy and therefore feel continual em-bitterment and reproach toward their mother.

My own clinical material deals with patients who have clearly and consistently felt exceptional and different, as well as outside of things and apart from others. They did not belong, did not fit in, felt terribly excluded, and longed to lose themselves in the larger group. Although they fit the superficial dynamics of the exception in having sustained a narcissistic injury that set them apart, there is also a distinct disparity in the degree of comfort with which misfits treat their difference. Some misfits relish the feeling of being a bit outside the ordinary. Others periodically long to belong. This dimension of indifference is one criterion of how one reacts to being different.

Misfits can also be seen as clustering at one end of a continuum of being exceptional and different. The eccentricity of strangeness that partially characterizes the misfit places this individual on the end of the line extending from absolute conformity to bizarre outsider. One's exceptionality can be treated as a vice or virtue, either appreciated or condemned by others. The relationship of the outsider to the inner group and its emotional tone further differentiate him or her. Nonbelongers may be talented, strange, freakish, but are further distinguished by their wish to be less so and by their longing for acceptance. The group that I have chosen to examine is thus characterized by a dual problem of eccentricity and exclusion. On some occasions, members of this group become resigned to this state of affairs and even treat their exclusion with a "sour grapes" attitude. However, for the most part, this is a protective façade and soon gives way to the painful longing to belong. In contrast to Freud's group, they feel both exceptional *and* underprivileged.

It appears most natural to approach this topic positively, that is, to examine how one manages to achieve a feeling of belonging or group membership, rather than how one fails at this task. Such a study would entail an examination of certain functions having to do with the adaptation and modification of one's infantile needs in response to the harshness of reality, much as Hartmann has suggested. It would also concentrate on the development of those capacities that allow one to perform adequately with and among others, as well as on the ability to control certain obnoxious characteristics and behavior.

This is not the point of view here, however. The feeling of being a misfit has a special meaning for people, and the elucidation of this meaning is the goal here. The feeling of belonging is a positive accomplishment that is part of most people's normal development. The experience of not belonging is an equal partner in many of life's sequences. However, the ever present sense of being an outsider who knows what to do and yet cannot do it, of being at a loss as to how to perform is peculiar to the misfit.

CLINICAL EXAMPLE

The clinical material that follows is used to develop a possible generalization about misfits. Even though the misfit's state can rightfully be viewed as a universal phenomenon not peculiar to any sort of familiar diagnostic category, it is hoped that this analysis will reveal some principle or set of relationships particular to this condition. The case to be presented also serves to differentiate the "misfit" from Freud's "exceptions."

This is a case of a homosexual man who despised his sexual orientation, who longed to be heterosexual, and who entered analysis primarily because of his unhappiness over homosexuality. He presented a blatant case of someone who did not fit in: he refused to belong to any sort of homosexual group, yet could not bring himself to an identification with heterosexuality. His sense of being "neither fish nor fowl" had its origin quite early in his life and went far beyond his sexual proclivity. Born into a blue-collar family of high school graduates, the patient was an only son, with one older and one younger sister. He was a strikingly unusual child. The patient became a professional with an outstanding college record. He seemed different from his family in almost every conceivable way. His father was a gruff, beer-drinking, television-watching factory worker. The patient loved music and fought with his parents for violin lessons. He was bookish and sensitive and totally at odds with the interests of his family. To this day, his mother is never quite certain what he does in his work, and she has an air of not quite comprehending that he is indeed her son.

The mother's difficulty in accepting her maternity seemed to be an issue early in this man's life. His mother seemed chained to her own mother, who seemed overtly psychotic and who was always at their home. That patient's mother had little time for her son. The patient always was fearful of his grandmother. He knew that he was intruding into the relationship between her and his mother whenever he wanted a little time and attention from his mother. He recalled being sent off repeatedly to play, at the early age of about four years, when this hardly was his desire or intent. Sometimes he would go upstairs to a neighbor's house to talk or to sit in the kitchen with her. He was a thin boy until about age seven and a half, when this neighbor moved away, and he then began to eat a great deal. Although his sister was eight years younger than he, he later insisted that he felt the eating change was not due to her birth but to his having nowhere to go and no one to talk to. Overall, he recalled being quite anxious all through his childhood and strongly insisted that no one supervised him or paid much attention to him. It was evident in the transference, however, that he felt only certain aspects of himself merited attention, while other parts of his personality were best left ignored.

The patient's sexual history seemed to parallel some of the key points of his life. He recalled the age of four years as the time when he looked at and touched little girls and the age of eight years as when he began homosexual activity of a sort by grabbing and feeling other boys. He described how a classmate in grammar school later involved him in mutual masturbation. He said that he was afraid to tell the teacher and unable to resist the advances of the other child. He masturbated regularly and continually throughout high school. Later in the analysis he revealed that when he was an adult, masturbation or going to pornographic movies was an almost daily occurrence. He was shocked to realize the all consuming nature of his sexual preoccupation.

Apart from the mutual fondling in grammar school, which lasted only a short time, the patient's first homosexual behavior did not occur until he was approximately twenty years old. His first experience was not a pleasant one, but he soon became involved with a young man who was his lover for several years before he started analysis. Shortly before treatment began, their sexual life became meager, and they drifted apart soon thereafter. The patient was unable to attend homosexual bars since he felt horrified at the idea of being identified as a homosexual. His sexual orientation was unknown to all save a few close friends.

During the beginning of the analysis, the patient revealed another form of sporadic sexual behavior that he found particularly distasteful. This consisted of going to a popular place in the park where a number of men congregated nightly. Sex there was flagrant, anonymous, and abbreviated. The people so totally lacked involvement that no one knew or cared who was doing what to whom. The patient was a completely passive sexual partner throughout the entire episode, which filled him with disgust, yet he periodically felt drawn to the place. This seemed to be a sexual display of his need to remain aloof and struggle against more meaningful involvement.

He described his family in bitter terms, with the exception of his older sister, who lived in California and whom he visited periodically. She was happily married and had a daughter and a son. The patient had less positive things to say about this younger sister, whom he described as needy and miserable. Next to his grandmother, his most negative description was saved for his father, who had died two years before our first analytic meeting. The father had sustained a heart attack some 16 years earlier (when the patient was ten), and had taken poor care of himself while relentlessly intimidating the family with his illness and possible death. The patient was extremely angry when discussing his father and commented that he had "not yet buried him."

The patient's mother was initially described as sweet, passive, and dependent on her own mother, who died shortly before the patient's father. This description of mother did not hold up in the analysis, since every conversation with her was reported in exasperated and frustrated words and tones. She had been ill for several years and could speak only about herself, her operation, and her suffering. There were few visits between the two, but they spoke on the telephone regularly. The patient did not see his mother as being much different than she had been during his childhood, except that his hateful grandmother was no longer in the way—but something else was. On the few occasions when they seemed close, it was because he was in the position of mothering her. As the analysis progressed, this relationship changed markedly, and he was able to create a situation in which his mother became more of a parent and even a friend.

This brief overview of the patient's history is intended as an orientation to the major points of the analysis that are pertinent to the consideration of the patient's picture of himself as a misfit. Similarly, the brief summary of the treatment will not be all inclusive, but will only highlight some salient points regarding the patient's character development.

The analysis progressed with relative ease. After a great deal of shame and embarrassment accompanying the exposure of the multitude of his sexual activities, the patient settled into a clear and intense father transference in which idealization played an important part. His relationships with others were passive and masochistic; and he complained bitterly about the mistreatment he felt that he endured from friends and colleagues. In the analysis he showed a deepening idealization of me and a quick change to incredible rage and subsequent sexualization at my failings and lack of concern. Missed appointments or weekend breaks usually resulted in homosexual acting out.

Over time, three phases of the relationship to the father were delineated. The first was periodic disruption of the relationship. This was most clearly related to the sexualization, which represented an attempt to harness severe excitement (Goldberg, 1975). Initially a rather common occurrence in analysis, the sexualization gradually diminished. When the patient was able to give up his daily, ritualized masturbation, he recalled for the first time an important experience that centered around the father's working nights and coming home in time to have breakfast with his son. When the father was late, the patient would be unable to wait because he would have to leave for school. At these times he would carefully watch the minute hand of the clock: and he would almost be in pain as the last minute ticked away, and he was forced to miss seeing his father. Often the father would bring home sweet rolls for breakfast and, on occasion, would bring a very special one that only the patient liked. The father did not always do this, but the patient remembered yearning for the special relationship with his father that that sweet roll represented. He also remembered that, for some reason, he never could ask his father to buy that special treat for him.

The second form of the relationship with the father was one of harmony. These recollections connected to increasing, long periods of equilibrium in the analysis. The patient recalled joining father on his many expeditions to sell certain wares, an extra business activity for the father, who wanted to be more than a mere factory worker. Some of the factors contributing to the patient's not fitting in are evident in the father's lack of contentment with his own lot in life.

The third relationship to the father was the most frightening for the patient and had to do with the lost or absent father. This issue always was in the air in analysis and was most likely to emerge during longer vacations. The patient likened his feeling about this to a feeling of falling apart and related it to both the father's heart attack and his death. The patient also recalled long periods of waiting quietly outside of father's door while he slept. The patient yearned for his father to awaken but feared his wrath if any noise woke him prematurely. This was the totally lost and then hated father. All of this was reexperienced and repeatedly interpreted in the analysis. After working through his paternal relationship, the analysis turned to the more frustrating one with the neglectful mother.

It may be of interest to try to explain why this man failed to gain a positive response from his mother. The interference offered by the grandmother was only one factor. Later we learned that his grandfather (the husband of this delusional woman) was an unusual person and perhaps even something of a misfit himself. He stayed away from the rest of the family, did his own work of carpentry in a private area of his house, and never seemed to be upset by the rantings of his wife. Her accusations against the grandfather were characteristic ones of jealousy and sexual betrayal; and it is small wonder that the patient's mother behaved in an unusual and apprehensive manner toward her father. She may have had a parallel transference toward her own son, considering him strange, unusual, and frightening. It would be too superficial an explanation, however, to say that the patient identified with the grandfather as a misfit and lived out maternal expectations. There is little doubt that eccentricity can serve to organize a personality, but such postures or "identities" are always social phenomena that need an in-depth psychological explanation. In this case, I concluded that the explanation lay in the fact that the patient was not properly mirrored by his mother, who could not free herself sufficiently from her own neurotic entanglements to do so adequately. Then, of necessity, the patient turned from her to his father, seeking an avenue for self-expression and development.

Coexisting with all the analytic work relating to the idealizing and disappointing relationship with the father was the patient's everpresent fear that the analysis and the analyst were forcing him toward heterosexuality. He experienced marked improvement in every other area of life, and he repeatedly faced his fear of and revulsion at being heterosexual. Although he had several women friends, he never had any intimate physical contact with them, and he could not manage much more than an occasional kiss.

For this patient, all sex was disgusting; he hated his body and felt ugly and awkward. As the material in the analysis shifted and revealed his secret pleasure in his own specialness, he recalled how his aunt and sister had dressed him as a girl when he was quite young. His mother made fun of his penis. He was laughed at whenever he was nude and the small size of his penis was emphasized. Later, everyone seemed to laugh at the possibility of his dating. He spoke about a fantasy in which he announced his marriage. His family would be shocked; it would hurt them. They thought of him as an eccentric, a weirdo. He would have especially liked to tell his best friend's mother, who had only contempt for him and who would have been crushed at his happiness. The analysis shifted to an intense feeling of hate toward those persons who might have responded positively to his achievements, his body, his masculinity, but who failed to do so.

At one point he reported a dream in which he felt as much in limbo in relation to his sexuality as he ever had. The dream report followed a session in which he told me how his father always belittled his masculine accomplishments and gloated over his failings. He dreamed of his French-made coffee maker, which has a plunger that separates the coffee grounds from the hot water in order to leave clear coffee floating on the top. He mistakenly added the coffee grounds to the top of the plunger and then stared at what he had done, feeling stupid because of his error, which would not allow the mixture to form. The patient associated to the evening before, when he had dinner with an old homosexual lover and the very attractive girlfriend of another friend. He felt very estranged from both of them and their relationships. The old lover was distant and still a little angry about his failure to revive a homosexual relationship with the patient. The sexually stimulating girl was filled with plans for her new marriage to their mutual friend. The patient felt very much a misfit since neither world seemed open to him, and the dream seemed to signify this inability to reconcile the separate parts of his life. The mix could not take place. Pushing the plunger (heterosexuality) would mix water and grounds and would be distasteful. Leaving it as it was would be unfulfilling. He felt just as he did when he could not be what he wanted to be for reasons unknown to him and was appreciated only for what he did not especially like about himself. He could not bring his worlds together, nor could he straddle them. The dream seems to graphically illustrate this failure.

From the early focus on sexual issues to the ever present failure to have recognition and appreciation from his parents, there was an extension to his overall brightness and talents. He recalled his graduation from grammar school and how everyone present seemed to feel that his celebration party was a burden. Every time he won an award in school, he was embarrassed and ashamed. He felt that his family was put out by his successes. As this feeling was examined in the transference, it became clear that his father especially had been afraid of losing him and experienced every difference between himself and the patient as a loss. The patient's homosexuality represented the sexualization of a self-presentation that could not otherwise evoke a positive response. Briefly, he felt his achievement hurt and angered others who would then be lost to him. His perverse sexual behavior took the form of being the passive partner in fellatio. Symbolically, this acted out his wish to maintain a relationship with his angry, threatened, unresponsive father by a sacrifice to the older man's needs.

In summary, the patient turned primarily to the father for fulfillment of both mirroring and idealizing needs. Although he seemed less traumatized in the idealizing aspect of his personality, he showed the dual problem characteristic of most perverse disorders. What was so telling about this patient's problem was his inability to reconcile these two sectors of his personality. His grandiose, narcissistic self was not responded to by his preoccupied or threatened parents. His need for an idealizing relationship was equally impaired. Each aspect of his self was sexualized separately. As one was repaired and reorganized, the other came more clearly into conflict with the environment and his selfobjects. A total solution to his problem lay in the analysis of the unresolved grandiose fantasy, which carried the seed of a masculine self that needed further growth through responsiveness. At every point in the transference, the developmental problem of "fitting in" came sharply into view. Neither a comfortable regression nor an easy road of progress was available to this man, for whom a happy union with his selfobjects had not been achieved. His temporary points of rest had to do with a fantasy of being "neuter," but this always was short lived, and he soon returned to feeling a misfit. No evidence of a twin-ship transference was seen. His problem was clearly one of fitting in rather than on of finding an alter ego.

DISCUSSION

There is an advantage to using the theory and models of self psychology to examine the phenomenon of the misfit, since it is essentially a very personal experience, albeit one directed toward an interpersonal or social state of affairs. The relationship between the self and other is, at times, less well depicted using the perspective of the self and discrete, separate objects than using that of the self and selfobjects. The latter perspective directly expresses the positive experience of fitting in and a concomitant feeling of unity and belonging. Thus, we might fruitfully study the attainment of such a feeling using a developmental approach to the self vis-à-vis its selfobjects. Such an approach would employ the models of the two poles of self development suggested by Kohut—the grandiose self and the idealized parental imago.

In Kohut's (1977) later discussion of self disorders, he emphasized the bipolarity of the self. Whereas initially we would follow development along either the grandiose self axis or the idealized parental imago axis, one or the other usually predominated, and this was the focus of the transference in analysis. Next Kohut urged a study of the relations *between* the two poles, concluding that the psychic health of the entire personality could be restored when functioning along one axis was rehabilitated; the archaic layers of the other would then fall away. Kohut emphasized less the content of one or another of the poles of the bipolar self than the relationship of one pole to the other. He suggested that development could be seen either as a succession of self-selfobject relations along one pole or as movement from one pole to the other. He also stated that later experience at one or another pole could compensate for an earlier defect. Psychoanalytic treatment would thereby heal a defect in one but not necessarily in both poles, since unipolar compensation could be wholly efficient in restituting a personality. The introduction of the twinship transference increases the number of possibilities but does not change the basic premise.

When Freud (1916) wrote about the "exception," he described the external and social manifestation of one type of disordered internal narcissistic configuration. In the exception, the relationship of the two poles is usually resolved in favor of the grandiose self; the misfit, however, remains in limbo. In terms of a developmental scheme, the misfit may represent a particular typological variation involving repeated incursions into a succeeding stage, which are unsuccessful but are not abandoned. Rather, the child (and later the adult) remains poised on the edge of a new developmental experience but has gone too far to be able to retreat. Successfully traversed, a developmental step allows integration of mastered behavior into one's personality; conversely, failure to participate in such a stage can lead to a lack of integration and mastery and the unique posture of being neither in nor out that is characteristic of borderline phenomena. In terms of later defensive arrangements, such a stance can be used as a strategy for secondary gain, and it can become so gratifying that it serves as a stalwart resistance to analytic work. Primarily, however, the misfit struggles at the door but, gaining neither entrance nor exit, remains unsatisfied.

For example, as my patient became more and more involved and interested in a relationship with a woman, he experienced intense humiliation at being *seen* as a suitor. At the same time, he was intensely jealous of any competitor for the woman of his interest. In this manner he seemed like a child who had had some relevant oedipal experiences but they seemed, for want of a better phrase, to have been truncated ones. He had no fantasies of actual rivalry, and, somewhat characteristically, immediately associated the idea of change with that of loss. I use this example here only to illustrate what seems to be the salient point about misfits: they do not achieve either successful regression or adequate progression. A recurrent dream this patient had seemed to reflect this condition. It was about an intricate violin piece, which he practiced but never quite finished. The dream was only of music, but it changed during the analysis to display shading and tones not previously heard. The associations to the dream indicated that the music was a symbol for heterosexuality, and the patient slowly mastered its performance as the analysis proceeded. When eventually his sexual and masculine self emerged, a new dream heralded the appearance of a vigorous male who was looked upon positively by others; that is, he was seen in context and in a group and with pride.

It is hoped that this general scheme will aid in the better delineation of the misfit. Certainly, every perverse individual does not feel like a misfit, and finding a congenial group allows many homosexuals to gain comfort and support from a feeling of belonging. The comfort of this particular form of ideals and values was unavailable to this patient, however. Perversions that exist in relative isolation from the main sector of the personality are often associated with a great deal of shame and humiliation, but they need not lead to the pervasive feeling of internal dissent that, unfortunately, this patient and misfits in general experience.

The misfit is at odds with himself. This kind of eccentric cannot fit in because he is unable to commit himself to the values and ideals of the larger group. Though he may fit in superficially, he remains unfulfilled much of the time, and he fails to gain sufficient mirroring response from the selfobjects around him. Thus, he demonstrates his internal dilemma in his conflict with the world. In order to adapt or conform, to join the larger group, one either must be compatible with it or one must subordinate oneself to it.

Returning to the "exceptions" of Freud, we see that these are narcissistically damaged people who feel "entitled" and who remain in conflict with the realities of the world. As Freud (1916) said, they "will submit no longer to any disagreeable necessity" (p. 312). They remain fixated or arrested at the primitive, grandiose levels of development. However, the yearning and longing that is so characteristic of the misfit is relatively lacking in these exceptions. This lends support to the idea that misfits are more aware of their internal dilemma and thus are more motivated to change.

As we examine the case of any misfit, ranging from the universal feeling that Freud attributed to all women to those few truly oustanding or talented people for whom fitting in would be disastrous, we can observe the crucial relationship between one's picture of oneself and the capacity to give oneself over a larger entity. The woman who feels damaged or unresponded to, for example, can reconcile herself to her fate by accepting the conventional woman's role or by embracing an aggrieved set of values. Likewise, she can achieve harmony by modifying her feelings about herself. She takes on the character of a misfit only when such a reconciliation is not possible for her. She cannot change her unhappy state and she cannot lose herself in or belong to a desired group. This combination leads to the chronic outsider.

The extremely talented or unique individual may experience the same dilemma. He or she cannot give up specialness, and yet may not be able to find inner peace by remaining in such an individualistic position. A longing for merger with an idealized other may be expected to result from the childhood of very talented individuals. Any person who is thrust into a new environment may find a period of fitting in to be painful or prolonged. This reflects the universality of developmental processes that are at odds with environmental supports. Such periods of disharmony are part and parcel of every normal growth pattern.

The so-called secondary gains that are to be derived from feeling estranged, injured, or abused are well known and have been underlined by Freud (1916) in his discussion of the feeling of privilege and/or compensation. The patient discussed above was obsessed with both the experience of self-pity and the complementary one of compassion for the underdog. He alone would befriend and champion the weak underdog. He recalled how in grammar school he befriended an ugly, limping, unfortunate girl and defended her against the jeers and scorn of his classmates. Such a position of specialness in the service of the outcast sometimes takes the form of championing causes and leading separatist movements. These supposed "gains," however, are not easily given up, inasmuch as they offer tremendous support and a necessary definition to a person seeking a place to stand. As my patient moved away from his homosexual orientation, he was met initially by an extraordinary hostility from certain of his friends, both men and women, for whom it was necessary for him to be a sexual deviate. As he wrenched himself free from these very needed others, he felt periods of extreme anxiety at being abandoned and alone, and vividly characterized the options available to him as a child of being alone or being what he did not want to be.

Thus we can see the secondary gains of the characterologic organization as offering further evidence of the needed but essentially more archaic selfobject relationships. The analysis of these gains and this character leads to intense anxiety unless the selfobject nature of character is comprehended. However, the developmental path of an individual who feels like a misfit need not always take the form of movement from one pole of self development to the other. By way of generalization, I have said that a misfit has tested a developmental stage and can neither advance into it nor retreat from it; the misfit thus can be seen as on the verge of developmental failure. From the vantage point of selfobjects we can study the movement from one pole to another or along one pole to delineate just where the individual failed to achieve a match with the needed selfobjects, so remaining in a perpetual state of limbo. Misfits thus can be found at every transitional point of development. They characterize a movement from one set of relationships with selfobjects to another, and as such the relationships can be primitive or mature. Thus we can see that their experience is more or less universal. To return to the view of the adaptation of the individual to the demands of the environment, we can again examine the shift in perspective required to move from the interpersonal to the subjective to emphasize that misfits are only to be diagnosed from an analytic vantage point of the personal experience of the patient.

CONCLUSION

A psychoanalytic examination of the misfit that concentrates on the subjective experience of a person fitting into a group is essentially a contribution to the consideration of psychoanalysis as a social science. The study of adaptation as an extension of psychoanalysis seen as a general psychology (Hartmann, 1939) runs the risk of removing the focus from an intrapsychic experience to an interpersonal examination of adjustment. Just as Freud's contribution to group psychology concerned itself with the experience of the individual in a larger group, so, too, should all psychoanalytic efforts at explicating social phenomena ideally proceed from and confine themselves to the data derived from the analytic process—the intrapsychic state. Misfits, therefore, are defined by the individual experience of feeling alien, and they are studied to determine what developmental issues lead to this complex state of affairs. The utilization of selfobject models is a felicitous conceptual aid to such an investigation. At the same time, such an investigation can also serve as an avenue for developing new insights regarding so-called social phenomena by considering the variety of personal configurations that go under the overall rubric of "relationships." The area between persons is a proper psychoanalytic study with the aid of conceptual models that concentrate on connections rather than on differentiations. Such linkages between persons are core units for a psychoanalytic contribution to the study of the social world of individuals. The investigation of the misfit as a form of character pathology can focus our study on the attainment of these ties.

12

The Wishy-Washy Personality

This chapter is intended to further develop and explicate a characterology of psychoanalytic self psychology. As with all character studies, it should be seen as highlighting traits that are ubiquitous in the entire population, while outstanding in some few individuals. It is thus to be considered as a lifelong pattern of behavior which in turn is tied to normal development. This linkage should not be seen as connecting a specific time or occurrence, but rather as one denoting a certain enduring quality of relationships. We may see the self through life as having qualities of coherence, firmness, harmony, continuity, and so on. This last point, that of a feeling of sameness through time and space, will be focused on as crucial to the emergence of the particular character to be considered here. In the previous chapter on the misfit, the developmental difficulty of that pattern was noted to be a failure to achieve a necessary transition from one stage to the next because of the lack of sustaining selfobjects at the succeeding stage. The present cohort of patients is differentiated on the basis of the failed sense of stability that would allow such a transit even to be considered. In a simplified way this would translate to the wishy-washy person's showing a defect earlier than the misfit, but such a simplification should not be read as being time-bound—for example, the first at 13 months, and the next at 21—or as reflecting severity of pathology. Since we see that people need stability and responsiveness throughout life, we should be able to highlight a character disorder that reflects the problematic state of these needs. The one that is selected here for examination is that of self-continuity. Once again it is necessary to examine this sort of organization primarily in terms of the emerging transference manifestations and not at all in a phenomenological or descriptive sense of social relationships, although these may conform to what is ultimately to be the prevalent transference. It is probably also necessary to present a disclaimer to the effect that even though one links a developmental problem to later adult psychopathology, it is not always the case that such problems inevitably lead to such pathology nor need it be true that the later pathology is always a product of the earlier difficulty, i.e., the linkage is not a rigid one.

DEFINITION

Not surprisingly, the term wishy-washy is listed in Webster's New World Dictionary and is an accepted phrase in our language. One could, of course, substitute a more scientific sounding word or phrase, but this one is unusually evocative. It suggests an unesteemed individual, and in turn one can often conjure up an image of such a person. In more cases than not, it is a woman who is surrounded by a network of similar words such as weak, insipid and flighty. Still, although such a vulgar phrase may hardly seem to be a fit topic for scientific inquiry, perhaps a case can be made for a more sturdy definition, one based on psychoanalytic evidence and principles. As such it will be enlisted in the category of character disorders and will be considered as an "habitual mode of adjustment of the ego to the external world, the id and the superego" or else as a pervasive subjective feeling concerned with adaptation (see previous chapter). The person possessed of a wishy-washy personality is seen in a particular manner in relation to the world and to himself or herself; such persons have a corresponding feeling about themselves and what they are, as well. It is, of course, the emergence of this form of appearance or adaptation in a psychoanalysis that allows us to consider it as representative of some particular significance and to differentiate it from the superficial evidences of this in ordinary social intercourse.

It is a rare person who has not had some experience that might correspond to this phenomenon and who cannot thereby easily identify it as an issue that may seem to dominate the life of some people. It is likewise a personality pattern that need not be associated with any sort of subjective discomfort or distress while on the contrary often leading to a medley of negative feelings in others. A common feature of the problem is this lack of awareness of it to the bearer and the relative ease with which it is rationalized with terms such as easy-going or flexible. In the course of analytic treatment, the basis of being wishy-washy may thus be experienced with a good deal of sadness and despair as the patient discovers what may be a profound deficit in his make-up. Indeed the thesis of this essay is that the malady is a reflection of a deficient structural organization that may be more prevalent than is ordinarily noted.

Though some might espouse a way of life that produces contentment by suspending judgment and thereby freeing the person from the problems and anxieties of searching for the truth or the right way of living, it is more that the wishy-washy personality has not opted for the way of skepticism but rather is robbed of that very sort of peace that a true skeptic may achieve (Stroud, 1984).

DIFFERENTIAL DIAGNOSIS

And Indecisiveness

The indecisive person is thought of as torn between one or another courses of life or ways to act or sets of beliefs. He is pictured as standing at the crossroads of a bifurcating road and so unable to commit himself to the one or the other presented path. Every step down one lane causes anxiety about forsaking the other. The neurotic counterpart for indecision is the obsessive-compulsive who must undo everything that is done, who begs others to decide for him and then rebels at the decision, and who is poised at indecision as a solution to the conflict below. Wishy-washy people, on the other hand, are not particularly concerned about going down one path rather than the other; they have no real regrets about the choice of one thereupon precluding the other; and they are more often relieved at a decision being made by themselves or anyone else. Their problem lies in the fact that they do not or say not that they really care. They may or may not be relieved by a decision being reached, but they are lacking in the feeling of true satisfaction in having arrived at one. Nor do they evidence much regret at having missed out on the alternative, since decisions and choices and options are of no concern or interest to them. At times they do regret the lack of enthusiasm that they see manifest in others over these issues, but they often mask this by rationalizing that they do not have the same degree of concern about some things that others seem to possess.

The ability to see both sides of a question is often the hallmark of an even-handed person and is at times associated with growing maturity and wisdom. This posture is linked as well to indecision but has been lifted away from the intrapsychic conflict of the obsessional individual to a more conscious deliberation involving the relative weights of one choice versus another. But wishy-washy people are overwhelmingly lacking in the capacity to consider one thing and then move on to contemplate the other, since the necessary firmness to take a stand seems nowhere present. If anything, they are bewildered by the effort expended to evaluate positions, since it seems of little moment if one decides one way or another. True ambivalence is filled with regrets, and the wishy-washy person has little of that.

To be wishy-washy is not so much to be unable to be decisive as it is to be unable to care about the problem. Something is missing or lacking that allows for the struggle to take place and this deficit so permeates the personality that one is more readily characterized as vapid and shallow than as locked in uncertainty. They lack the solid state on which one plants one's feet as contemplation over choice proceeds.

And Compliance

The compliant person is a master of agreement and conformity and readily adapts to situations and to others. Though seen as weak at times, they fit themselves into situations with a minimum of discomfort and distress. Such an attribute is thought of as revealing a flexibility of personality and thereby a lack of rigidity and stubbornness. It is also felt to complement the more dominant and perhaps more rigid person, who cannot so bend to meet the demands of people and the world. On occasion, compliance is seen as a nuisance in its eagerness to still dissension and debate, and it may thus reveal a defensive posture against stirring up heat and discord. As such it can reveal a fear of anger and discontent and a protective façade against the pain of such affects. No doubt much compliance is of this nature, but in this light it retains the elements of a developed organization which is goal directed and in the service of maintaining a personality. There is nothing to this that suggests that the person is beset by anxiety over what to do or by resentment at having so chosen or at being forced to do something. Regardless of the defensive nature of compliance and its subsequent hidden hostile intent, it is often only a problem in the area between personalities, for example, one wanting, with some degree of intensity, and other going along, with some pleasure in agreement.

Aside from the compliance of hostility and hidden resentment, there does exist one form that reflects genuine ease of adjustment and conformity. There are people who have a nonconflictual life of fitting in with a minimum of strain or struggle, and it seems apparent to all that this can be accomplished with no evidence of uncertainty or wishy-washiness. Thus, complaint people need not be, and usually, are not wishy-washy.

And Passivity

The passive position, whether or not associated with femininity, is defined in opposition to that of aggression. It is receptive rather than direct and reactive rather than initiating. It usually has few earmarks of indecision as long as someone else takes the lead or dictates the direction. It is undoubtedly seen from outside as a posture of compliance but seems to restrict its evidence of this to a modicum reflecting passivity, that is, one can imagine a compliant, yet aggressive individual.

Like the compliant person, the passive person may appear to be indecisive, but he or she only is waiting to be told and directed. There is no necessary conflict about doing, as long as it is in a favored passive mode. And though passivity may be defensive or otherwise, it need not be evidence of a weak and vapid structure. Passivity as well is often looked upon as an admirable and positive way to live, but this is never true of wishy-washiness which always has negative connotations.

PHENOMENOLOGY

A description of the wishy-washy person must focus on the peculiar status of concern or care in their lives. To do something or to be something or someone need not be simply a matter of indifference to such a person; rather, one avenue seems to have no inherent advantage over the other. This circumstance leads such people to say that they care not, when in truth, they more likely cannot care. Thus they are neither carefree or careless, both words that reflect a capacity that may or may not be exercised. They wish, sometimes openly and often secretly, that things mattered more. Such a longing often reveals itself in treatment, and the façade of ease gives way to puzzlement over how others can feel so committed to things. When change does occur, it may be a wrenching experience that disturbs the people around as well as the wishy-washy person. It leads to a realignment of relationships and strong fears of being disliked by those who counted on the person to be flexible and undemanding. No doubt there are degrees of wishy-washiness, and it may dominate a personality or else reign in but one segment of behavior. Our clinical material should therefore describe a person for whom it was a pervasive feature as well as one who had it occasionally. The developmental issues that will be touched on should therefore reflect the sort of problem that can be seen as varying in its import. One of the patients to be presented felt it to be a major aspect of functioning; the other manifested it alongside another characterological problem. One could correlate these differences to the different transference reconstructions.

DEVELOPMENT

Though children are often described as stubborn or obedient, difficult or easy going, determined or easily persuaded, it is rare to hear of anyone characterizing a child as wishy-washy. That term is usually reserved for people old enough to know what they want, those of an age that corresponds perhaps to an Eriksonian achievement of identity though certainly the etiology of the difficulty is not of that period. Since this is so much a social concept, it remains to be seen if there can be a corresponding psychoanalytic explanation to the state of knowing what one is and what one wants. It would, however, be a banality merely to say that the developmental step that is necessary is essentially that which corresponds to a firm self or sense of self. To be sure, firmness is the basic requirement or essential ingredient that combats wishy-washiness, but the infirm self can be seen to manifest any variety of difficulty and pathology. The question to be addressed is that of a particular deficit in the structural integrity of the self; one that accounts for an inability to feel strongly about a choice.

At the risk of speculation, there may be some general ideas that could be suggested as indicative of the source of the problem that, in turn, might be studied for verification in a clinical setting. One is that of movement or transition. It seems that choice always involves change from one state to another and likewise demands some reorganization of the self as it moves from the first stage to the second. Children need a continually supporting relationship in order to effect such transitions and will have maximum anxiety if the caretaker or selfobject is unavailable or lost to them over the change sequence. Such anxiety tends to make change frightening and lends safety to staying as is. Thus, one scarcely invests interest in what may lie ahead, since any aspect of stepping forward is frightening and potentially disorganizing. Because this is a general delineation of development that could well fall into the catchall of separation-individuation, it needs a better detailing if we are to see just what is required to enable one to invest in something new without fear and with interest and enthusiasm.

To pursue the problem of firmness and transition, we can isolate the subjective feeling of sameness or continuity over time as one essential complex emotion that merits attention. One can move freely from one point in time or space to another as long as there is the security of some stable and unchanging self experience. Developmentally this may be offered by a sense of being able to return to touch base for refueling or reassurance or comforting. Soon the next step becomes a source of comfort and reassurance, and one may pass into it by something akin to a mourning process for what is left behind. There is a developmental push to new stages of growth and achievement that, although initially frightening, are likewise gratifying and fulfilling. The self is thus expanded at developmental progress and at any point one is capable of a view that looks backward and forward and which, of itself, assures the feeling of continuity through time and space.

No doubt the sense of sameness is a continual developmental accomplishment, but probably there are points in life when it begins, is fostered, and needs maximum nurturance. To ascertain these nodal moments, psychoanalysis must turn to a reconstructive approach that reflects best why and when the disorder comes about.

CLINICAL MATERIAL

Much has been said about the value of single-case generalizations (Edelson, 1984), but the one that follows is primarily illustrative. A brief mention of similar cases will be attempted for contrast, and, furthermore, one assumes a host of such cases in any clinical practice.

Case Report

This is the case of a middle-aged woman (of chapter 10) who entered analysis for extreme hypochondriacal preoccupation of near disabling proportions. Her analysis was not especially noteworthy. After several years of work, she reported the following dream:

> She was walking down the street and saw her friend Sylvia. She was unable to see Sylvia's face however either because of fog or a cloud or hair obstructing it. She tried to push whatever it was away so that she could get a clearer glimpse of it but did not seem satisfied that she had accomplished this. She awoke frustrated from her efforts at getting a clear view of Sylvia.

Sylvia was a good and dear friend of the patient's. As she thought and talked about her, she centered on the fact that Sylvia was an uncomplicated person, that Sylvia knew what she wanted and just did it, not beating around the bush and waffling. The patient recognized how much she wanted to be like this, but came to realize that this ability had long been lacking in her life. She usually did not know what she wanted to do or be. For instance, this weekend her husband was to be away on business, and she was free to do whatever she pleased. Whenever this happened she would plan her time down to the minute. Her plans did not necessarily involve events and activities that especially pleased her but rather covered a total schedule of her time; she did not concern herself with whether she wanted to do one thing or another, but rather that all the time was accounted for. She was married to a man who was a model of discipline, time allocation, and duty; and she was content to go along with him on whatever he had planned. But she never particularly liked what they did together, nor was she particularly displeased. She just went along. She felt that the dream was an indication of her wish to find herself as a more determined or certain person.

In the patient's work as a poet, she began by first constructing some form of solid structure which she would later freely fill in. She likened this to her planning her weekend and to having a husband who planned everything. Left with too much uncertainty, she felt unable to perform creatively until a minimum decisive step had been made.

The dream coincided with two events in her life. The first had to do with a scheduled reading of her poetry. She was asked to share the podium with another poet and friend, and she had agreed, or perhaps it might be better to say, acquiesced. She did this readily, but only later had misgivings about it. These increased in frequency and intensity until the patient had a fantasy while riding on the expressway. She thought of seeing a horse belonging to Louis XIV from the rear, quickly identified this is as a horse's ass, and soon thereafter decided that this was her image of herself for agreeing to share the program. This led to a decision to recant her agreement and flooded her with apprehension about what would be thought of her along with an accompanying positive feeling of pride in having made this decision. She announced that she had to have the program to herself in spite of feeling that she would be exposed as selfish and fearful of competition. The uniqueness of this experience of clearly knowing what she wanted was literally overwhelming.

The correlative events in the analysis surrounded her missing a single session to join her husband for a long weekend. Separations were always difficult for her, and although this was no different in its potential fearsomeness, it was of some distinction in her planning for it. In the history of this particular analysis, there had been a sequence of negotiations about missing sessions. The analysis had begun with a fairly clear contract that the patient was responsible for all of her sessions and would therefore pay for any she missed, for whatever reasons. She had no questions about this point, although admittedly she was a patient who rarely took issue with anything. During one long vacation her husband had protested mightily about paying for missed hours, and so the patient asked if we might renegotiate the agreement to something like a friend of hers had with her analyst, who tried to fill hours that were vacated and so relieved her partially of responsibility for all of them. The issue of missing hours and payment was subjected to long and repeated scrutiny in the analysis until I felt that there was little more to be gained from this work. The pressure from her husband for a change remained intense. I agreed to the change, and during the patient's next absence she was beside herself with anxiety about the hours that were taken away from her while she was away. She had to feel and know that her hours remained hers. We tried to connect this to her childhood feelings concerning the birth of a brother when she was four years old. He turned out to be a very sickly child who required the concentrated attention of their parents until he died when he was eight years old. For some reason the patient felt this explanation was unsatisfactory inasmuch as she was already in school when her brother became ill, and she could recall no feelings of her position's being usurped. Rather her fearfulness about losing her hours seemed more clearly evidenced in a general fantasy of hers about dropping from sight in terms of me and my memory. She once noted that I turned away from her as soon as her hour ended to tend to some papers on my desk. She elaborated this fantasy that I wanted to be rid of her or perhaps that I forgot her as soon as she was gone. She wanted to keep her hours even while she was away in order to stay alive in my mind, not to be forgotten, to establish a continuity of presence. She had decided on this shortly before the time of the poetry reading and the decision that *that* had promoted in her.

I privately compared this fantasy and fear of my turning away from her to another case in the literature (Goldberg, 1978), that of a man described as a procrastinator and a voyeur. He, too, showed severe separation anxiety and related it to wanting to be retained in the mind's eye of the analyst. His case report detailed how he drew a picture of the analyst's face during a weekend separation and painted miniatures of himself where the eyes, nose, and mouth of the analyst should be (p. 272). The reconstructive work in this analysis had to do with an exhausted mother who was unable to fully respond to her son. It was felt by both analyst and patient that this was never an absolute absence, but rather that her limited energies did not allow her to respond in accordance with the timetable of the child's needs. A minor note in the case report indicates that the symptom of procrastination disappeared as the analysis progressed.

The patient was described as always studying his mother's face, which was inscrutable: like a mask. He said that no matter what her mood, she showed but one face. He also said that thinking of her face gave him the creeps. In contrast to the first patient, whose mother seemingly had no steady, even if inappropriate, gaze, this man felt an irritating sameness to his mother's mood and expression. The patient was disturbed over the inappropriateness of the response of his mother and longed for something else. This is in contrast to the patient who said that her mother had no particular feeling about anything and who therefore had nothing for her to scrutinize.

My own patient did not have an exhausted mother so much as an elusive one. There was no evidence of depression in the mother but rather a sort of restlessness or flightiness of preoccupation, much like the analyst who wants to be rid of a patient in order to get on with other things of real interest to him.

With this patient, as with most of the others with similar problems, after a decision was reached, there occurred a period of relative tranquility. As a rule this is often short lived and ushers in a new state of severe anxiety. This latter phenomenon is due to the feeling of total abandonment and aloneness as one marches down a chosen path. The patient soon reported a dream:

> I am in G's department store and feel good but want to go home. A phone call informs me that I must go through a pass to get home. The pass is surrounded by trees and ravine. There are horseback riders on the path but the horses are under control and I am not afraid. But soon the horses get larger and riderless and I am afraid. Suddenly a tiger leaps out and I wave a white towel and awake in terror.

The associations to the dream were to a feared attack by a critic of her work. G's store was probably the comfort of the analysis when she had reached a decision. She realized then that she wanted to go home, and the phone was a warning. The pass was like one that she used to go to the beach as a child. Now she recalled all the fears that she had as a child: of shots by the doctor, of all the people throughout her life who had power over her. That was the whole thing: that she really did not have control, people were unpredictable, and she was not in control of her life. She then turned to the analysis and saw the dream as approaching termination with the conviction that it would be done to her rather than being under her control.

The conceptualization of this patient's difficulty in not having a sense of sameness and solidity through time can be illustrated in many ways. Mahler (1972) might have seen it in terms of separation-individuation, wherein the child becomes anxious when she feels too distant from the parental figure and so must repeatedly return to refueling. Others might visualize it in terms of some needed introjection of "holding objects" that allow more autonomous function. I (Goldberg, 1983) have suggested using a metaphor of ownership for the sense of something being owned and therefore under one's control. Such a metaphor removes the boundary between persons as psychological entities and allows an idea of shared ownership, i.e., something had by both mother and child without the usual connotations of transitional objects as "things" such as blankets. The idea of the child, the image of the child, shared by mother and child is then illustrated in a new form of representation. Just as ownership is an issue over the analytic hours, it is likewise one of the same form about one's person.

Let me illustrate this point of ownership with another clinical example of the patient previously mentioned. She had gone to a lecture on poetry given by an eminent poet and had sat enthralled and elated by what he had to say. Some of it was difficult to comprehend, but much of it was especially meaningful to her because it so resonated with her own feelings and convictions about the subject matter. The audience was a mixed one, and afterwards several friends who were not very learned about the subject approached to ask her questions since the lecturer was surrounded by other interested inquirers. She felt bewildered and unable to articulate her thoughts, and as the next day approached, she felt more and more uncertain as to whether or not she had really understood the man. Her husband was irritated at the lecturer for giving so erudite a talk and demanded that the patient, his wife, translate it for him. She became dizzy and begged off. When she came for her analytic hour, she was able to describe the lecture and its content fairly coherently but saw her position erode as she described the events of the previous evening. She likened this to a difficulty in school that likewise had made her always feel uncertain and unsure of her position and knowledge. In her words, she said how hard it was for her to own something, some fact or idea, as her very own. She so quickly lost the base of certainty that she stood on because other people could not reinforce the sense of sureness, often because of an innocent ignorance of their own. Her wishy-washiness was reflected in this easy erosion of the sense of conviction, which seemed, in itself, so unsettling to her because it intensified a sense of abandonment.

The essay of utilizing new metaphors also suggested a change in our concepts of representation, which, at a minimum, are problematic (Boesky, 1983). A static picture or idea of the self cannot do justice to this issue of the self in transit. The earlier mentioned dream is a representation of movement and thus paints a picture of sequences and development over time. In her creative activity, the patient moved from static or cross-sectional icons to those that moved through space as well as through time. The act of creating makes a claim for mastery, control, and ownership and also delivers a presentation to another person to share. This may also be the child's attempted solution to the inability of the mother to retain the child in her mind. We shall note later how the creative product aids in a solution of the problem.

The "representation" that we are outlining is not seen as residing in the mind of the patient; we must momentarily dispense with the simplistic notion that inarguably every thought does indeed sit somewhere in the brain. Rather we see this representation as necessarily shared between mother and child, and so the child must feel that he or she exists in a shared or mutually constructed reality of mother and child. The child is seen as one in his own eyes as well as in the mother's eyes, and this is carried on as he feels carried by others in the same manner. Coexistence is a different kind of representation from that of singular image of oneself.

With the achievement of a feeling of shared reality by way of her decision to have her hours remain hers while she was gone, she seemed able to leave on trips with less anxiety and even soon thereafter to contemplate a termination, something that had previously filled her with dread. She ceased to feel so uncertain about what she wanted to do and to be and feared that she would be seen as obnoxious and a pest by family and friends. Knowing what she wanted seemed such a new and different sensation that she felt it as nothing that she had known before. It may be noteworthy that the patient did not have much trouble or conflict about making decisions since as noted earlier, she had not ever been an indecisive person, and, with her newfound sense of certainty, she merely enjoyed the state of deciding. In a sense, she felt confirmed about herself in a way that had been previously unknown to her. Whatever had been lacking in development before now seemed to be behind her.

There still seems to be a need to unpack this very large and cumbersome term of responsiveness or mirroring to see if there could be more specific defect in the relationship between parent and child that on occasion leads to this characterologic picture of wishy-washiness.

SPECULATION

Adler and Buie (1979) have described the difficulty borderline patients have in maintaining an image or memory of the therapist in their mind over periods of absence or expectable separations. Such patients seem unable to conjure up a picture of the missing person and, in this manner, to effectively think about the person and to use that thought or image for comfort, soothing, or planning. They lack a developmental achievement of what Piaget (Furth 1981) has called evocative memory, and this cognitive deficit is responsible for the unstable, erratic, emotionally labile personality and the overall difficulty in treating such patients. They provoke uncertain and unpredictable reactions in therapists, who are troubled by the intensity as well as the irregularity of the patients' affective stance. Therapists often behave in an indecisive manner in dealing with borderlines, or they attempt to become a stable and reliable selfobject to patients. Phrases such as the patient has an "insufficient internalization of holding objects" are said to describe the central defect that the therapist aims to ameliorate or correct. It is important at this point to emphasize that the patient just described is not to be considered borderline.

One maneuver sometimes used in the treatment of borderlines is to allow them to phone over weekends or to carry a picture of the therapist in order to handle periods of separation. In marked contrast to this, my patient gave me a picture (actually a number of pictures ranging from snapshots to portraits) so that I would remember her. Her fantasies about the pictures had to do with whether I would display them in such a way that they would be readily visible or would secret them away and hid them from sight. Essentially the transference seemed to disclose a relationship to someone who seemingly suffered from the defect that Adler and Buie had described i.e., a borderline personality disorder with a failure of evocative memory. It was not one that represented the exhausted and depressed mother who potentially participated in the formation of a child who later developed mixed procrastination and perversion inasmuch as we do see perverse symptomatology arising from the spasmodic unavailability of the parent. Rather we see a chronic failure of the parent to respond in a manner that should be a routine part of any interaction: the child being treated as the same person from day to day. The feeling that she would not be remembered emerged in the transference with the patient's conviction that I was always sitting on the edge of my chair waiting to be rid of her. She had a variety of fantasies that turned on my wishing to wash my hands of her, to forget her. The countertransference reaction probably echoed this, since she was a woman in her fifties who claimed that life was over for her. I myself felt it painful to struggle with the fact that I would also be forgotten one day, as indeed all of our wishes for immortality resonate with this early wish that the world will not lose sight of us.

Robert and Edna Furman (1984) discuss a certain form of child-parent interaction that they call intermittent decathexis. Such parents seemingly become so self-absorbed that they periodically lose contact with their offspring. Children of these circumstances are said to identify with the use of this "primitive defense mechanism," to develop a false self caused by continuous decathexis of parts of the child's personality rather than intermittent total parental decathexis and a lasting lability of their own cathectic investments. It is interesting to compare such nonanalytic data with analytic reconstructive material inasmuch as it has such a ring of truth yet often is lacking in some individual details. The clinical experience reported here does not confirm the identification with the parents or some of the material about the parental cathexis. This is not to deny that very correct and cogent observation that parental interest is a sine qua non for a child's development. But something is certainly missing in ascribing it to investment of energy and saying that such investment "determines the harmonious functioning of the personality" (p. 432). We probably need to concentrate more on the particular nature of the interactions.

The male voyeur noted earlier told of giving his mother some pottery he had made, but she soon gave it away. The gift of the child is an effort to have some place in the mother's life, and here the mother was unable to provide that niche for her son, and he was disappointed. The female patient told of never knowing what her mother wanted and felt her father was someone who had only one correct response for anything; nothing could be negotiated, if you hit it right you were lucky and more often than not you were wrong. She did not offer gifts for remembering until she had progressed somewhat in analysis, since she did not feel secure enough to make a try. Interestingly the male patient gave a picture to his analyst as well; a picture of someone watching someone else.

It takes no great leap of imagination to speculate that a profound uncertainty about one's sameness or continuity from one time to the next time would be etiological in the formation of a personality of uncertainty, indecisiveness, and wishy-washiness. Likewise the potential fragility of the self reflects the hypochondriasis of the patient (Kohut, 1971). Perhaps the steady recognition of this patient by her mother was what was missing in her growth. Such recognition is a shared ownership and a shared communication. It is represented over time and space in dreams, enactments, and creative work.

DISCUSSION

The need remains to delineate better just what such terms as "mirroring" mean at different developmental levels in a child's growth. In particular we should try to know what different forms of pathology can result from failures of such needs, and especially to clarify that a host of factors such as timing, consistency, intensity and substitution of one parent for another play crucial roles in the emergence of such pathology. To be sure, one may posit something like a "failure of mirroring" and insist that it was a lifelong problem, or that it was responsible for all manner of difficulties. But this seems too close to the problem that all psychoanalysis has had with reducing every instance of pathology to oedipal struggles and then insisting that it is indeed such a multivariate phenomenon that it is capable of covering all pathology. There is a certain poverty of explanation in saying that a neurosis comes from a conflict between instinctual drives, superego prohibitions, and ego strengths just as there is in stating that all trouble is due to emphatic failures from a selfobject relationship. These are but general pointers to particular forms of disordered development that should be re-evoked as specific transference configurations. It likewise seems unsatisfactory to label parents as narcissistic or depressed or even borderline since these appellations need carry no specific form of behavior except in the most general sense. Certainly we need generalizations to categorize our clinical data, but for a true developmental psychology we must aim to place our findings on an axis of development and deviations thereof.

Patients who are wishy-washy or whose wishy-washiness is revealed in treatment suffer from not knowing where or how to move forward because of a lack of the necessary structure to ensure self-continuity. This deficit may arise from a failure to achieve temporal continuity in the child's development by way of parental recognition and responsiveness. In the transference this is manifested by a feeling of being forgotten between hours, of losing one's hours, or of having to terminate before one is ready. The analyst is experienced as one who cannot hold on to a permanent image of the patient, an attitude attributable to borderline patients as well. This may well reveal that the patient's mother was a borderline personality or at least suffered from this sort of cognitive defect. Wishy-washiness disappears as the patient creates a temporal bridge in the analysis, one that allows continued existence over periods of time by way of the analyst's memory: the patient is alive in the mind of the analyst.

CONCLUSION

As we move from concepts of people as independent units in time and space to those of selves composed of sets of relationship (Goldberg, 1978), we need different metaphors to describe our clinical material just as we needed different theories (Kohut, 1971) to explain it. People seen in networks of relationships can also be seen to manifest certain forms of pathology only revealed vis-á-vis these matrices (Goldberg, 1983). One such form of pathology is that of the wishy-washy personality. This individual is unable to choose a course of action or to care about such a course because of a defect in the structure needed for such transit. The defect does not lie within the subject but is one of a shared concept between the self and selfobject, and possibly has to do with a failure of the maternal caretaker to hold the child in her mind, much as the borderline patient fails to manifest evocative memory. The metaphor of shared ownership seems best able to deliver this deficit, which may be healed in treatment by devices that allow transit in time and space.

A revisiting of much nonoedipal pathology in terms of the varied construction of networks of relationships might widen our considerations of psychopathology and better differentiate what have heretofore been but large and amorphous forms of equally obscure categories of developmental failure that are responsible for these problems.

IV

CLINICAL PAPERS

13

Comments on Rules and Psychotherapy

Often when I am asked to present a paper for a meeting, the invitation offers me the freedom to speak on any topic that I choose. Under such circumstances my mind races around to all sorts of topics that I always felt were challenges and that required discussion and answers. Not surprisingly, I often find myself quite unable to find any great (or small) new insights. The very generous and gracious offer of the committee soon becomes a burden for me, and I begin to wish that they had told me exactly what I had to talk about. Such freedom is often a chore, and, once, as I shuffled around for a reasonable topic, I finally realized that I was living one. I was in the midst of not knowing which way to go and of not having enough constraints or directions— no rules—by which to live. Once I realized the dilemma of this momentary, unregulated life, it was a fairly easy task to think about it in terms of psychotherapy and the governing rules of that vague enterprise. We are, all of us, engaged in an activity that begs for clear and definitive ways to proceed, and we also spend a great deal of our time pondering these fuzzy areas where we seem mainly to live by the seat of our pants.

Everyone has anecdotes about such times of vagueness and uncertainty. I would like to illustrate and explore some of them to see if perhaps I can extract a principle or even a rule to govern these ruleless parts of our lives. Of course, Freud (1923b) gave us one: that patients

175

should say whatever comes to mind. And countless other scholars have offered a wide variety of others. To step back for a moment, I would like to note what one of the great philosophers of our age, Wittgenstein (1953) had to say about rules in general. He observed that rules do seem to bind behavior, but that the very term "rule" has many different roles. Some games are played "according to the rules," but certainly following the rules, say, of tennis will not teach you how to play the game. However, if one follows the rules in cooking, one will often end up with a good finished product. Rules are guides at times, instructions at others, and imperatives at still others. I cannot go much more deeply into the philosophical issues involving rules except to say that we are all rule-following animals who define our lives by our rules, who become social beings by way of our rules, and who always appeal to some rule to rescue us from the many uncertainties of whatever we may be doing.

Rules of human behavior, of course, are quite distinct from natural laws, which in the physical sciences are felt to be rather complete descriptions of the behavior of physical objects. Though the laws of nature themselves run the gamut from universal applicability to specific contexts, they are felt to make reliable statements of regularity and relevance. The Law of Gravitation says something about all objects in a constant and universal way. If one could devise laws about human behavior in a comparable manner, then one might approach a more scientific description and prediction of human beings much like, for example, the work being done in artificial intelligence. If, on the other hand, we recognize that even though people agree upon and more or less follow the rules of behavior, it soon becomes apparent that one cannot supply all of the many rules that are required for a complete description and prediction of such behavior. People revise rules as they go along. They have rules for how to break the rules as well as rules for making up new rules. In the field of language, for example, we see the full range of creative activity as people intuitively understand how one may use a word or a sentence in a new way that is contrary to the established rules. Our capacity to understand one another is, however, quite dependent on our ability to recognize what rules the other person is following.

Meaningful exchanges between persons depend on an implicit awareness and acceptance of the rules governing their behavior. We are confused when we either do not know the procedure as, for instance, when we are fooled on April 1; or when the rules are simply not followed and we therefore cannot devise an explanation or a "metarule" about what has transpired. Such an event is marvelously illustrated by the conduct of Jacque Lacan, the French analyst who took to stopping some analytic sessions after five or so minutes (Schneider-man, 1983). His patients were dumbfounded and enraged, until they learned that this was a planned part of his radical analytic procedure. Thereafter they were able to participate in the new set of rules perhaps a bit apprehensively, since the new rules were set by a rule-maker who seemed a bit daft. It is in this area of a mutual recognition of the rules of conduct that the psychologic treatment of patients can be seen as an exercise in rule recognition, rule following, and rule changing.

When one first trains to become a psychotherapist, there is nothing so helpful as a set of rules. I remember clearly one of my first patients in my residency: a depressed young man who had been completely devastated by the death of his father and thus was unable to work in this job or to continue to function as a husband or father. Pitiful and forlorn, he came to our clinic and soon became a dependent, cling-ing, and very difficult patient. I saw him a few times, and soon he and I were locked in a problem about appointment times and schedule. He never seemed to be able to meet at the times that I offered him but insisted on all sorts of irregular (for me) hours. I went to my super-visor. I remember my visit quite clearly; it was ostensibly to find out what to do, although I was fairly sure that I was doing the right thing and following the rules. My supervisor (like all supervisors) lived in a palace. He was, or was about to be, an analyst and thus knew just about everything and had just about everything and was supremely happy. I told him about my patient, and he told me about a patient of his, a successful corporation president, whom *he* saw on Sunday afternoon. I explained to him that my patient, who was unemployed, had absolutely nothing to do all week *except* to keep his appointments and therefore hardly qualified for a Sunday afternoon time. I wanted to know just what to do to enable the patient to be a better patient, but my supervisor seemed lost in the intricacies of corporate life. I left the supervision quite unsatisfied, still determined to have the patient conform to the rules of my schedule. He shortly thereafter dropped out of treatment.

Over the years I did not modify my conviction that my supervisor (who, by the way, is now a colleague who lives in a modest home) was dead wrong and the patient was simply untreatable. I did, however, puzzle over the multitude of fuzzy areas that pervade our practice. They range from simple issues, such as schedules, to calling patients by their first name, to charging for missed appointments, to a host of more complex social interactions with patients. There are a number of therapists who are uniformly rigid and strict about the procedures of therapy and treat any deviation from the standards as evidence of countertransference problems or worse. There is another group who feel that an ease of intimacy with patients is a sine qua non of successful treatment and who encourage all sorts of so-called open and human responses. We might here recall that Freud (1909b) not only fed the Rat Man before sessions but also had Marie Bonaparte and her children visit at his house every evening one summer while she was in analysis with him. He did, however, refrain from playing cards with her; he said that that was too intimate. I recall a friend of mine who was in analysis with Therese Benedek telling how one day he left his hour, which was at the end of the day, only to encounter a severe snowstorm. Dr. Benedek also was leaving at that time, and my friend offered to drive her home since they lived quite close to one another. She adamantly refused, saying that it would interfere with his analysis. I thought that quite fitting and admirable—but was it?

Heinz Kohut used to quote Glover as advising: "When in doubt, do what come naturally." Otto Kernberg once told me that one must remain equidistant from the id, the ego, and the superego. I confess that I saw (and see) merit in each position, and I could often understand some individual cases; but I sorely wanted some sort of general rule, and I could not easily comprehend any of them. I was convinced that almost any action could be rationalized by a therapist. Though there are certainly moral and ethical reasons why we draw the line at certain forms of outrageous behavior, they are not so easily explained from a psychological perspective.

When one speaks of rules, it should be clear that they range from the seemingly meaningless to the profound, from shaking hands with patients to sleeping with them. When a moral injunction is obvious, then we are relieved to avoid a struggle over propriety. As depth psychologists, however, we have learned that nothing is meaningless. I have a colleague who tells me that he calls all his patients by first name, and they do the same to him. When I asked if that was not a false intimacy, he replied that he felt very intimate with his patients. But another friend and colleague told me that he never calls patients by their first name because it erodes the doctor-patient relationship. Now I think we would soon agree that this is not a question of right or wrong and that both therapists give spurious rationalizations. Intimacy is not a desirable trait on all occasions, and it is not the same as chumminess. A Catholic in the confessional is participating in one of the most intimate of life's moments, but he hardly wants to call the priest Fred or Sam. He *needs* the dignity of the priesthood. So too are we often offended by the cheerful waiter who introduces himself by his first name and assumes a closeness that simply is out of place. But those of us who deal with adolescents know full well that my overly dignified colleague is equally off-center addressing one and all by their surname. I bring this point up now not to belabor the idea that first-name calling can be as defensive as it is helpful, but to alert us to the issue of rule changing, which I shall pursue later in discussing the use of rules that are sometimes appropriate and sometimes quite unhelpful.

It seems that certain sets of rules do well for some people but not for others. The rules are based on some sort of theory that is felt to approach the status of a law. For example, we might say that one should not have prolonged physical contact with a patient because it is so grati-fying that it prevents later interpretation. But we recognize that there are equally well-intentioned therapists who would say that one should not reject the honest overtures of a patient for such contact, since they may feel abused and narcissistically injured and so become resistant to interpretive work. Of course, any discipline that seems secure with a theory allows it to function more or less as a set of laws. It can offer the best process of rule making; and here is where one turns to psychoanalysis.

Psychoanalysis is often seen as restrictive in its form in order to allow a relatively uncontaminated transference to emerge, whereas psycho-therapy seems burdened with all sorts of permissible parameters. Of late, however, I think we have witnessed the erosion of the analytic posture by a variety of allowances ranging from occasional phone calls, to shared coffee, to the full range of doing what comes naturally. Psychoanalysis seems to approach psychotherapy in its looseness and flexibility in some cases; in other cases, therapy seems to borrow heavi-ly from analysis, such as charging for missed hours.

Jonas Robitscher (1980) cited charging the once-a-week patient for missed hours as an example of an overall abuse of power practiced by psychiatrists. He felt that the reason advanced by Freud to insure the continuity of psychoanalytic treatment, as well as his own income, was exploited by psychotherapists who are not practicing analysis in order to safeguard their own interests. It is a fascinating exercise to review just what analysts and therapists do about this issue. Some never charge for missed appointments, and some always charge. In the mid-dle are those who forgive misses on 24-hour or 48-hour notice, or for supposed good reasons, or if they can fill the time with someone else. Some allow a quota of misses. One strange compromise I heard of in-volved not charging patients if they cancelled appointment but insisting that the schedule time was now available to anyone else who might want it from that time on; hence, the hour might not thereafter be available. That event seemed never to arise, but the pride of the doc-tor did seem to be benefited. I submit that there is no absolute correct position in this regard. It is no more right to charge than not to charge. It is not a moral position at all, but rather a problem of proper psychological inquiry. It is a fine example of a fuzzy area that seems to beg for a rule. The host of rules that has grown up in this area is, I think, witness to the lack of agreement on just what we are attempting to accomplish by our rule-forming and so ranges from points of personal greed to personal comfort to personal generosity. Now, of course, there is no reason why these cannot be the principles or metarules for what we do. They do, however, bear rethinking.

Allow me to illustrate this issue with another case. A professional person in his thirties entered analysis because of severe marital problems in his current (second) marriage. He was a pleasant and agreeable person who struck one immediately as someone who was well-meaning and who tried very hard. The latter description aptly fit his role as a husband, since his chronic problem with his wife was that she was, on occasion, a fairly impossible person. There was no good way to tell in advance what would please or displease her, what she would or could not tolerate, and what might send her into an episode of dark depression or lighthearted frivolity. He spent much of his time trying to figure out this woman, and much of their time together was devoted to his being told what he should or should not have done—always too late and seldom with any assurance that next time things might go differently. He insisted that he loved his wife deeply and dreaded the idea of a second divorce, and so he was very eager to seek treatment.

He was soon able to link up to the feelings he had toward his mother, whom he described in terms similar to those he used to describe his wife, but with a layer of disdain for his mother's generally unrelenting critical stance. He told of returning home from school after final exams that had been preceded by several nights of cramming, and so he fell, exhausted, into bed. When he awoke the next morning at noon, his mother was hurt and angry because he had not spent any time with her. He described his father as being resigned to the personality of the mother and so he rarely intervened or was available for support. The patient's childhood was characterized by successes in school and athletics. He was on the swimming and tennis teams, got good grades in high school and college, and was currently a well-paid and well-performing professional man. Vignettes of his childhood seemed to form around his being torn between two paths of action. One story he told was of working on a project with his dad and wanting to leave to practice his tennis. He worked as long as he could and then had to leave, but not without a feeling of guilt reinforced by the look in his father's eyes. He had a full suitcase of such stories, and we used to characterize them as "red tie/blue tie." This referred to the story of the mother who bought two ties, a red one and a blue one, for her son. When he came downstairs wearing the red one, her only response was "You don't like the blue tie?'' The patient loved that story because he felt it captured his life's theme of survival.

This patient began analysis with an immediate compliance with the rule that he was responsible for every hour with no exceptions. He felt this was a reasonable contract and hardly blinked an eye in agreement. The analysis initially was experienced very positively by the patient; he felt he had a willing and sympathetic audience for the outrageousness of his wife. He soon noted that their conflicts seemed to diminish as he began to achieve a little distance from what had been an urgent need to be on the best of terms with her. As the transference began to develop, the patient was behaving in the mode of an exemplary analysand, who brought interesting dreams, worked hard at understanding them, and felt easily abused if his efforts and achievements went unnoticed. Soon he wanted to take a vacation and commented on the fact that he would have to pay for the hours that he would not use. There had been perhaps one or two missed appointments before this planned vacation, and some early signs of his anger at the unplanned and expensive events. On one occasion, he asked for and arranged an alternative appointment and was delighted with this way of avoiding a feeling of exploitation and its concomitant rage. The vacation was something else. He tried mightily to put it to rest, but it seemed to dominate his dreams, and the theme of doing his best though being unappreciated or downright ripped off seemed to crop up everywhere. Interestingly enough, he developed a certain forthrightness among some colleagues at work and was able to improve his financial and managerial position by standing up to people whom he had heretofore allowed to get away with certain minor but irritating abuses. As his feelings became focused in the analysis, he reported a dream of coming up with a solution to a problem that had baffled him and his colleagues for some time. He associated soon to the problem of the vacation and suddenly arrived at a solution of having make-up hours for all those he would miss. When it was pointed out to him that there weren't enough days in the week for an analytic patient to accomplish such a solution, he recalled the multiple efforts he had made as a child to resolve the seemingly unresolvable. Indeed his capacity to persevere and struggle with situations that others gave up on was one outstanding and welcome part of his overall personality. He soon demonstrated a part of himself that had not been immediately apparent: an image of someone who had Herculean abilities of performance and who could indeed do the impossible. But along with the emergence of this heretofore inaccessible part of himself came a readiness, against great resistance, to start to see his analysis as something for himself and not solely for his wife and the problems of his marriage.

As we concentrate on the transference we can see that the patient's fantasy that I was angry at him when he left town or misses an appointment for any reason is easily analyzed, since he admitted that I should not mind at all from a financial perspective. Either the anger was a projection of his, which he easily saw, or else it was a way of concealing how much he wished me to care, which was less easily recognized. He thus by the clear limitation of the rules became a more active participant and saw his own involvement in the transference, and he hesitantly began to investigate his own participation in the childhood and later life history of the person who triumphed over the raw deal visited upon him by the real world. His problem was to live with a task that is beyond his ability to conquer, and he made my rigid rule equal to that conundrum. I was the victimizer at times and the helper at others, much like his mother and sometimes his father. When he was away from me, he felt relieved, abused, and, at a deeper level, forlorn and depressed. This came alive in the transference through the issue of who benefitted from the analysis: him, his wife or his analyst. The rule seemed not to hinder but even to aid this reenactment.

I do not present this case example as a unique clinical event, but rather as one that seemed fairly well suited to the imposition of the rigid rule of payment. It seemed to me that no great harm was done by the initial contract, and it appeared, at least superficially, to facilitate the progress of the treatment. Of course, one cannot say what might have transpired with an agreement on a different sort of rule though we might guess that it would have effected only a minor variation. But it does seem to serve as a warning that so-called leniency or flexibility, or what is often called humaneness, has no direct bearing on the conduct of treatment. There is no inherently special therapeutic value in a stance that seemingly espouses kindness, and, certainly, what is natural for one person is not so for another. I personally felt that the patient was, if anything, more accessible and better understood by way of this rule. But if rules are to be judged neither by moral nor ethical nor therapeutic standards, then what can be the principle that we hope to divine for the proper conduct of the uncertainty in our profession? Is it that anything goes, or is it all up to the individual; or does it simply not matter at all? My first case seemed ruined by my rigidity; but the second appeared to profit from a similar sort of stance. I have known people to come to grief over the struggle over charging for missed hours, and I have known therapists and patients who insist that it is never an issue of consequence. However, I cannot speak to those fortunate ones who have mastered the problem, and so to try to resolve the dilemma of my two cases, I must now turn to a third.

This particular case, the last I shall mention, had to do with another rule of treatment, one promulgated by Freud (1918) in the case of the Wolf Man, that of setting a date for termination. It is a rule that, in contrast to some of the others mentioned, seems to cause little difficulty to most therapists and, for the most part, is looked upon favorably in the literature. When I first became interested in it, I found little of controversy about setting a date save for the change over the years from its being decided by the analyst to its being a negotiated and mutual decision by patient and analyst. It has been borrowed in a wholesale fashion by psychotherapy, although here a great deal more latitude is given to patients who change their mind. In general, it is felt that termination of treatment is best handled by a mutually agreed upon date to end, and that this ushers in a termination period characterized by work that is comparable to that of mourning. Freud's (1937) famous "the lion springs but once" dictum supports an unwavering attitude on the part of the therapist, since it is essential that the patient confront the reality of no longer seeing the therapist. The literature seems of one mind in stating that termination is something that must be worked through in any successful treatment and that most patients do not know "how" to terminate. The patient who on bringing up termination say, "Okay, let's stop today," is always cautioned to wait a bit, even just one more week in psychotherapy, in order to judge the effects of the decision. So too the patient in analysis is given sufficient time to master all the gains of the treatment in the final resolution of the transference neurosis.

In brief, my case was of a man in analysis who began talking about termination and wondered, but did not ask, if he could do so without setting a date. I decided to see what would happen under these circumstances, since much of his analysis had to do with his struggle with an erratic and unpredictable father who was alternately fearful and loving; and it had seemed that he had successfully worked out his relationship to him in the transference. For him, setting a date was an indication of one or the other of us imposing something. I shall not go into the details of the end of that analysis except to say that it seemed to come to a reasonably successful conclusion with all of the ingredients deemed necessary for a good termination. The interesting part came some time after the analysis, when I, along with a colleague, presented the idea and the case to an analytic seminar. The group of analysts present seemed on the whole to react with a certain degree of discomfort. One belligerent member of the audience dismissed the effort as a failure on my part to decide on a date with the patient. Other, less antagonistic listeners suggested that although this particular case seemed to sound all right, I certainly was not advocating the suspension of the rule of setting a date for every case—or was I? Some, even friendlier colleagues pointed out that a presentation such as mine was clearly an attempt to handle my own countertransference problems with the patient, and I was to be commended for this effort. The nicest of the group said that the paper was obviously unfinished, that I seemed to be leaving it up to the group to finish it, to decide what to do, and that my decision to do that was interesting but troublesome. The funniest comment came from someone who said the government would never allow such open-ended cases, since they would soon require all treatment to be time-limited.

The lack of a clear rule or a change in a sacrosanct rule is unsettling to most people and often creates even more anxiety than do rules that are unfair or unfeeling or worse. My presentation had been designed to open up the question of rules, and it was a fine demonstration of the binding and reassuring quality of implicit rules. I mention it here because it is in sharp contrast to the rigid rules of the other cases and seems to make a brief for a most liberal application of rules. Here was someone who did well in the absence of the usual rule, although I would not argue with the fact that a new rule of "no set date" was now in operation. Intriguing to me was that this exemplified a constructed rule that offered an opportunity to investigate what rules meant to us. The analytic seminar stood out in my mind because it dwelled on the practicability of a particular rule—Is it a good one or a bad one?—and sidestepped the point of what rules are for anyway. I think that if one rests with the fact that some things work for some people and some for other, then one settles for an essentially unscientific and even trivial statement that breeds contempt in our students. We need a place to stand on that is neither a cookbook for procedures nor a set of blank pages.

DISCUSSION

Leaving aside for the moment the problem of whether we are or will ever be able to formalize or program the rules for all of human behavior, it does seem that we approach other people with an initial effort to ascertain just what rules they are following. Goffman (1974) has beautifully illustrated this in normal social intercourse, and Spruiell (1983) has echoed this assumption in psychoanalysis. Once we can determine just what the rules are, we begin to understand that person. This formulation of understanding someone by way of determining what rules are being followed was first described by Plato (see Flew, 1979) who wondered whether the rules required to understand someone else were necessarily followed as well by the person, with or without that person's awareness. Of course, we now believe that people unconsciously behave according to some sets of rules, rational or irrational, and we like to believe that the way in which we make that behavior intelligible to ourselves is a true explanation of what is going on with that other person. Essentially we achieve an understanding of others by figuring out just what rules they are following. When the rules escape us, we fail to understand others, their behavior is inexplicable. Do patients learn in similar fashion, how to be patients by learning to live with the rules of therapy?

What does it mean to understand another person? We say that we try to be empathic with others by getting inside their head, to see why they do what they do and how they feel about things. In a sense, we attempt to determine the reasons patients are what they are by determining the rules they live by. We may feel they are dumb rules or silly rules or crazy rules, but understanding proceeds by way of such an effort. We may decide that a person does a self-destructive act to punish himself or someone else, and in this manner, we form a procedure of the internal working of that person. Empathy is assuredly the method of data gathering required to achieve understanding, but the step that stands between empathy and understanding is the determination of just what rules are directing the life of the other person.

Once we "catch on" to the self-destructiveness of that other person, he or she starts to make sense to us, and some sort of therapeutic intervention becomes possible. Until that moment, we often are unwitting participants in the rules of life of the other person. Understanding someone else therefore releases us from the need to act along with that other person.

Adolescence stands out in development as a period of rule upheaval. Those who spend time debating the phenomena of adolescent turmoil are probably misled not only by the question of manifest turmoil versus internal reorganization, but also by the fact that a very specific step seems to take place in adolescence in terms of rules and behaviors. Every observer of children knows the incredible attention paid to rules during play, and it is no secret that younger children sometimes devote their entire playtime to outlining and defining the rules. Throughout latency there is no diminution in the safety and security of rules, and rule conformity is as much a sign of health as overconformity is of psychopathology. I offer as a developmental suggestion that adolescence is a time to assume the role of independent rule-maker, and that this new function must, of necessity, lead to a period of turmoil, manifest or otherwise. Some adolescents are terrified of making rules for living, and they beseech us in a variety of ways to help them with this struggle. Some of these attempts provoke us into imposing rules and some into abandoning rules. I would venture to say that the "normal adolescent" term is one that should be reserved for those youngsters who are able to shift from following the rules to creating and developing a set that seems most appropriate to their owns lives.

Since adolescence is a period when the rules of conduct are in flux, the changes of development require a constant trial of new sets of rules. Therapists of adolescents use a wide repertoire of flexible rules to understand their patients. They act until they understand; they change rules in order to understand; and they sometimes say that there are no rules for treating adolescents. But there is a rule to follow that probably does qualify as the principle or metarule that gives license to the range and maneuverability required of all adolescent therapists: a rule is but a device to understand someone, and it is allowable only as long as it so functions. My own failure in the first case I described was certainly not a failure to schedule that man when he desired to be seen. With my limitations as a therapist and my supervisor's equally limited ability to help, I doubt if anything I did or did not do would have helped. I simply did not understand what it meant for the patient to come at the times he requested. Over the years I have made a lot of guesses as to its meaning, but I suspect the first step to helping that man would have been to admit to myself what I can now freely say. I did not know what to do because I did not and still do not understand him. I needed to embark on a process of negotiation, of presenting my dilemmas to the patient so that we could mutually work it out (see chapter 14).

We likewise require to learn and conform to our rules, and although we comfort ourselves with the idea that these rules facilitate treatment, we usually also admit that they serve a variety of purposes for us. I do not mean that we must hold up reality to patients in order to teach them what life is like. I have nothing against this stance, but it is now of secondary significance to my point. Rather, I think it an error to consider empathy and understanding to be a complete investment in another person devoid of our own baggage of theories, prejudices, and rules. Patients learn to live with us as well. Together we negotiate a set of rules, and patients do so by understanding us as being different from them. Sometimes we call this recognition of difference "breaks in empathy." But these disruptions are the stuff of growth and maturation as they lead us to further negotiations. The process of constructing explanations for why patients manage the world the way they do results from this sequence of empathy, negotiation, and understanding. And so I offer this principle of "negotiating to further understanding" as another basic rule of psychotherapy.

This issue that faces us is to expand this principle as a guide to seeing what to make of rule-following and rule-breaking in psychotherapy. A first instance of our scrutiny can be of the therapist who feels that his or her patient requires some extra measure of care or concern or action to effect treatment. Whatever the bit of behavior may be—and it ranges from minor adjustments in the setting of the treatment to major acting out outside of the treatment—it is always a sign of both an inability to understand the patient *and* an effort to achieve such an understanding. The well-meaning therapist who must go beyond the usual rules is probably engaged in a struggle to negotiate a new set of rules by which he and the patient can manage. The trouble with these maneuvers is that they tend to substitute for a later explanation of what is understood. If one indulges a patient in order to comprehend the rules, it can be only a temporary measure on the road to our primary principle of understanding. In like manner, the assumption of rigid rules is reasonable and necessary only if we thereby understand our patient. Otherwise it follows the same fate as indulgence.

Negotiation is the process by which persons exchange individual positions or theories or prejudices or convictions for shared ones. Since I believe that it is the basis for all meaningful human interaction, which, in turn, leads to mutual understanding, I can hardly do more than point to it. In its trite form, it is no more than saying "Let's talk about it" when a patient wants a response to a question. But in its major role in therapy, it is the process by which people hammer out the set of rules for living with one another. It is not that all we need do in therapy is to understand the patient. That seems to be just the half of it. The rest is that they understand us as well, and, in the rules of treatment, we see that process at work.

CONCLUSION

I have a patient who tells of his childhood talent to do "word problems," the kind that often start with; "If a train leaves Chicago at 100 miles per hour and twenty minutes later one leaves at 110 miles per hour . . . ." He said that he never really knew "how" he did them and became frightened in adolescence that he would therefore lose this ability. The same sort of thing happened to him in his baseball pitching, which he would at one moment get perfectly under control, and then inexplicably he would lose it. He managed to recreate this issue of control and mastery in his treatment and to connect it to sudden and unexplainable mood swings in his mother. He recognized that he needed to know the rules in spite of a talent that sometimes allowed them to be disregarded.

This patient stands in sharp contrast to another, who had a marvelous talent for making money. He said he could always do so without concern for the rules—referring not to the ethical dimension, but rather to the ways his peers operated. He came to treatment after a series of financial setbacks and sadly announced that he would now have to follow the rules—which he had always known—in order to stop losing money. He resented this imposition on his freedom and creativity. It made him feel constrained. We soon learned that this had more to do with a childhood position of specialness than with creative potential.

In a way these patients stand at polar opposites in their contrasting wishes for and disdain of rules. Both were gifted; but one needed the rules, and the other resented them. I think psychotherapists as well often cluster around these poles, and I know adolescents do so as well. My thesis is that we cannot afford to be complacent about rules, and, as much as we respect those talented therapists who live by "the seat of their pants," they can also be a pernicious influence in our field. Mine is not a plea for a manual of "how to" steps either, since I hope to have demonstrated that no such set of procedures can or should exist. Rather we need to expand our awareness of just what implicit and explicit rules have been imposed on our enterprise. And we need always to be prepared to modify, change, or even reverse our rules in the primary effort to negotiate the "meeting of the minds" that should underlie all our psychotherapeutic efforts. Such a meeting is not merely a conscious agreement, but rather must aim at a full comprehension of the unconscious rules of behavior. These are never obvious and have no inherent or intrinsic value or humaneness. Rules are made, and we are their makers.

14

Psychoanalysis and Negotiation

The technique of psychoanalysis has not followed a clear advance from a simple set of principles to a deepening and elaboration of these tenets. At times there seems to be a pluralistic approach to technique that borders on "anything goes" or at least "everyone does things different-ly" (Lipton, 1983). A study of technique should focus more on the method or form than on the particulars of the content, and so it suggests that we separate what is said from how it is said (see chapter 10). Thus two analysts may share a set of theoretical ideas but differ in their conduct of an analysis primarily in terms of their personal style, and this difference determines much of the conduct of the treatment. This point of form over content, the music over the words, the way it is said rather than what is said is often felt to be a distinguishing mark but not necessarily a crucial difference between analyses. One analyst's style differs from that of another in ways that are often assumed to be idiosyncratic or personal and often more facilitating or enhancing to the conduct of an analysis than central and primary. However, we soon become forced to look at the manner and form of analytic interventions as an integral part of the transaction since periodically it does appear to take precedence.

This chapter will attempt to bring the issue of "how" into a more central position by considering it as inextricable in its effect, if not in its study, from content. This claim can be supported by seeing it as

189

operative at every level of an analysis although often relegated to a secondary status. It thus demands its own theoretical underpinning and its own principles of activity. The latter may be subsumed under the process of negotiation.

WHAT IS NEGOTIATION

The word "negotiate" is so linked to adversarial situations, such as labor versus management, defense lawyers versus prosecution, and foreign powers in disagreement, that one might balk at considering it at all as a part of psychoanalysis. A less disagreeable definition considers it as communications made to arrive at some settlement of a matter and, this definition may relieve the negative note that is so often a part of the image of opponents trying to hammer out an agreement. We shall define it in the positive sense of a sharing of meanings.

On reading the notes of the Rat Man (Freud, 1909b), one sees that Freud fed his patient without feeling in any way that this hampered the analysis. Yet present-day psychoanalysts cannot but wonder about the effects of feeding or any other intrusion of the analyst into the process of analysis. This whole question of the analyst's input into the analytic work has undergone a series of scrutinies, arguments, and resolutions in the history of the technical management of an analysis. Positions range from the extreme of espousing noninvolvement to whatever degree is possible with a careful examination of any inadvertent intrusion or action considered under the rubric of countertransference (Silverman, 1985), to the other extreme of literally claiming the analyst's input as constituting the main form and content of the analysis (Tower, 1956). Some, like Laing (1967), might hold that the patient is correct in his or her perception of a crazy world that is recreated in treatment. Some, like Klein (1952), would point to the child's impulses as primarily responsible for the pathology, which is then recreated in the neutrality of the analytic setting. But, whether or not one includes the notion of responsibility in this consideration of the reappearance of the life of the child in the transference, there remains the question of whether the analyst can indeed be both a transference figure and observer of the situation or must inevitably be a participant, witting or otherwise. Thus Freud's feeding the Rat Man can be seen as so involving him in a real interaction that the posture of detachment and its associated word, objectivity, is temporarily abandoned. This would correspond to the sort of intrusion that might interfere with a transference based primarily on the patient's psychology: it might interfere more with one that is a compound of a two-person relationship. The issue to be addressed is whether one can conduct an analysis with the desired objectivity of a detached yet interested participant, or if every analysis is a mixture of the analysand's productions and the unpredictable input of the analyst. The first position at least allows for the hope of replicable and predictable data; the second portends a variable product that arises from a mixture of potentially idiosyncratic responses. Regardless of one's position on this matter, the method of exchange or interchange seems to warrant a study of the process of negotiation that goes on between patient and analyst. Only that term seems to capture the situation of two persons with distinct and separate interests working toward an agreement of sorts, and the nature of that agreement seems to depend on how it is arrived at. Thus consideration of psychoanalysis as negotiation would stand in contrast to it as an unearthing and so would modify the archeological metaphor to one of mutual construction.

Most psychoanalysts would agree that some minimal negotiation does take place in the treatment process but that it need not, or perhaps should not, be much of a factor in the conduct of the analysis. We negotiate such issues as appointment times, fees, and vacation schedules at the start of treatment and often assume (or hope) that they will cease to be problems later. As Freud (1913) said, "The conditions of treatment having been regulated in this manner, the question arises at what point . . . is the treatment to begin?" (p. 134). However, the conditions do not remain static. On occasion these points become major conflicts in the conduct of an analysis, and we view then as caught up in the unconscious conflicts of the moment. They are subsequently handled less by negotiation than by interpretation and so belong more properly (and comfortably) within the activities allowed to psychoanalysis.

In truth, negotiation is such a symbolic carrier of action that it is felt to defeat the proper stance of neutrality that is asked of the analyst. When Eissler (1953) discussed the introduction of parameters into analytic technique it was clear that, as necessary as they might sometimes be, they were always something of a nuisance, and one should as speedily as possible return to the single allowed activity: interpretation. The question to be posed is not only whether we have the obvious sorts of negotiations that are familiar to the conduct of the analysis, but also if the word properly belongs to the realm of interpretation as well.

NEGOTIATION AND RULES

Although there is but one basic rule in psychoanalysis, that of saying everything that comes to mind, in fact our patients must conform to a variety of rules in order to participate in the process. We set the fee, fix the time, determine the place, and talk when we desire. It is a rare patient who submits to all of our demands and constraints without some sort of reaction, and even a too willing compliance is seen as a sign of concealing a more profound meaning. It is probably also a rare analyst who has not either lost a patient because he or she could not fit into the analyst's constraints (regardless of their legitimacy) or bent the rules in order to allow an analysis to begin or to continue. Indeed, we often learn a great deal about a patient over this very issue of rules. Here is a clinical illustration:

A psychiatrist in analysis showed an intense interest in the time of starting and stopping his hours. The rule of a 45-minute session was not a problem for him, but he became enraged if he felt short-changed by as much as a few seconds, although he fought vigorously to squelch his expression of anger. He told of several of his supervisors who took advantage of him in the time allotment, and on more than one occasion had confronted a supervisor with an accusation of exploitation. He himself was quite reasonable about the supposed pettiness of his position but could become almost paranoid about his victimized position. Much of the analytic work was directed to his feeling of being deprived as a child, and this particular trait was readily enlisted in that category. As the analysis proceeded, the countertransference issue of being intimidated by the patient if the clock was not strictly attended to became significant. The question of deprivation changed to one of control over starting and stopping the hours. With this point raised for scrutiny, the patient recalled the times he had been left in his father's care as a child while mother was on an errand or otherwise away. He may have been five or six on the first remembered occasion when he asked his father about bedtime. The father, a rather preoccupied man, announced that that was entirely up to the boy. The father was pleased, but the son was dumbfounded and then frightened. It now seemed to him to have been totally incongruous for a little boy to have such a position of power, since he had not initially posed the question as a challenge to the rule. From his feeling of lack of control there ensued the one of victimization: He concluded that the father's liberal stance really reflected a lack of care and concern for the boy. He mused over whether he was somehow a co-conspirator with those supervisors who had so mistreated him and saw how the absoluteness of the rule had offered him a hope of keeping these feelings hidden. Of course, the rule of the analytic and supervisory hour was a ready vehicle for investigating the special individual meanings that it held since it quickly became caught up in the analytic process.

Examples of rule-setting and rule-changing can do no more than lend support to the idea that there is nothing inherently good or bad about any rule, save how we learn what it means to us and to the patient. We may feel that a good rule follows Freud's (1913) suggestion that it is effective—and I take that to mean that it does not impede the development and resolution of the transference—while a bad rule works against the goal. This seems in keeping with the theme of Freud's recommendations, as opposed to good or bad having some moral or ethical connotation. Even the fixed rule of free association was explained by Freud (1913) to a patient as being something quite beyond his control, and so he was relieved of insisting on conformity for his personal sake. We often wish to extend a host of similar rules in psychoanalysis as belonging to the same category of "it's not up to me but is part of the rules," until a rescrutiny of these points betrays our personal investment.

Rules such as length of hours, frequency of visits, and personal contacts between patient and analyst are handled in a separate category having to do with facilitating the treatment. The story told of Jacque Lacan ending some sessions after but a few minutes (Schneiderman, 1983) is reacted to as a breach of ethical standards much akin to that of the analyst who becomes overly familiar with his patient. Indeed it is usually true that, because of a rule's institutionalization in our profession, it becomes a part of the right way to do things. Without pursuing the matter of such moral imperatives, it seems clear enough that rules soon become our way of our world. They determine what should be done, how it should be done, and why it should be done. In short, they make up much of the analyst's reality. This particular view of the world meets that of the patient and thus does the situation come about for a meeting of the minds and re-evokes our concern with the matter of negotiation.

NEGOTIATION AND PSYCHIC REALITY

Once the matter of the rules of performance is put aside, we usually feel that we can step outside of participating with the patient in anything like an educative manner. Imagine a patient who tells you that he feels that the world is an awful place, filled with dirt and disease, peopled with evil individuals who wish only to hurt and exploit you, and destined to end in some sort of justified apocalyptic way. If we choose to treat such a patient, it is assumed that somehow we must be empathic with him and thus must enter his world and experience his reality. We cannot, however, be but another in a line of those who wish to set him straight or cheer him up or talk him out of it. Neither can we totally immerse ourselves in his problem and share his view of misery and sadness. It is folly to say that we must completely shed our own preconceptions of the world in order to really understand another person. Our very preconceptions that insist that the world is not such a place allow us to try to begin to disabuse the patient of his forlorn picture of existence. Thus, we neither totally agree nor totally disagree but seek a workable stance for our later interpretive efforts.

If that patient or another patient tells us of a world of brightness and sunshine, happiness and joy, peopled with those who have only our best interests at heart, we should be equally skeptical and equally caught between reality and empathy. It seems that we always weigh the disparity between a sympathetic identification with the patient and some other background concept of how people should or do experience the world. Though we may choose to allow the optimistic viewpoint to go unchallenged, we cannot fail to match our own world view with the presentation of the patient. In short, we cannot listen to anyone except against a background of our own traditions and beliefs, and we pick and choose our interventions on the basis of what we consider proper versus what we feel is deviant. That is how we decide a theory of psychopathology as well as normality. Somehow we know just how people should feel about things, and we act accordingly.

But of course no analysis is a process of argument anymore than it is one of suggestion. It is in the crucible of the transference that we determine whatever we choose to see as deviations from a norm. Psychoanalysis claims a unique window on the world by assuming that patients will inevitably and irresistibly bring their childhood into the treatment and the disparity between that set of experiences and the reality of the analytic situation will enable ameliorative interpretations. Ideally we should see a transference that follows a set program responding to a process of interpretation that allows only a minimum of latitude.

TRANSFERENCE AND NEGOTIATION

It soon becomes evident that the ideal equation of transference and interpretation is not easily achieved or readily manifest. One analyst told a story of seeing a patient who had had two previous analyses. She described to her new therapist a series of awful mistreatments bordering on malpractice in these analyst encounters. She professed her great relief that she had at last found a trustworthy person to help her. The about-to-be christened third analyst informed his patient that although he could not defend the analysts who had abused her, he had no doubt that he too would join the ranks of the oppressors. Being a profound believer in the repetition compulsion, he knew that a fixed program was operating in this patient's unconscious and that he must allow this to unfold in a nonprejudicial way. And indeed he tells the story in the manner of one whose good judgment was confirmed. He inevitably became the rascal and villian that this patient's psyche seemed to require. Thus the replicable and predictable feature of the transference.

But not all transferences are alike. The very fact that the analyst "knows" what to expect makes him a different person than the naive or untutored partner in a similar such transaction. Another analyst might be more willing to mistreat the patient, given her proclivity to call this behavior forth in others; still another might even have kept these feelings to a minimum. Only in the most ideal of transference enactments are we able to claim a pure form of emergence of the childhood, and even if that is the case we do not all attend alike to what does emerge. Sooner, rather than later, every analyst seems to direct or focus the patient's productions by way of his own history and traditions, his transference and countertransference, and his theory and convictions.

Here is an illustration of an analytic intervention taken from The Two Analyses of Mr. Z. (Kohut, 1979). It concerns a dream interpreted differently over a period of years:

> A dream occurred. . . .In the dream his associations pointed clearly to the time when the father rejoined the family. (He was in a house, at the inner side of a door which was a crack open. Outside was the father, loaded with gift-wrapped packages, wanting to enter. The patient was intensely frightened and attempted to close the door in order to keep the father out.) . . . Our conclusion was that it referred to his ambivalent attitude toward the father. I stressed . . . his hostility toward the father, the castration fear vis a vis the strong, adult man: and, in addition, I pointed out his tendency to retreat from competitiveness and male assertiveness either to the old preoedipal attachment to his mother or to a defensively taken submissive and passive homosexual attitude toward the father [p. 8-9].

In the discussion of the second analysis Kohut wrote:

> The new meaning of the dream as elucidated by the patient via his associations . . . was not a portrayal of a child's aggressive impulse against the adult male accompanied by castration fear, but of the mental state of a boy who had been all-too-long without a father; of a boy deprived of

the psychological substance from which, via innumerable observations of the father's assets and defects, he would build up, little by little, the core of an independent masculine self . . . the dream constitutes a tame replica of a traumatic state [p. 23].

This is not the place to discuss the many reactions to this set of dream interpretations, which range from outright agreement to serious disagreement. The latter holds that the two interpretations are really one, that the second should have preceded the first, that either the one or the other was unnecessary, and so on. It seems of little moment to the critics that for the analyst the dream had a "new meaning," which was in opposition to the previous one. Thus, at a minimum, this dream or any dream means nothing except as seen in the context of the timing, the transference position, and, most importantly, the theoretical stance of the analyst. Kohut would probably modify the last by insisting that the patient's association led to his revised interpretation, but, contrary to Kris (1983), there are simply no observations of the mind possible without a theory of the mind to direct, guide, and elicit them. One never sees a pattern or follows a theme of mental phenomena without a preexisting schema, and it is simply impossible for any so-called theory-free data to emerge. Therefore one influences what is seen by the very act of seeing. Alas, we are not and never can be neutral observers. The associations of the patient seem more in the nature of a dialogue than a monologue.

Although the analyst may never openly direct the flow of associations, he participates in two ways. The first has to do with his choice of one meaning over another since any given dream or bit of analytic material has multiple vantage points. This, of course, is the nature of overdetermination. The second is due to the fact that every intervention resets the communication just as every conversation is made unpredictable by virtue of one's need to respond to the input of the other. If we choose to keep our interventions to an absolute minimum by silence, we soon learn that such absences are a significant form of input. We may thereupon choose to move the arena of our scrutiny to studying the effects of intervention or nonintervention on the associations. In one sense this concern with form rather than content, a concentration on how things are said rather than what is said, is a natural member of every analyst's armamentarium and, as was demonstrated in chapter 10, is really a theory about a theory or what we called a metatheory.

Thus we see that psychoanalysis exists on two levels. The patient talks and we listen, and the patient makes something of our listening. We study what the patient says by way of our theoretical inclinations.

We study *how* the patient reacts to our silences or our interventions via another sort of theory. If a patient speaks of a common-sense term such as an apple, we assume we know what it stands for until we learn of the very special personal meaning it has for that patient. Much of our own sense of the term "apple" is shared by the patient, but some part is always special and individual for each of us. In Rangell's (1985) words, "The analyst, by a more informed theory than the patient, produces in the latter further insight and understanding" (p. 83). The how of this process, the manner in which our theory, whatever it may be, is able to change that old apple to a new one, is the process of negotiation. But now the question of just where the change takes place arises.

NEGOTIATION AND CHANGE

The theory of negotiation is also a metatheory, one that concerns itself with the communicative process that goes on between persons to achieve some sort of shared reality. It stands in marked contrast to a theory of indoctrination that has associations to submission, compliance, and lack of participation. Results of negotiation are quite apart from fixed beliefs, which permit no form of alteration from either indoctrination or negotiation. Rather, the negotiating process is based on a modification of beliefs and, in analysis, consists of the interpretation of the unconscious content plus the process of working through. Merely naming the unconscious content before the patient is ready is of no import, just as doing it only once likewise has a minimal effect. Psychoanalysis also has a variety of ways to determine the effectiveness of interpretations by way of further associations, increased or decreased resistance, or the like. As Rangell (1985) indicated, the achievement of insight is essentially the capacity of the patient to gain conviction of the truth of the "more informed theory" of the analyst.

There have been many attempts to explain the nature of the therapeutic change in psychoanalysis. It is important at the outset to differentiate such efforts at explanation from those that are more descriptive in nature. Statements such as "Where id was there shall ego be" (Freud, 1933 p. 80). "Corrective emotional experiences that occur are crucial . . . and may well be the single most important aspect of psychoanalytic effectiveness" (Peterfreund, 1983, p. 251) are not so much an explanation of a causal relationship as they are a rephrasing of an event. This may be sufficient for many, but usually we look for causal explanations.

Hartman (1951) offered such an explanation by positing the lifting of countercathexis from repressed material and the subsequent neutralization of the released energy which then became available to the ego. The satisfactoriness of this idea may be reduced by the general lack of acceptability of the entire energy concept.

Kohut (1984), following Freud, utilized the model of mourning to explain the acquisition of structure that occurred in treatment. He stated that the two-phase process of understanding and explanation allowed a partial merger followed by a disruption. This sequence leads to minute internalizations of functions and this is, in turn, explained as a furtherance of the process. Thus change resulted from structural growth.

Basch (1981), following Piaget and theories of cognitive development, considers the cause of change in treatment to the progressive movement from one state of cognitive development (say sensorimotor) to another (e.g., concrete operations). He relies on the Piagetian (see Furth, 1981) theory of a fixed program that will unfold in an appropriate environment. This formulation is similar to those suggested by analytic developmental theorists who liken analysis to a developmental experience.

Barratt (1985) argues against the curative factor in psychoanalysis lying merely in the new knowledge acquired. For him, the knowing of psychoanalysis is a change in one's being. He insists that one cannot approach or comprehend these changes within the framework of logical positivism. Rather the method sets in motion what he terms knowing as being, and being as knowing. A change in knowing changes who you are, and a change in who you are alters what you may come to know.

Those, including Kohut, who see analysis in developmental terms feel that the analytic situation encourages the maturational processes to unfold. They range along the continuum depending on what they feel are the proper conditions for development. Thus, the analyst must create the climate, lend the language, or correct the deviations in order for the inherent program to be realized. But even the most austere of analytic approaches recognizes that the analyst affects the patient by his presence, his interpretations, and the state of the transference.

The rules of the process, the theory of the analyst, the communicative exchange or metatheory employed, all contribute to any psychoanalysis, and all may be quite different from analyst to analyst and from time to time. It would be foolish to say that anything said by the analyst can be considered therapeutic and therefore the words are meaningless; but it would also be naive to say that there is but one true way to proceed. Different analysts do say quite different things at different times, and that these diverse ways of analyzing seem to work demands some explanation that goes beyond the options of nihilism (anything goes) and fruitless comparisons (mine is better than yours). Spence (1982) asks for some naturalization of our data in an effort to pin down some empirical facts. Schafer (cited in Spence, 1982) speaks for alternative narratives that may share equal claims for true historical records. What is being suggested here is that every interpretation and intervention is an *approximation* of some true state of belief and feeling of the patient. It is couched in the therapist's language, guided by the therapist's theory, colored by the prevailing transference, and open to correction by the therapist's capacity to negotiate. Patients and analysts learn a shared social reality, learn to communicate in a shared language, and learn what one another's expectations are. Inasmuch as we have a sometimes startling and bewildering array of therapeutic interventions, we should attend less to the truth of these propositions than to the way some sort of agreement is reached between patient and analyst. This is negotiation, and this is what merits study.

THE PROCESS OF NEGOTIATION

A cursory study of the notes of the Rat Man (Freud, 1909b) case demonstrates the nature of the negotiating process that goes on between Freud and his patient. Freud asks him to bring a photo of the lady with him in order to give up his reticence about her. No matter that a modern-day analyst would himself be reticent about such a request, the words reveal the motive and goal of the analyst. Every page demonstrates some action of Freud's ranging from "I could not restrain myself" to "I explained to him." Freud persuades him to reveal things, suffers with explanations that mean nothing to the patient, and even delivers a lecture on perversion (p. 283). These notes are not presented as exemplars of good technique, but many of today's analysts would do away with all but the interpretations. I suspect that is both a foolish and impossible goal since we too persuade, suffer, and lecture but are perhaps a bit more alert to the consequences.

Many analysts have attempted to divide the components of treatment into what may be termed the therapeutic, or working, or real relationship, and the transference, others say it all belongs to the transference (Brenner, 1985), and perhaps still others claim the relationship encompasses everything. So too do some wish to have this therapeutic relationship assume a background presence so that the real work of analysis may proceed. Putting this feature of analysis into such a framework and seeing it as a positive feature or an impediment seems to minimize the complexity of the process that goes on in every analysis and that underscores how patient and analyst agree or disagree about anything at all.

Brenner (1985), recently presented a vignette of a woman who argued with him over everything in her analysis. As an analyst, he appropriately considers whether *what* he has said infuriated her and then studies the peculiar state that makes *whatever* he says or does not say serve as a stimulus for her irritation. The second consideration, which is essentially about the first, is of a different logical type; that is, it is on a different level of inquiry from the first, just as the word fruit is of a higher order than the word apple, pear, or orange. The study of the content is the first level, whereas the study of the exchange irrespective of the content is on a different level. We also say that the second is a metastudy, which means no more than a study about something studied.

Brenner does not tell just how this impasse was resolved, but he does mention that the patient tried mightily not to so disagree. She ultimately realized the motives for her persistent arguing, and so, we assume, it dissipated. We might also assume that interpretation alone was effective, but one can only wonder about the intermediary steps involved in getting the patient to listen, in convincing her of the truth of the analyst's interventions, in achieving a state of agreement that was so antithetical to her nature. Just how was this negotiated if not by sheer repetition of an interpretation? At one point, the patient is said to have resolved to keep quiet until her analyst had spoken. In truth this was an attempt at a negotiated peace, but one that was unsuccessful. It seems that over time the patient was able to see what she was doing.

Kohut (1984) tells of a similar case of a patient who could not accept any interpretation from him even if it was a correct one (as the patient would later agree). He says that this pattern of refusal by the patient had to do with his own failure to see that the patient felt incompletely understood. When *that* was interpreted, then the analysis could proceed. This is more by way of a commentary on the transaction between analyst and analysand and coincides with Kohut's conviction that an understanding phase must precede the explanatory phase. But does recognizing that something is wrong and interpreting why it is so always lead to such prompt resolution of the impasse? The question seems to have shifted to how one achieves empathy, that is, how one manages to make the explanation effective. For Kohut there seems to have been a more immediate attention to this level of disagreement, and the analyst seems to be more active in its lifting. But this likewise seems to assume an ease that leaves something out.

To tease apart the factors involved in having the arguing (negative, resistant) patient accept an interpretation, we must recall that negotiation is a two-way process regardless of whether the analyst is silent or verbose. The patient responds to silence or to words by accepting either as some sort of a negotiating position of the analyst and carries on from there. The silent analyst may be felt to allow less room for maneuver, but in the exchange between patient and analyst some acceptable compromise is achieved. Over time, the angry patient may agree to the analyst's repeated interpretations or to the supposedly new and more empathic ones, but ultimately we hope to achieve agreement. What seems to transpire is that the patient, perhaps sooner rather than later, must learn to understand (be empathic with) the analyst. Empathy is operant on both sides, and surely patients learn to comprehend their analyst in a manner similar to what we usually say is required of analysts. The intermediate steps may consist of the patient's rephrasing the analyst's interpretation or modifying it or accepting a part and rejecting another part. The analyst, in turn, may learn to present only certain parts or to put it in different words or to change the meaning in response to later associations. Together they aim to arrive at a shared meaning. It is a rare analyst who forms and delivers interpretations that need little reshaping, and a patient never ends a successful analysis with the same view of his life and the world with which he began.

NEGOTIATION AND THE CHANGE
IN THE ANALYST

If the analyst is a participant in the negotiations that aim at a change in the patient's view of and theory about himself, can the analyst emerge untouched? Participants in any negotiating process usually give and take except for those infrequent involving fixed beliefs and indoctrinations. Analytic patients change in diverse ways, but we usually assume that the analyst gains only in experience, wisdom, and skill. Yet most of the elements of analytic change do require some, at least temporary, ability to see and believe something differently. It probably is difficult, if not impossible, to grade the potential changes in the analyst in a positive or negative direction, but one can offer the suggestion that every patient offers a world view that demands some sort of accommodation by the analyst. Sometimes this is in the direction of changes in rules (Goldberg and Marcus, (1985), or in theory (Kohut, 1984), or in technique (Freud, 1909). It takes no imaginative leap to realize that these components are also aspects of a total personality, and so we might say that every analysis does indeed cause us to remake ourselves (Gadamer, 1975). The levels of analyst change may be primarily cognitive, as when we simply learn more about something from a patient, or affective. The latter may be severe enough to warrant some personal analytic work. But another level would combine these to bring out a change in our science that corresponds to Freud's change of mind and heart about the seduction theory. Perhaps it is not too revolutionary a stand to insist that effective analyses are such meaningful negotiations that they demand that a new analyst emerge. We may or we may not be wiser, but we are (or should always be) different.

Of special moment here is the change in the patient's empathy for an understanding of the analyst. It would be naive to withhold credit to our patients who teach us how to understand them, who are patient with our mistakes, and who tolerate some of our outlandish interpretations and theories—who sometimes even are quite therapeutic to us! Given the two—way street of empathy, it probably means that we too are undergoing new experiences, in being understood if not always having things explained to us. Unless we grant this form of the potential for change in analysts then we fall back on a mechanical version of offering interpretations that are universally and eternally valid; and that position may not be acceptable to many analysts.

DISCUSSION

We negotiate the rules of the analytic procedure, our shared version of the world, the meaningfulness of the analytic transference, and the goals and method of cure. When Freud wrote up the case of the Rat Man, he decided, as does every analyst, to present certain facts and to omit others. Among those omitted were the host of personal contacts that were felt not to be a part of the analysis. His friendly feeling toward his patient was noted but mainly discounted or subsumed under present-day concepts of the therapeutic relationship. But every analysis operates on at least two levels: what we talk about and how we do it. When the latter becomes the focus of interest, as often occurs in the analysis of resistance, we assume yet another level for that discourse. We can never escape the process of trying to reach common ground with our patients. We should agree that no part of the transaction between patient and analyst is ever immune from the effects of the one person on the other, and no part of the analyst per se does not matter for one or another patient. The history of psychoanalytic technique makes much of the particulars of allowing a patient to see things and understand things and master things that were heretofore unknown to him. Since we must choose never to suggest or to indoctrinate, we appeal to reason and good judgment in order to move from transference to reality. Each step of the process is suffused with our rules, our theories, and our world views, and each step must entail a negotiation to achieve a shared meaning. Thus the process of negotiation is another way of looking at the technique of psychoanalysis. There is no inherent essence to release what a patient is "really like"; rather it is a mutual construction.

At its simplest, psychoanalysis is an effort to change someone else's mind. It is, of course, not confined to the level of conscious decisions but rather aims to reach to the depths to effect such a change. Merely seeing the truths of the world never seems to be sufficient to convince people of the folly of their position, and psychoanalysis lays claim to a powerful tool that expands one's vision: the transference. It would be a great relief if that were the sturdy platform on which we could all stand to enable insight to emerge, but it seems that our convictions about the transference are as contaminated as are all of our other truths and convictions. (Bird, 1972). Thus we should move on to a study of just how mind changing takes place (all the while knowing that this as well will be a prejudiced pursuit). The process of persuasion or understanding or gaining insight is a fruitful study in its own right. It consist of all the factors that we study about negotiating a meeting of the minds, that is, examining the steps that allow one person to reach agreement with another. This process essentially comprises the technique of treatment, which in turn includes the whole of our ideas about reality, psychopathology, and analytic theory. No step of the process of negotiation is free from this baggage of prejudices, cultural background, and training with which we enter the room; and it is probably equally simplistic to think that we are able to leave the room unchanged. Rather, the job of getting another person to change involves an empathic exchange wherein each participant becomes aware of the other's position. In this manner the technique of psychoanalysis demands that we not only understand our patients but that they understand us as well.

15

Selfobjects and Self-Control

The term selfobject, which usually connotes another person who is experienced at performing a necessary psychic function for the self, certainly would include the range of functions that have to do with impulse control, limit setting, and others dealing with the containment of action and behavior. However, for the most part, the illustrative clinical material in self psychology treats selfobjects as primarily gratifying or enhancing, using terms such as mirroring or consolidating and avoiding those that are suggestive of prohibition or injunction. To pursue an inquiry of the latter would lead to examining the question and determining just when and how a selfobject becomes a true object in the sense of being *an independent center of initiative* that controls or affects the self and thus is truly experienced as an "other" and vice versa. It seems that self-control is a ready function for the study of whether such an action belongs to the self or to another. It would thus allow one to determine when and how such "control" becomes transformed in the eyes of the observer from external to internal and would begin to answer such knotty questions as the role of the superego in self psychology. Control is the key word in unlocking the range of problems that deal with the feeling of coercion that is experienced as coming from outside oneself, in contrast to the feeling of mastery that issues from within.

Questions about the range of psychological material that deals with prohibitions and the superego will also raise the problem of guilt. Self psychology has had little to say about this affect and has emphasized the shame experience as more central to its primary concerns. Yet self psychology can make no claim to going beyond its concern with a narrow group of psychopathology unless it includes the guilt affect in its explanatory domain. Such explanations should also go beyond the usual assigning of control to the ego or superego and the detailed and sometimes meaningless arguments of such categorizations that are based more or less on the feeling of guilt. We need to say why guilt emerges in one set of constraints and not in another, and whether we are essentially dealing with selfobjects or have shifted to a concern with other sorts of object relations.

SOME METAPSYCHOLOGICAL GROUND RULES

The taking over of functions is often considered under the general rubric of internalization, but that is a word that is sometimes a subject of confusion and uncertainty. Any psychoanalytic perspective whatever must concern itself as a necessary first step with what is within the mind. Thus the first form of internalization that we meet has to do with events, things, and persons of the external world becoming represented or taking up residence in the mind. This is not so simple a process as would be explained by a mere transposition of the outside to the theatre of the mind, since we know that certain developmental achievements must take place before one can in any manner represent the world. Added to this is the fact that our sensory organs are selective in their apperception of the world. The problem is then made more complex by the knowledge that not everything that *can* be perceived *is* perceived. Rather things, persons, and events of perception must carry a certain charge or significance in order to be registered. We know from tachistoscopic experiments that much may be registered in the mind without awareness, and we also know that much that is perceived may be denied. However, regardless of the conscious awareness of such registration, there remains a selective reading of the external world, and this reading becomes the first level of internalization for our consideration. Thus, a person may enter a room filled with people, being aware of a handful and unwittingly register perhaps more; by no means can we say that the entire room has now assumed a position within his mind. Psychoanalysis uses the shorthand of object representation for the transposition of the world to the mind, but we should be cautious about even that, since once we move to the mind we find other levels of organization that need to be delineated. Psychoanalytic studies are thus confined to the intrapsychic, which is derived from, but is by no means equal to, the interpersonal.

Once within the realm of the mental, the arrangement of events, persons, and things takes place along a variety of axes having to do with their special significance and meaning. Those that have minimal unconscious valence or are without much affective charge may often be forgotten or used as day residue in dream formation. Those that have standing in their own right, but remain separate from the self, are classified as true objects. Those experienced as part of the self are termed selfobjects. The passage from internal representations of selfobjects to the "transmuting" of the selfobject function into a part of the self is noted as yet another level of internalization, where the object per se is dispensed with and the self assumes an equal or analogous function. Since it is part of the lore of self psychology that selfobjects are never totally forsaken, one must assume that there is something in the nature of the link between the self and the selfobject that determines how we shall consider it—just what allows us to feel that a selfobject is needed for sustenance versus its being expendable? It is clear that the nature of these relationships between self and selfobject cannot be evaluated under the single axis of internalization. Other metaphors (Goldberg, 1983) should be emphasized here to describe these connections. The description should follow a developmental scheme and so, for example, would differentiate an archaic selfobject from a mature one. They should also highlight the dimensions we consider in self-selfobject linkage such as physical presence, intensity of attachment, interchangeability with similar relationships, and so forth. Thus the mental map that we draw will show a selective view of the real world and a complex set of connections of varying significance to those aspects of the world to which we do attend.

A nice example of what is seen as internalization is given by Stern (1985) in his description of a two-year-old girl who is put to bed every evening by her father. He speaks to her of the day's events and the plans for the next day. The girl participates in the dialogue and goes through maneuvers to prolong the visit. When finally he says "goodnight," her voice changes into a matter-of-fact tone, and she begins a monologue. Over time she moves closer to a "satisfying verbal rendition" of her thinking and thus "internalizes" the relationship with the father by reactivating his presence and carrying it with her. In this manner we follow the steps of a child who perceives and reacts to her father (one form of internalization) and then supposedly transfers the relationship to a theatre of the mind by way of different representations (another form of internalization) and, following this, proceeds to modify the dialogue in terms of language and gestures (a form of identification with the father that would suggest even another level of category of internalization). Thus the father "out there" is perceived "in here' and then takes up residence "in here" in a special way (what Stern seems to feel is an essential or basic internalization) and then proceeds to influence the person or self, which is also represented in the mind, even to the point of modifying that self. Certainly this schematic view of the workings of internalization cannot begin to accomplish more than a sketch, but we need to focus primarily on the nature of the influence between self and other once such residence is established. Since we wish to concentrate on self-control we must elaborate the way the self assumes those controlling functions which initially are outside of its domain. Thus, the dialogue between child and father, once internal, must be examined in terms of how the child assumes ownership of what was once the father's, that is, how what was yours becomes mine.

In summary, our ground rules have to do with an abandonment of the external-internal dichotomy and a focus on intrapsychic phenomena. These phenomena then are examined in terms of the manner of linkage and influence between self and other, in particular that of seeing how an object becomes a selfobject and how that becomes a matter of self control. This is not to diminish the significance of all the steps that precede and influence this focus, since the process is probably not sequential but involves feedback influences and multiple modifications with development. The child represents the world, organizes it in categories of significance, and lays claim to a special category of personhood in a continual circle of mutual influence and interaction.

THE SUPEREGO

Glasser (1986), writing about identification and perversion, states that "the relationship between the pervert and his superego, is that the superego, while clearly an internal object, remains quite distinct from the self" (p. 12). Aside from what seems to be an unfortunate mixing of mental models (see *Models of the Mind*, Gedo and Goldberg, 1973, for a differentiation of these psychic concepts), the author suggests a continuum of internalization. This ranges from a simple copying of an object at one end to a thorough incorporation of the object into the self at the other. The latter step is called identification. Of course, this runs counter to the usual picture of merged self- and object representations (Jacobson, 1964) that are ordinarily held to be rather primitive states of affairs, whereas separation of self and object is something to be achieved. In order to rescue himself from this dilemma Glasser suggests that the superego is an introject that may become a part of the self-representation or may be involved in pseudo-identification, or "simulation." He is seemingly representative of a whole spectrum of confusion about just how and why the collection of standard and prohibitions that constitute the superego is sometimes felt as alien, sometimes as fearful, and sometimes as comforting.

AND GUILT

The clearest form of self-restraint or control lies in the physical presence of the prohibiting other. In infancy and childhood, the parental restraints become assumed over time with the initial occurrence of the "inner voice" of control seen to imitate the parent; but this inner presence is clearly experienced as apart from the self. If the child disobeys, the child is punished by the parent or the internal parental surrogate, and this is the precursor of guilt. If, on the other hand, we postulate a mutual relationship of child and parent or of self and other, then the mere disruption of this relationship by the child's misbehavior causes parental anger or displeasure, and this is experienced by the child as a potential albeit momentary loss of the parent. In a manner similar to a sexualization of a relationship in order to maintain it, there may occur an aggressivization with a similar goal in mind. The relationship between parent and child becomes charged with anger. The child experiences a narcissistic injury and in turn responds with anger. This is turned upon the self, and the guilt experience is born. The requirement for this lies in the sequence of the parent serving as a necessary selfobject to the child, the child acting in a manner to threaten that, a disruption of the selfobject bond, a reactive anger to the potential loss of the selfobject, a turning of the anger upon the self, and a restitution of the parental selfobject relationship by way of and resulting in guilt. Thus the guilty response serves to capture and maintain the sustaining parental selfobject. It regulates the nature of the bond between self and other in that it obliterates the threatening separation evoked by the child's behaving in too separate a way. It seems not available in the mere interaction of the self with a "true object" but rather demands the sort of connection seen between self and selfobjects. Thus, our requirement for superego is a strongly linked relationship demanding a certain conformity. We shall later sketch its development, but first we postulate the guilt reaction as one designed to handle separation.

A CLINICAL ILLUSTRATION

A patient in analysis delayed payment for a small part of his bill for several months. During this time he complained of feeling burdened and oppressed and behaved in a manner corresponding to a suffering and unhappy child. When at long last he paid the bill, he felt relieved and lighthearted. He then recognized that he had begun this mild form of delinquency at a point when he began to feel excited and over-stimulated about the prospect of improvement and thus of terminating his analysis. He had defended against the painful feelings of such overstimulation by an act that bound him even closer to his analyst. He had felt terribly guilty about not paying. The burdensome guilty feeling had been a common one in his childhood; the more joyful and stimulated one, exceedingly rare. The fantasy that predominated during this period was of the analyst rising up in anger and ridding himself of the patient. One sequence that would explain this consisted of (1) a wish to be rid of the analyst; (2) a fantasy of defeating the analyst by not paying; (3) a fantasy of the analyst's retaliation by way of the superego in order to curtail the offensive wish; and (4) a feeling of guilt engendered by the punitive stance of the superego. Another sequencing of this would be (1) a wish to be free of an archaic selfobject relationship; (2) a fear of losing the binding and coalescing quality of the selfobject; (3) an act of aggression to reconnect to the selfobject; (4) a turning of this aggression to the self with a concomitant narcissistic injury; and (5) a guilty feeling composed of the injury plus a reconnection to the selfobject.

To reconstruct this behavior from the different points of view we could contrast the explanations as those of a classical stance versus one based on self psychology. The first suggests that the active act of sexual or aggressive behavior is associated with an unconscious fantasy. If this then becomes associated with regression and subsequent symptom formation, then we have neurosis; if not, we have the normal affect of guilt. This is a complex affect that somehow derives from the basic affects present at birth. It is a fact of every human experience that involves feeling guilt over acts of commission that somehow connect with the forbidden.

The alternative, self-psychological view is constructed around the nature of the self-selfobject relationship. It posits a linkage that is somehow unstable because of a developmental push or because of a regressive move. This instability is the key to the affective charge that is to result. The action on the part of the self threatens the relationship and initiates a process of self-fragmentation. The selfobject reaction to the movement is experienced as a narcissistic injury because of its open hostility and contempt. In our clinical example this may be little more than the analyst's unwitting reaction to not being paid, i.e. the bond is loosened and the patient is frightened and hurt. The resultant rage from the narcissistic injury binds the self once again to the selfobject, halts the regressive and fragmenting process, and allows a reintegration of the self around a masochistic or depressed posture that is suffused with the guilty affect. This sketch of the nature of the pathological nature of the guilt reaction allows us to formulate a program about the developmental issues involved in the emergence of self-control and self-restraint.

And Development

Examples of early self-controlling relationships have to do with an external object. In our metapsychological considerations we recast this as another object that is experienced as separate (albeit represented in the mind) but given significance in that it is capable of inflicting a narcissistic injury. Some external objects are incapable of this action and so can be relegated to insignificance. Exactly what gives an object the power of such personal hurt should yield a clue to just what constrains and controls the self. For a start, we should allow for the definition of "significance" to carry a sense of some self-investment in the object. Objects cannot hurt us or control us unless they mean something to us. Thus, the child's emotional investment or tie to the object binds him or her to the other, and injury becomes linked with loss of such adherence. The linkage of self to object is once again modified by the concept of selfobject inasmuch as that other is both capable of hurting and simultaneously needed to sustain the self. Some may say that the division is an arbitrary one and insist that all objects of significance are selfobjects, but we must momentarily put that problem aside. Development does seem to proceed by a strengthening and widening of self-selfobject relationships and to be composed of the increased investment of the self in the selfobject. Investment here is meant to be an increasing importance of the selfobject, an increase in the similarity between self and the selfobject so that danger of disruption (difference) is diminished, and an increased sense of control over the selfobject.

The process of establishing, enhancing, and making enduring the self-selfobject relationship can also be seen as one of identification. This is not a case of merger between self and object or selfobject, but rather one of mutuality. Similar aims and values permit the stabilization of the self-selfobject linkage whereas differences breed disruption. Parental control is exercised to enhance such similarity, although this is a process filled with unconscious and distorted communications. The advantage of this self-psychology model over the usual superego model is primarily one that helps to explain the nature of the linkage by an examination of the idealization of the superego. The self may share the same contents as that of the other (i.e., superego or selfobject) but unless these are idealized, that is, suffused with narcissistic libido or charged with emotional value, then there is no real relationship of meaning. The relationship of meaning allows the positive affect of enthusiasm to be experienced while it also allows the negative affects of guilt and shame to issue forth. It is in the gradual shaping of the self-selfobject relationship that one sees the formation of stabilizing links between self and other whereby the external object becomes an internal selfobject not by a process of bringing the outside in but rather by one of mutual accord. Disruptions lead either to further efforts at compliance and similarity or else to further painful states of alienation and prolonged guilt or disintegration. Guilt becomes the carrier of parental blame and proceeds by the sequence of misbehavior or noncompliance→selfobject estrangements→narcissistic injury→rage and reconnection→turning against the self→guilt and compliance and the reconnecting to the selfobject via remorse.

GUILT IN AN ANALYSIS

A twice-married professional man in his late thirties entered analysis primarily because of increasing marital difficulties and a wish to avoid another divorce (see chapter 13). Over time his marriage did become more solid and satisfying, although he continued to be plagued by conscious wishes to leave his present wife. Although many of these wishes could be seen to emanate from his realistic assessment that she was (according to almost everyone who knew her) a "difficult" woman, there was an added feature of his penchant for philandering. Many analytic hours were spent over his urgent desire to be rid of a part of himself that was errant, out of control, and bad. He dreamed of a troublesome boy whom he wished to banish or lock up and flee from, but inevitably the scoundrel would reappear. Sometimes the bad boy would be connected to the analysis and would be seen in his preconscious wish to terminate his treatment. Sometimes it would emerge outside of the analysis, and thus cause him to look forward to his hours for help in quelling this disruptive factor. He, of course, would readily feel guilt over misbehavior and transgressions, imagined or real, and would try mightily to be a good and honest and well-behaved husband and patient.

Though his bad feelings in the marriage had to do with sexual behavior, in the analysis it took a different form. Part of the patient's exemplary behavior in all aspects of his life carried over into the analysis in the form of a certain diligence of patienthood. Much of this lent itself to an ease in the conduct of the analytic procedure, but one resistance was soon evident in terms of his missing hours. It seemed that all of these misses were unavoidable—they were necessitated by his job—but he usually experienced them as causing me grief and anger. He, in turn, felt abused and exploited if made to pay for the absences. He felt himself to be an innocent victim of uncongenial rules although he had readily acquiesced to payment when he started treatment. He associated these feelings to many moments in his childhood, when he felt that there was no way to satisfy his parents. With his mother, this took the form of her persistent dissatisfaction with him over issues that were inexplicable. He had many memories of incidents with her when it was never clear to him just why she became angry or disappointed with him. The situation with the father was a bit different; the patient could see that he had done something that displeased his dad, and there was never much doubt about the particulars of his transgression. Mother would get mad if he wore the wrong tie to dinner; father would be angry if the patient chose to go bowling with friends rather than helping his dad paint the garage. Both parents made him guilty, but one was easy to pass off as crazy, while the other left him feeling like a bad person. This was clearly reenacted in the transference over missing appointments: those which he innocently missed and yet met my displeasure and those which he wanted to avoid and felt punished for. In a similar manner the marital situation gave him reason to feel unjustly maligned as well as rightfully accused. His wife would periodically become irritable and enraged at him for no obvious reason, much as his erratic mother had; he, in a similarly unpredictable manner, would be overcome with lustful feelings toward a neighbor.

One can easily see the admixture of feelings coming from within that lead one to feel guilty, along with those accusations from outside that contribute to a like emotion. So too does the child have to sort out a sequence of events that lead to the guilty feeling with the necessary sense of responsibility for his transgression. Just what did he do that was wrong? This patient's childhood experience followed the form of some action on his part that led to parental blame. The action is unclear at times but not so for the blame reaction. Such blame is translated into alienation and subsequent narcissistic injury. In the transference, the patient periodically felt estranged from the analyst, and he regularly felt that his analyst was angry. In turn, he responded with anger of his own, more noticeably when he could claim to have been unfairly hurt; but ultimately all such disruptions evidenced some narcissistic rage on his part. The sequence then evidenced a turning of the rage against the self or an aggressivization of the relationship with the analyst, which in turn produced a cessation of the regressive disruption by way of guilt. His guilty reaction was marvelously effective in binding his wife and his mother, and later his analyst, closer to him. Soon a communications network became established between mother or wife and patient that made guilt a crucial component of the relationship. The child becomes controlled by guilt, which ensures a tight link with the selfobject. But this should properly be seen as requiring a participation from the parental selfobject. This patient illustrates the necessary role of the parental input, since one cannot simply restrict the guilt to an unconscious forbidden fantasy. Indeed one may, of course, concentrate on this fantasy, but equal credit is due the parental reaction that leads to guilt with little regard to the particulars of the patient's behavior or fantasy. One certainly may tie the parent's blaming the child to an unconscious fantasy of the child, but this linkage can be also seen as an attempt to explain or justify the behavior of the parent rather than as an appropriate response to a forbidden wish.

The analysis of guilt, therefore, need not follow the sequence of an act that represents a universally forbidden fantasy and in turn leads to blame. Rather, blame comes from a variety of actions that are defined as bad or wrong by way of parental reaction. This particular patient showed an easily distinguishable set of bad versus innocent acts, but further analysis revealed that the real affront to the parent was the effort to emancipate him from the restrictive selfobject, or, as in all development, to move on to a different (e.g. more independent) mode of behavior. It is in the progressive developmental process that inevitable breaks in self-selfobject relationships occur, and it is at these points that a parent can evoke guilt by way of narcissistic injury to the child, who is seen as acting in an untoward manner.

SELF CONTROL

The objects of our life control us by threat of punishment, which becomes transformed in our minds into a threat of withdrawal. The so-called superego of the pervert, which is involved in abovementioned (Glasser, 1986) pseudo-identification is essentially an archaic object that exerts control by coercion. The gradual idealization of this object permits the formation of mutuality between self and selfobject: a situation that we can call identification. In that sense, there is a sameness between self and selfobject, which become indistinguishable by virtue of their shared meanings, values, or goals. The threat to this sharing is the stuff of the guilt affect.

An example of the process of idealization should demonstrate how one can transform do's and don'ts of life into action patterns that are felt as natural rather than as alien. It is the change from superego to ego control or from abstract values to idealized ones. As the patient to be described dreamed, "The sun screen that I had applied in the morning was now absorbed into my skin, and I felt protected against the prospect of the glare of the hot sun." The hot sun was the disruptive issue in his life over which he now had control.

CLINICAL ILLUSTRATION

Let us return to the patient in chapter 5 who highlighted for us the point that the selfobjects of one's life are essentially the structural components of the self. They do not live outside of the self, but rather traverse a road from a fragile sense of control and sameness to a sense of being the very fabric of the self. We noted earlier that that patient experienced the analysis as protective and supportive and likened it to the paternal relationship,which had not always been reliable and predictable. The clinical illustration of a missed hour was connected to sexual activity as a substitute behavior aimed to fill in the self-defect. This defect is notably equivalent to a defect in the relationship with the father as well as one in the father's personality. The reliability and regularity of the analytic hours become experienced as a sense of reliability of the self and echoed the search for the reliable and dependable father.

As this patient planned to terminate his analysis, he had to exercise a self-function that was gained through the interpretive work of analysis: self-control. His entire treatment had turned on his concern for his hours, his agitation over losing them, his planning for holidays and vacations months in advance, and his desperate anxiety over the possibly cavalier disregard of their significance by me. As analysis progressed, he was more and more able to predict the moments of disruption, which were paralleled in the calendar and in his feeling of integration. His feeling of self-control was seen both in his control of his sexual behavior and in his ability to predict what might upset him. Times away from analysis were now seen in dreams and fantasies as dark periods, which reflected the sadness of the lonely child whose father had forgotten or neglected to pick him up after school. After the divorce, the father had lived alone; but my patient had never visited his father at his new living quarters, nor, he insisted, did he have any curiosity about the father's living arrangements. As an adult, he imagined that his father lived in a tiny single room in something close to abject poverty. In the transference, he began to experience more curiosity about me during periods of absence. The curiosity, however, was not filled with fantasies about my sexual life while I was away but could more properly be considered examples of discovery, of new interests, of a literal self-expansion. They arose in the transference but became activated in the patient who, for example, was able to read novels for the first time in many years. The solidity of the selfobject transference was the stepping-off point for the more solid feeling that resulted from his new-found and newly exercised self-control.

At one point in the termination phase of this analysis, the patient renewed an acquaintance with a younger man who had been a homosexual lover of his. There was no sexual activity, but he did give the young man some money to get him out of debt. He felt that I would be angry at him for this and was quite guilty and frightened at what he felt would be my displeasure. He insisted that I would be very critical of what he had done; but when this criticism failed to materialize, he readily saw the behavior as a capsulized version of the control being offered to me in the old sense (i.e., early in the analysis) of his submitting to a quasi-external object. Now he could control his own actions, and the lover of old quickly faded from consideration.

As he next turned to a curiosity about heterosexuality, he reported a dream: "There were four beds. They were occupied by his two brothers, himself and his father. They were all waiting for the mother, and the father was wide awake." His many associations led him to his anticipation of heterosexuality—that is, waiting for mother—but he felt that the necessary precursor of this was a stabilized self. Only after he had achieved sufficient self-control, something that could be said to consist of (say) an identification with the father or else a relationship with a stable, idealized selfobject, could he venture to begin a sexual relationship with a woman.

DISCUSSION

The narcissistic investment of one person in another is a lifelong deployment of all of the components that constitute a self. The achievement of self-control seems to demand a particular set of qualities in the idealized selfobject that enable feelings of mastery in oneself. These qualities of predictability, reliability, and dependability must reside in the selfobject, but inevitably they become shared by the self in a process that some call identification but that is really the mutuality of a mature self-selfobject relationship. Breaks in the establishment of this relationship lead to narcissistic injury and an aggressivization of the relationship, which is then sometimes retained and sustained by way of guilt. A good selfobject relationship aids in self-consolidation, and this lends itself to a feeling of self-control. Fragile or tenuous relationships lead to fragmenting experiences that give the appearance of an impulse disorder, which, however, is basically to be seen as a secondary phenomenon.

16

Some Notes on the Mirror

When Alice stepped through the looking glass, she fulfilled a desire to see if there was a fire burning in the fireplace—and there was. Psychoanalytic concern with looking glasses or mirrors has seen all sorts of things associated with them and has given rise to such speculation that it has been suggested that the mirror is really a metaphor for the mind, in which one can see conflicts, structures, functions, and even psychic agencies (Shengold, 1974). Yet a review of some analytic writing about mirrors (Bornstein, Silver, and Poland, 1985) yields a paucity of information and a sameness of conclusions about the role of the mirror in development, the place of the mirror in clinical issues, and the significance of the mirror in theory. This chapter is an attempt to categorize some of these ideas and to suggest some broadening of the concept.

A REPRESENTATIVE LITERATURE REVIEW

The first significant discussion of the mirror was by Lacan (see Schneiderman, 1980), who discussed the mirror stage in children and whose overall set of concepts depended largely on what he concluded about this stage. Of course, every discussion of Lacan must take into account how difficult he is to comprehend. The only exception

217

to that proviso to be offered here is that the meaning of the mirror for Lacan seems to correspond to this lack of total understanding; that is, it means frustration and discord.

Lacan states that the mirror stage occurs between six and 18 months of age, when the infant first recognizes his or her image. The child experiences this recognition as pleasurable and is fascinated with the image. An effort is then made by the child to control the image. Lacan compares this behavior with that of the chimpanzee, which likewise is delighted with the image; but the human goes beyond the chimp, progressing from being confused between the reality and the image to realizing that the image is actually his own. When the child is around six months of age, he first, according to Lacan, becomes aware of his body as a totality. Whereas previously he had erotic relations with fragments of his body, he now can take the image of the whole body as a love object. For Lacan this stage is associated with a movement away from the simple reflection of the mother's gaze to an active perception. With the imagined mastery of the mirror image, as well as with the fascination with it, the child inevitably experiences alienation. "Alienation is the lack of being by which his realization lies in another actual or imaginary space" (Bevenuto and Kennedy, 1986, p. 55). For Lacan, this feeling of apartness remains with the child forever, and he posits the formulation of the ego at the very point of alienation from and fascination with one's own image. The mirror image organizes and constitutes one's vision of the world. And this vision is one of feeling apart. The ego is then formed on the basis of an imaginary relationship of one with one's own body. Any discord between the fragmented self and the unitary image is experienced as "an aggressive disintegration of his own body" (p. 57). This discordance also determines the discordant nature of the relations with others who occupy the space around one's mirror image. Thus Lacan considered the individual to be in permanent conflict with his surroundings; and, though the ego gives one a feeling of stability, this is an illusion. For Lacan, life is an effort to capture the unified image, but one always somehow remains separate and at odds. The elusiveness evoked by the mirror stage seems reflected in the analogous experience of trying to understand Lacan's writing.

Winnicott (1974) credits Lacan with his own awareness of the mirror stage but does not think of it in the same way. Like Lacan, he felt that the precursor of the mirror is the mother's face. The baby sees himself in the mother, and the mother appears to the baby as the baby looks to the mother. It is important that the baby does see himself, or else he suffers what Winnicott terms an atrophy of the creative capacity. Since the mother's face is not yet a mirror, the baby may see a face that fails to reflect, and thus this perception takes the place of a significant exchange with the world. Winnicott illustrates this "mirror-role" of the mother with those women who "put on a face" or wish to be seen in a certain way. Essentially Winnicott feels that the mother, by way of mirroring, gives the baby's self back to the baby, and so, seeing leads to existence. The normal girl studies her face to reassure herself that the mother-image is still there, and the mother can see her and maintain rapport with her. For Winnicott, psychotherapy is a long-term giving back of what the patient brings. The patient will find his own self and be able to feel real. The actual mirror thus is significant mainly in its figurative sense, and all other family members help personality growth by reflecting back to the child.

The need for mirroring and its role in identity formation was taken up by Mahler (1968), although she does not attribute the origin of the idea to Lacan. Rather she credits Elkisch (1957) and Lichenstein (1964) for suggesting the ideas of the echo phenomenon through magnification and reduplication. For Mahler, the primary method of identity formation consists of mutual reflection during the symbiotic phase. The narcissistic, mutually libidinal mirroring reinforces the delineation of identity. Optimal "mirroring" involves the acceptance of the child's separate identity by a loving mother. Mahler (1972) notes that the need for mirroring persists throughout life.

The clinical material presented by Elkisch (1957) has to do with borderline and psychotic patients who use a mirror for defensive or therapeutic reasons and try to retrieve the ego, or self, or identity they have lost. Shengold (1974), on the other hand, presents clinical material from neurotic patients. He feels that neurotic conflicts can be enacted in the mirror, which maintains the magic that stems from the narcissistic period at the time when identity and mind are formed through contact with the mother. Feigelson (1975), in a similar vein, has discussed mirror dreams, and Bradlow and Coen (1984) have presented cases of mirror masturbation. For them, such activity is a dramatic play that defends against castration anxiety. Others (e.g., Elkisch, 1957) have commented on the wide and varied clinical significance of the mirror. It seems fair to say that no aspect of psychoanalysis has escaped the pull of the mirror.

The only original idea after Lacan, however, is Kohut's (1971) introduction of the mirror transference. Kohut appears to be the only analyst who has described a stable configuration between patient and analyst, which he called a mirror transference. In this he seems to follow the advice of Brenner (1985) to depend primarily on data derived from psychoanalysis, although he does speak of child-mother interaction. Although the clinical vignettes in most of the other literature do tell of patients reports, they do not delineate a coherent transference that could be said to correspond to a definitive period of development. For Kohut, this transference is a repetition of a developmental period wherein the child needs a responsive person for self development. Kohut terms this a selfobject function, and he describes the particulars of the transference and countertransference phenomena that correspond to this issue. He also differs from Mahler and others who liken this behavior to echoing or mutual reduplication. For Kohut, the mirroring object does not in turn feel mirrored but rather has specific and sometimes troublesome reactions to such an assigned function. Thus he delineates a set of countertransference reactions to this phase.

The foregoing is but a sketch of the pertinent literature on mirroring and is not meant to be comprehensive or all inclusive. Rather it is aimed at highlighting some points of differentiation and separating out some categories of how the word and the concept may be used. It should be clear form this overview that there are both similarities and differences in its usage.

Some Distinction of Use

The concept of the mirror in psychoanalysis appears to cover at least three ideas: the mirror as an object; the act of mirroring that occurs between persons; and the emergence of behavior in analysis that speaks for a specific kind of psychopathology along with a set of technical suggestions or rules for its interpretation.

The Mirror As Object

There can be little argument with Shengold (1974) that the mirror is a metaphor and that fairly free reign can be given to its use. That he saw it as a metaphor for the mind is no more than his particular deployment of his theory about psychic functioning. Some other patients and therapists see it as representing the mother; some see it used to master various forms of anxiety, that is, as a defense; some as the self; and some as a void. As in all of psychoanalysis, we have no readily available one-to-one correlations of symbol and meaning or referent and reference. There is, however, fairly good agreement that patients who are involved with mirror symbolism evidence narcissistic disorders or more severe pathology. But usually this becomes obscured behind vague phrases like "retrieving the ego that is lost." Thus, the literal use of or concern with the mirror in dreams, masturbation, or daily behavior is but a pointer to its figurative role. Its literal role is emphasized by Lacan to be the carrier of a special moment in development, and much of his theory of alienation derives from the elusiveness of the mirror image. Many authors conflate the real mirror with the mother's reflection and proceed to concentrate on that category. And it should come as no surprise that interpreters of Lacan (e.g., Ragland-Sullivan, 1986) insist that Lacan did not mean it to be literal at all.

Mirroring Behavior

One person is mirrored by another by way of a response that is read as pleasing or supportive, encouraging or uplifting, or some other positive affective experience. Although Western culture seems to prefer smiling for this response, there must always be a wider context for the appropriateness of what occurs. Thus, mirroring at funerals and at examinations is of a different form from that at weddings and graduations. If we chose to unpack that term, it would immediately be revealed that mirroring is not pure reflection: the gleam in the mother's eye is not a duplication of the baby's gleam, nor need the baby "gleam" in response. Rather, mirroring seems at a very early age to be a complex kind of communication that should lead to certain states or feelings. When Winnicott (1974) described the lack of responsiveness or the false face of the mother he seemed to suggest that there are some essential ingredients to proper or positive mirroring that go beyond a simple reflection. When Lacan described the child's fascination with the image, he was indicating that the sight of the image lends a certain new dimension to the child and that this, in turn, proceeds to a "discordance" between what the child's illusion is and the real world. For both of these writers, mirroring adds something, and because of this— or because of its lack—there may be difficulties in later development. To determine just what mirroring behavior in infants does, we can ally ourselves with efforts such as those of Stern (1985), who preferred to restrict his study to what he called affective attunement. He felt that mirroring encompasses three processes: the behavior of imitation, the sharing of internal states, and the verbal reinforcement or validation of such states. His attunement is confined to the second process, alignment of emotions. Since the clinical usage of the term seems to go beyond this, we need to turn to that setting to see if some more uniform meaning of the term is possible.

Mirror Transference

The many references to attunement, empathy, intersubjectivity, and a host of other words that suggest a harmony of thoughts and feelings all fall short of the concept of an enduring psychological configuration that we call a transference. Although introduced by Kohut (1971), the argument as to the existence of selfobject transferences seems to have been stilled by the words of Wallerstein (1983): "I think we analysts can (almost all of us) agree on the importance of Kohut's clinical formulations of the selfobject transference, the varieties of mirroring and idealizing transferences, and their characteristic colluding countertransferences. . . .These are indeed significant and enduring additions to and widening of our psychoanalytic vistas" (p. 25). If there is some kind of consensus about a mirror transference, it then becomes the task for analysts to see what it means in terms of recognizing it, interpreting it, and connecting it to development as a whole.

For Lacan, the mirror is "a metaphor for the alienation that first forms the ego from the outside world through identification with others" (Ragland-Sullivan, 1986). In the clinical setting this is seen when the subject's "sensible discourse is suddenly interrupted, and signifier and signified are revealed in their separateness. The subject comes into being at this point, when he experiences a lack of cohesion, a moment of discord (the mirror stage), where his own words and knowledge of himself fade away" (Bevenuto and Kennedy, p. 169–170). To be sure, this is but a hint at a transference manifestation, but it seems that the mirror stage is experienced in the analysis in this particular manner of separateness and discord. Schneiderman (1980) says that the mirror stage ends when the child can recognize that its parents are not entirely responsive to inarticulate demands. We might say, then, that the effective use of language allows the discord of analysis to replace imaginary things (like mirror images) with real feelings. Ragland-Sullivan says the stage ends when real jealousy arrives, and the child wishes to destroy anything that threatens the union with mother. One can hardly do justice to the labored versions of the mirror stage offered by the many interpreters of Lacan, but there does seem to be some general agreement on the points of alienation, discord, and the passage beyond this to a postmirror stage of different identifications. In a sense, the postmirror stage actually seems most like the mirror stage of Winnicott, Kohut, and others, but one is always on treacherous ground in translating from one theory to another (Goldberg, 1985).

The clearest exposition of a mirror transference is by Kohut (1971), who detailed an exchange between himself and a patient, Miss F., who wanted him to reflect exactly what she said without any omissions or additions. His theoretical position was that one does not pass out of or grow out of the mirror stage, but rather that the mirror transference is resolved by moving from archaic mirroring selfobjects to more mature ones. In accord with most authors, he felt that mirroring needs are lifelong ones, also that the self performs the functions of the selfobject. Thus, whatever mirroring needs may arise are satisfied by an inner or internalized set of responses that qualify as mirroring. This set of functions is experienced as pride in one's exhibitionistic fantasies, when grandiose ambitions become realized in an acceptable manner. Here there is a step toward saying what mirroring does, but the clinical example of Miss F. seems more restrictive than the wide use of the term in other contexts.

It is not possible to illustrate examples of mirror transferences from Mahler and Winnicott, because they restrict their descriptions to infant and child observation. Indeed, Pine (1985) goes so far as to say that the self-experience is organized around the capacity to do (i.e., to act), and thus will not appear in the database for psychoanalysis, based as it is on patients' associations and fantasies (p. 115). This rather startling and unusual statement seems to restrict psychoanalytic data to patient reports, i.e., what they do and say they did, and to rob it of its very essence: the transference that is necessarily an inference of the analyst derived from what the patient says and does. Only a readiness to see a mirror transference would allow one to achieve that perception.

Mahler, Pine, and Bergman (1975) do allow this action of mirroring to effect the self. They state that one can observe the demarcation of the self from the other by way of the "mutual mirroring mechanism" (p. 53). She joins those who see the self as a structure, and it is to this that we turn in order to determine better what is achieved in analysis by way of mirroring or with the working through of a mirror transference.

THE EFFECT OF MIRRORING ON THE SELF

If we accept the self as a psychic structure that has certain qualities, then we can employ it as an object of study and can observe changes in it. The thesis to be entertained here demands this minimum assumption of a self-structure and then states simply that mirroring is what mirroring does. There seems no clearcut kind of behavior that would uniformly qualify as mirroring, although one might claim that it is easily discernible in infancy. Nor does the use of the mirror in dreams or associations lend itself to a ready correlation with the state of the transference or the needs of the self. Rather, one's theoretical approach tends to dictate how one evaluates the meaning of the mirror and one's response to it. If we feel that conflict plays a central role in all psychopathology, then the mirror would appropriately be seen, as do Bradlow and Coen (1984), as a device of defense. One seeks to master or control the castration anxiety that underlies the neurosis or psychopathology by way, for example, of the drama of mirror masturbation. If, on the other hand, we feel that the use of the mirror represents a defect or problem in the self, then we see it as some reparative effort, much as Winnicott (1974) does in his description of finding oneself in the mirror. The same would hold true of our evaluation of mirroring as behavior. One's theory determines if any bit of behavior qualifies. With this in mind, it is suggested that a beginning categorization of such behavior will be a division into stability versus change.

STABILITY

In chapter 12, a case was reported that centered on a mirror transference in which the patient suffered from a feeling of a fearful loss of continuity. Analytic reconstruction of her development showed a lack of the necessary structure to ensure a feeling of being the same person over time. In the transference this was manifested by a feeling of being forgotten between hours, of losing one's hours, or of having to terminate before ready. The analyst was experienced as someone who could not hold on to a permanent image of the patient, and it was inferred that the patient's mother suffered from a personality disorder or even a cognitive defect that led to a similar perception by the patient. The achievement in the analysis was the creation of a temporal bridge, one that permitted continued existence over time by way of the analyst's memory; that is, as the patient remained alive in the mind of the analyst, she felt a stable sense of existence.

If we assume the self to be a structure that exists over time, then it possesses the quality of sameness that allows one to feel that the person who wakes in the morning is the same one who went to bed at night, the person who graduated from grade school is the same one who got married. And so on. With all the qualifications that one may introduce to the concept, one retains that essential sense of a continual something over time that results in a continued someone. That this is a psychological event and a developmental achievement is evidenced by the pathology of those unfortunate persons whose personal history seems to have no such sturdy base and by the resultant amelioration of this condition with proper treatment.

In the transference one sees the mirror as adequately describing an exchange between patient and analyst as she tries to read her presence in the analyst's eyes. In this way, she does indeed find herself, as Winnicott put it. But we must go further to underscore the fact that such a finding is necessarily sustained over time so that she is able to find again the same person who remains alive in the parental eye. The sad tale (chapter 12) of another mother who did not recognize her toddler who had wandered away and been returned by a neighbor seems to bear testimony to the potential defect in the parent who is unable to retain an unchanging image of the child. Thus, one may conclude that one aspect of proper mirroring is that of allowing self-development to unfold in a setting that provides for these elements of continuity, sameness, and stability: a sense of living over time.

CHANGE

In sharp contrast to the image of a stable self that somehow remains the same over time, we also have a picture of an ever changing structure. There is no static self except for a single slice of time that captures such an image. We see the self of the child as evolving, and we conceptualize treatment as evoking a modification in any of the forms of a fixed pattern that our theory demands. Thus, we need to introduce a seeming contradiction to the issue of sameness, and we need to see if mirroring warrants a place in this process.

Kaye (1982) discusses the interplay between mother and child and notes that there is always a disparity between the mother's image of the child and the infant's or child's true capacity or ability. The baby seems to try to catch up to where the mother is, and there is usually some mutual negotiation between the two that allows for some resting place until the next spurt of development.

Beebe and Lachmann (1987), in their presentation of a mother-infant mutual-influence-model, state that mothers and infants do not exactly match one another. "Instead, they match the direction of engagement change, both increasing or both decreasing. That is, mother and infant match where the other is going, tracking the process as it is happening, moment-by-moment" (p. 13). They also discuss the lack of matching in a process of the mother's "chasing" and the infant's "dodging." They suggest using two models for structure formation: one of interactive regulation and one of disruption and repair.

Indeed, the very notion of development demands an unfolding of change that strains the very idea of mirroring as echoing. Today in our analytic treatment it is as true as it was when Freud (1909a) said about Little Hans

> that during the analysis Hans had to be told many things that he could not say himself, that he had to be presented with thoughts which he

had so far shown no signs of possessing, and that his intention had to be turned in the direction from which his father was expecting something to come. . . . In a psychoanalysis the physician always gives his patient (sometimes to a greater and sometimes to a less extent) the conscious anticipatory ideas by the help of which he is put in a position to recognize and to grasp the unconscious material. For there are some patients who need more of such assistance and some who need less; but there are none who get through without some of it (pp. 103-104).

In a like manner, the child and the patient literally, require a certain degree of disparity. This is clearly seen as the child's wish *not* to be seen as the same person. We exhibit ourselves to others as much to be an object of difference and surprise as to be the opposite. The child who has achieved a new step of development does not want to be treated as yesterday's child, who was incapable of such mastery. The child delights in the surprised reaction of the parent to a new accomplishment. But this still seems to remain within the domain of mirroring when the reflection confirms a new image that is at odds with the old. Such disjunctions and lack of sameness are the heart of growth, which demands a continual lack of pure symmetry on the part of each participant. The mother and analyst are ahead of the child and patient. The patient and child need a moment of the delight of difference in the reflecting person.

This is not to be read as a pathological need to be different as much as an affirmation of one's capacity to move beyond the static. To see the self as a structure is to see it as both enduring and evolving over time. The developmental pattern that is pursued delivers fresh images. And the mirroring function of the mirroring selfobject enables or assists such a developmental unfolding. Thus, the mirroring behavior is a dynamic series of matching and mismatching efforts as child and parent or self and selfobject move between union and disjunction.

The corollary to this in treatment is a similar state of match and mismatch. The analyst does not reflect the patient in a fixed and unchanging manner, since the regressive and progressive movements of the patient do not allow this. So too there is a necessary need for mismatches or disjunctions that enable both patient and analyst to catch up. This supports the notion that sustained empathy with or understanding of a patient is never a sufficient therapeutic action; rather, the fundamental need for the analyst's interpretation is evidence for the work of bridging the discord. That seems to be how the self-structure repairs the organization that was faulty owing to the lack of proper mirroring.

DISCUSSION

The mirror was alienating for Lacan, a site for conflict for classical analysts, and a place for self-formation for the developmentalists such as Winnicott. In the clinical setting, these theoretical positions are noted or interpreted in an analogous fashion. If we pursue the mirroring issue to its possible place in a bona fide transference, then we extend the concept to the same sort of multidimensional form that we might apply to a father transference or other overall category. It is, then, not merely a moment of analysis, but an extended process that moves back and forth on a time dimension and so has many different faces and intensities. A mirror transference over time has all the nuances that are associated with a proper reflection, among which are varied perspectives, problems in focusing and adjustment, times of poor imaging, and times of great clarity. So too would a mirror transference over time require a multiplicity of changing reflections as the process of development unfolds and thereupon reveals a new set of images or presentations that are offered up for confirmation, admiration, or simple affirmation. The idea of transference extends the mirror concept and makes sense of the lifelong need for mirroring that has been noted by Mahler and others. In so doing, it confirms the notion that there may be more infantile mirroring and more adult versions of this particular behavior.

The mirroring function enables a self-unfolding that gives it a sense of continuity as well as of difference. The sense of difference makes for a relationship of disparity or a sense of levels that can be seen as another dimension of the self-structure. For example, I (Goldberg, 1983) have suggested that use of the concept of ''control'' and its development would enhance our notions about self-selfobject relationships. This would enable us to do away with the idea of a separate object that is acted upon or taken inside and, instead, to study the middle ground between the self and the selfobject. Hints of this are also seen in Lacan's emphasis on the child's wish to control the mirror image. The ability to move from being controlled by another to a position of being in control is a stepwise advance in the structuralization of the self. It goes on to issues of self-initiative that we feel belong to the picture of a fully developed self. And these sorts of interactions likewise seem to be part and parcel of a mirroring relationship. This richest psychoanalytic category for the mirror seems to lie in the full elaboration of the mirror transference.

CONCLUSION

The place of the mirror in psychoanalysis may be seen in its significance in development, its appearance in the productions of the patient in psychoanalysis, and in its broad category of a mirror transference, which is an inferred category of the analyst. One's own theoretical bias tends to focus more on one than on the other, and various authors have stressed one over the other. On the whole, it is agreed that it plays a significant role in development and that this role continues to a lesser degree throughout life. Its appearance in the ordinary data of analysis seems more prominent in patients with narcissistic disturbances, but it can be studied as a significant issue in neurotic conflicts. The fullest treatment of the mirror lies in the elaboration of the mirror transference. In this context we can study some elements of how the self is structured. One part of mirroring seems to offer the self a feeling of stability or continuity over time. Another seems to suggest a capacity for difference and a beginning form of self-initiative and self-control. It is to be hoped that further unpacking of the term will lead to more detailed aspects of self-development.

17

The Place of Apology in Psychoanalysis and Psychotherapy

What must count as a minor classic in the psychoanalytic literature is the "Say You're Sorry" article of Kubie and Israel (1955). It is there that the power of apology is seen in what may be considered a pure form. In that clinical presentation, a child of five who was hospitalized for an acute syndrome of mutism, anorexia, and other signs of severe regression is over heard to be making a sound that a nurse interprets as "Say You're Sorry." In meeting room filled with many people, the examiner of the child begins a refrain with the apology, "I am sorry, I am very, very sorry," and this is taken up by a series of participants in the conference room. The child brightens, begins to talk, and a week later is recovered.

This case is presented as an illustration of the magic of unlocking unconscious processes with precision; the instantaneous cure is likened to that gained from hypnosis. The article fills out the history of the child's illness with some speculations about her recovery, but one should read on to a follow-up presentation of this very same girl, who is hospitalized again some six years later and followed as an outpatient for several years thereafter (Ravitch and Dunsten, 1965). Her initial improvement was maintained for a while, but over time she deteriorated and needed to be re-admitted, this time with symptoms of multiple school phobias and hypochondriacal complaints. Her second hospital course focused on the use of the word "enema," and the reporters of the second article present the case as one of a core conflict over the forcible administration of enemas from age one-and-a-half to four-and-a-half. Her treatment was suspended at puberty (at age 12) with the note that she was not communicative in the sessions. Not much more can be said about the case, but it is striking and memorable more in terms of the technique employed by Kubie than it is revelatory of this particular child's malady and recovery. It seems to make something magical of an apology.

Of course, apologizing per se in not considered a normal part of psychotherapeutic or psychoanalytic technique. The foregoing case speaks of an apology offered by a nonoffender. In order to move into the realm of the use of apology in the normal conduct of treatment, we must define the term better and survey the literature to see if it is at all applicable to such an inquiry.

DEFINITION OF AND SOME LITERATURE ABOUT APOLOGIZING

Apologizing has two components: acknowledging a mistake or error and expressing regret for it. If we momentarily confine our inquiry to the acts of analysts or therapists rather than to those of patients, we will probably note that only the first half of the definition is met. That is, some therapists and analysts do, on occasion, admit that they have made an error. They seem apt to make an explicit acknowledgment of a mistake but to allow the second half, involving remorse, to remain implicit. By merely recognizing the validity of a patient's grievance, they sometimes embrace the further legitimacy of the entire scope of an apology. As in every case of human communication, a set of unspoken rules can be seen to govern what ia allowable and what is taken for granted; and so for one person a simple acknowledgment may equal a very eloquent apology.

The inclusion of both psychotherapy and psychoanalysis in this review is necessary because some of the writers in this area claim that the distinction between the two is not based on technique (Goldberg, 1981), whereas others (Gill, 1984) seem to say that something akin to a therapist's acknowledgment or apology allows the differentiation between therapy and analysis to be made. For the moment, we shall lump together the therapist and analyst and put aside whether one or the other is more relevant to the subject.

At one end of the spectrum of therapeutic misdeeds is the position of Langs (1982), who seems to feel that much treatment is in error because it avoids the therapist's unconscious needs and wishes. He says:

> In the psychotherapeutic conspiracy between patients and therapists, it is the therapist who is the main perpetrator of harm and distortion. The patient is the willing victim. The conspiracy is largely unconscious, outside of the awareness of both participants. Adorned with sincere wishes by therapists to help their patients, the cure—if it does occur—is by collusion and victimization or traumatic stimulation for growth [p. 55].

Newman (1985) examines in detail those analytic failures that do not allow the treatment to progress. He feels that the countertransference reactions of the analyst can be used to facilitate treatment and overcome stalemates if these analytic "failures" are employed in the service of making "a new object" available to the patient. He says that the analyst, having entered the patient's inner world of objects and having *accepted responsibility* for repeating an aspect of the failed primary relationship, can function as a potential selfobject. Newman reminds us that we are asked to see our failures from our patients' vantage point and to endure considerable distortions arising from these internal encounters. He notes that much depends on how well we are able to take responsibility and acknowledge that our own injured self-esteem can influence our negative attitude toward the patient. Essentially Newman seems to isolate a special group of patients who require a sharing of blame for their pathology. He calls for a reenactment in the transference to allow it to deepen and suggests that we, as the parents, inevitably visit our problem upon the patient.

Such a heavy burden to be borne by therapists is seemingly relieved by Langs (1982) when he urges a stance that allows one to be truthful and honest and so to escape this conspiracy. Part of that effort does seem to lie in the use of apology. Often this takes place following grievous errors, such as overcharging (p. 266), but there seems no inherent limitation on the use of "admitting one's mistakes." No doubt most therapists do separate real mistakes from unacknowledged ones. If we discharge a patient 15 minutes early or if we make a mistake on a bill, we probably will apologize. The dividing line gets blurred, for example, if we forget the name of an important member of the patient's family or allow our own emotions to be inappropriately expressed. To consider "mistakes" merely as examples of countertransference still leaves us with the problem of dealing with it in treatment. Racker

(1968) holds that the telling of one's countertransference is an entirely undecided issue, but we know that one can apologize without explaining. Indeed, one of the foremost proponents of alerting the analyst to his or her contribution to the transference (Hoffman, 1983) insists that the analyst need not "admit" actual countertransference experiences. Rather, he or she should allow the patient to realize the "plausibility" of certain reactions.

Gill (1982a) has developed a strong thesis for considering the here and now transference to be most significant and so to raise the claim that the patient's view of the analyst always has a core of reasonableness to it. The differentiation of treatment into psychoanalysis versus psychotherapy is said by Gill to depend on how rigorously one analyzes the witting and unwitting suggestions offered by the analyst. He claims that the situation is eased for the analyst who is disabused of the idea that an uncontaminated transference can develop. He skirts the issue of self-disclosure, but says that an atmosphere must exist that allows the patient's point of view to be acknowledged. He (1984) says that this is in contrast to the viewpoint that argues that, in effect, to acknowledge the rationality of the patient is to confirm his belief that his experience is fully due to the behavior of the analyst. We are also told:

> If the analyst has given the patient cause to be angry, for example, and the patient is angry, at least some aspect of the anger is neither a transference or cooperation . . . . We do conceptualize inappropriate behavior on the analyst's part as countertransference, but what is our name for the analysand's realistic response to countertransference [p. 4].

This seems to recreate the burden of determining what is expectable and what is regrettable. We are cautioned not to say *why* we feel the way we do. We should accept the patient's perception of something as true to some degree, and sometimes we are even chastised for doing or saying the wrong thing or even for remaining silent (Gill, 1982, Vol. II, p. 4).

Kohut (1984) has made the problem into a solution by considering the tenet that meaningful interpretations occur around points of empathic breaks or misunderstandings by the analyst. These inevitable disruptions are, of course, failures on the analyst's part and are to be treated as the sine qua non of effective analytic intervention. He says:

> In a properly conducted analysis, the analyst takes note of the analysand's retreat, searches for any mistake he might have made, nondefensively acknowledges them after he has recognized them (often with the help of the analysand) and this gives the analysand a noncensorious interpretation of the dynamics of his retreat [p. 67].

Now, this is clearly an objective appraisal of the normal analytic process, but one cannot help but see that it is a mistake that ushers in a retreat and an acknowledgment that halts it. The mistakes are those of the analyst and would (probably) range from the inadvertent and inevitable ones of everyday life to the gross mistreatments that a more sensitive or seasoned analyst could avoid. From the analyst's transference or countertransference or innocence, a failure seems still to rank as such and is hardly more forgivable if it carries an explanation with it, unless the explanation likewise comes with a plea for forgiveness.

If we choose these several contributors as points in the field of scrutiny, we see that they espouse a position that relieves the patient of the burden of error and shifts it to the analyst. This is much like the move that places the seed of psychopathology first in the child's drives and fantasies and later in the parents' mistreatment of the child. We reenact our theories or psychopathology by moving from patient blame to therapist blame, and we redress the error by saying we are sorry for our witting or unwitting folly.

INTERPERSONAL ASPECTS OF APOLOGIZING

In considering a communicative exchange between two persons, one can utilize a variety of theoretical constructs to map the field in order to realize some data. These range from fields as diverse as information theory to speech act theory. The theories are devised to explain how one person manages to influence another, to inform another, to move another. In an ordinary conversation, a multitude of phenomena present themselves for consideration, but in a psychoanalytic exchange we single out an appropriate pattern in terms of some stable transference configuration. That configuration may be familial or otherwise, object-libidinal or narcissistic. Interventions of any sort tend to disrupt the transference. They especially do so if they are designed to alter the explicit and implicit roles that are assumed. Thus, when two people are dancing and one complains that his or her toes are being stepped on, the dance becomes something different from what it was before. So too if a patient is pouring out a tale of woe and the therapist interprets this as a childhood reenactment, there is a momentary bracketing of the content, as it is subject to a different level of scrutiny. Apologizing does the same: it resets the nature of the ongoing relationship and forces it to become a different sort of relationship. It is a form of action that is tantamount to doing, rather than interpreting in an analysis or treatment, and thus forces us to consider a necessary alteration in the transference. Apologizing is not always what it seems to be, since it can be employed for a variety of motives. In the most general sense, it does seem to lend an advantage to the apologizer, who is able to redirect the communication to his or her own ends. Thus, there is nothing inherently worthwhile or ameliorative about apologizing, anymore than there is about not apologizing.

CLINICAL ILLUSTRATION

This patient, a middle-aged man who had had a long and successful analysis, was once again in treatment for a recurrence of symptomatology. During one hour, he told of a relationship with a woman who wanted him to behave in a certain way but whom he could not accommodate: the situation was something like agreeing with her about the worth of a movie. I said that perhaps he wanted to be free of the woman, but the patient protested that I was wrong, that it was not that. Soon after, he began talking of Christmas and wishing to have a tree. He and his childhood family had celebrated Christmas in Germany even though they were Jewish. He could not enjoy such a celebration here in America. I asked "Why not?" since they were not particularly religious Jews. He became quite angry and told me that I simply did not understand what it had been like for him as a child. I responded with what I felt was a neutral comment about how this sort of effort at understanding, which I had seemingly failed to achieve, was what makes for the effectiveness of the treatment process, that is, that I was trying to comprehend. He told me that it was just stupid of me to suggest that he have a tree, and it probably related to my own shaky ground as a Jew who probably did now have a tree, but that was nothing like the Jews of Germany who had trees. I responded in a louder voice that that may well be true, but it did not make me stupid. He became contrite and said that he felt horrible that he had made me angry, and that it was very much like the relationship with his wife and his brother, who would make him angry and then attack him in turn. He felt loathsome and awful.

I asked more about people being mad at him. I felt bad and wanted to apologize for raising my voice. He had been right about my reacting to being called stupid, but I allowed him to continue. He told me that, on the rare occasion that his father had yelled at him, he had, indeed, apologized. I asked how he felt about this, and he said that it was wrong of the father. He had a right to blow off steam. He did not do it that often and apologizing diminished him in his eyes. I suggested that we talk more about the apologizing and whether he would want it of me. He said it was different, that my apologizing would help with his own sense of reality, that he was not such an awful person who managed to enrage others. I felt like apologizing but did not. Instead I began to wonder about the nature of our interaction.

To begin with, there had clearly been a misunderstanding, one which by itself was of minor significance, but another one rapidly followed it. The patient had also sensed something in me that lent plausibility to his perception of the scene—that I did not know what Christmas meant to him because of my own defensiveness or perhaps even naivete about the event. Once he felt the second, more severe or intense misunderstanding, he was even more distraught and by calling me stupid managed to get me to respond angrily; that is what he experienced, and it was certainly plausible that I was defensive and angry. The reactions thereafter were typical of the old masochistic posture that had been part of his first analysis but had long been away and, we had hoped, gone forever.

That stance did dissipate in the next few hours as we talked more about his feeling about people who are difficult or self-absorbed or crazy and whom he felt he had to placate since he could not cut himself off completely from those few souls who were so much a part of his life history. He still needs to work out an accommodation between submission and independence. Much of his first analysis was connected to this point of reluctantly accepting the reality of his life without despair or depression, the judgmental condemnation that Freud (1923a) espoused. In this illustration, we see several points that apology raises: a specific transference reference to the father, a countertransference reaction of the therapist, and interpersonal transaction in the treatment. To unpack this clinical vignette and examine the issue of apologizing, we can follow it sequentially:

1. The first illustration, about the woman who wanted the patient to agree with her, could be a transference allusion to the patient's wanting to differentiate from the therapist (as was suggested) or could be an example of the therapist's failure to understand per se. Either way, it sets the stage for "the effort to understand" that should follow.

2. The Christmas tree material was begun by the patient with a tone of regret and sadness that evoked a sense of loneliness. That reinforced the therapist's idea that the patient was telling himself that he could never separate from the people who were so burdensome to him. The therapist probably wanted to challenge this idea with his question, but it only widened the gap of misunderstanding. He then tried comment about what they were doing. The strength of the patient's response is significant because he felt misunderstood on both levels—in the transference as well as in terms of the particular content of his communication.

3. The therapist's anger and the patient's retreat from him may be less significant than it might appear. It did evoke an old characterological response in the patient, but that was short lived. More important, it was the impetus for the therapist's wish to apologize. The reference to similar childhood situations did allow him to delay his wish. The final wish for an apology leads back to the original theme of two people seeing the world differently (e.g., the movie), but neither having to submit to the other in order for the relationship to be sustained.

The following hours showed a shift in the content of discussion. The patient began to see a pattern of interaction in a number of his relationships. The sequence was (1) an intense involvement with someone who expected him to behave in a particular way (2) his refusal or reluctance to conform, and (3) a withdrawal by that person from him. The time of such withdrawal or alienation was experienced as very painful by the patient, who would manage to effect a rapprochement by some sort of apology of his own. With the review and overview of such occurrences, the patient connected it all to a familiar childhood experience of being "frozen out." This phrase described the mother's way of punishing the patient for anything and everything. Mother would stop speaking to the child for one or more hours in order to let him know how angry or disappointed she was. The patient, feeling a desperate pain, would do anything to win back the mother in the form of her attention and communication. This always necessitated some form of apology and forgiveness. As an adult, he could readily see that the wrong person had done the apologizing. Thus a deeper transference issue of apologizing was elucidated.

Once the foregoing material was examined and discussed, the patient felt relieved and free and determined to work out relationships that allowed him to feel connected without feeling controlled. The alternative solution of leaving behind the people who interacted with him in this manner seemed untenable to him, just as his first analysis had ended with his putting up with his wife rather than contemplating a divorce. But first he felt that he had to get someone to apologize to him. He did this in the next few days in a very acceptable manner, but immediately after the wrongdoer (who was easy to find) told him how sorry he was, he felt depressed and frightened. He knew that he had only succeeded in making that person feel guilty, and he would soon avenge himself for that discomfort. And so he completed the circle of injury, apology, and a repeated cycle of injustice.

Apologizing made the patient feel abused and enraged, much as he had felt while enduring his mother's perverse form of punishment. Being apologized to made him feel guilty and frightened because he recognized the rage behind such social proprieties. In parallel fashion, the analyst or therapist at times wishes the patient would apologize for his mistreatment of him and, instead, apologizes and then must endure his own feeling of mistreatment.

DISCUSSION

Our assessment of the analytic management of a patient's productions and associations ranges from the belief that the analyst can process pure data in the manner of a blank screen to the realization that the therapist's own unconscious may occasionally intrude upon, and even victimize, the patient. The first position allows interpretation of the patient's drives and fantasies as they are developed and expressed in the transference. The second encourages a view of a traumatized person forced to live in a crazy world and forever seeking redress. Certainly psychoanalysis has always embraced the first and has segregated the second into the lesser class of psychotherapy, and, more particularly, into therapy of nurturance and support. Apologizing seems to be nonanalytic.

The problem seems easily approachable by eliminating the extremes. Is there not a host of egregious mishaps in therapy for which an apology is due? And do these not correspond to the position of the victimized patient that can be readily dismissed? If we let a patient out very early, or overcharge on a bill, or completely mix up one patient's life with that of another, obviously we are wrong and should apologize. Or should we? There certainly are patients for whom this amenity would be uncalled for or unnecessary. If the patient does not care, should we? Is there any generalizable rule to follow that clarifies what is to be considered as an apologizable error of the analyst or is each error to be evaluated against the backdrop of the patient?

On the other hand, there are the seemingly trivial errors of everyday life that for some people are momentous. Forgetting the name of a favorite uncle, ending the hour some 30 seconds early, not understanding what something meant to a patient and feeling certain that no one else would possibly do better. These are all events that could beg for apologizing from a certain set of patients but would feel forced and unreal from the side of the therapist.

Now, one conclusion that can be offered for the dilemma is to let the patient determine the rule or to invoke certain nosological or process-related criteria. The categorization could be that sicker patients get apologies, whereas healthier ones do without. Or the differentiation could be that an apology is called for if it allows the treatment to proceed and is to be suspended if it does not serve the resistance.

Unfortunately, as our clinical case tried to show, one cannot tell what an apology will do or what it means until long after the fact.

Another escape from the problem would be to conjure something like the "average expectable analyst or therapist." This would create a community standard of propriety, whose borders would determine what is and what is not a mistake. Thus, we apologize for deviations from an expectable therapeutic performance and turn it back to the patient if the feeling of mistreatment prevails in spite of our conviction that we did what everyone might do, Indeed we often operate this way in the sense that our patients learn just what to expect from treatment from just about anyone.

The extremes of patient as victim to parent as provocateur are sometimes handled simply as a problem of an appropriate match. For instance, rather than blame the child or the parent, we say that this child could not be appropriately raised by these parents. But they need not be seen as evil or malevolent. They simply could not fit the needs of this particular child. This posture allows us entry into a possible solution to the problem of apologizing.

THE TWO WORLDS OF TREATMENT

The patient and the analyst live in different worlds. Patients arrive with a life history and a perception of life that the analyst tries to comprehend by some sort of gathering of data that perhaps can be subsumed under the umbrella of "prolonged empathic immersion." In this manner, he may attain a state of intersubjective agreement or an ability to see the patient's world as the patient does. If he is successful, then the analyst can be said to understand the patient, and, in this sense, every patient can claim a right to be so understood. If one is capable of maintaining a level of intersubjective agreement by resolving whatever discord may emerge, then the patient and the analyst are truly of one mind. Moreover, if the analyst assumes the major burden of achieving and maintaining this state, it follows that the failures of intersubjectivity also become the responsibility of the analyst. It takes no great leap of logic to see that an apology might well be forthcoming from such a failure. This is not to say that one must employ apology to repair discordance, but it does make a case for the logic of this response. To the degree that one feels that understanding is essential for any given patient, then that logic becomes more forceful and determinant of one's response.

The reverse side of the two worlds of analyst and patient holds the analyst to be the carrier of a more informed reality. Although every analyst aims for the development of a workable transference, this is always also considered, by definition, to be a distortion regardless of the "plausibility" of its content. Such transferences are studied and interpreted in order ultimately to correct them or to make the patient understand the analyst's view of the world. With all the tact and sensitivity that may be called for as a prerequisite to this effort, the work of analysis is to dissolve the transference and have the patient disabused of his view of the world. Thus, the differences in perception of patient and analyst never call for apology from the analyst. Rather, apology is an indicator that the analyst is not being faithful to his own world view, much like the analyst who overcharges the patient and so sees a discrepancy between what he sees of himself and what he would like to see. These "errors" of analytic practice do, of course, lead to an occasional act of apology, but they are not a part of the normal conduct of treatment. To admit them as such is equal to making countertransference the essence of treatment. Certainly errors and countertransference are significant guides to doing treatment, but most practitioners are not ready to make them the whole of treatment.Thus, in this view, the logic carries us to the conclusion that there is no routine place for apology in analysis.

Between the viewpoint that the major task of analysis is understanding the patient and the stance that it is that the patient renounce his fantasies and accept reality, there should be a possible compromise or resolution. Such a resolution is made possible only if one sees these polar positions as basically untenable.

The first position, seeing the patient's world as it exists for the patient, demands that we put aside our own preconceptions and convictions for the time being. To understand someone means to forego prejudgment and put ourselves in the other's shoes. Although this is an admirable goal, it is also an impossible one. We cannot effectively merge with another person in a total way. Rather, we move from misunderstanding to understanding by way of a negotiating process. No matter how much we may be able to see what it was like to be that child and that patient, we are also simultaneously aware that we are not that other person. We share the patient's experience through empathy, but we do not become that patient. In the clinical example, it was necessary that I understand what having a Christmas tree meant to that patient, but my understanding could never have reached the point where having a tree meant the same to me as to the patient. My suspension of my own beliefs and judgments allows access to the patient's inner world, but there always is a gap between us. No matter how intensely I may persevere in my effort to understand, I know that I can leave the session and return to my own norms and standards and reality. That gap, which is never erased by our merger efforts, by our empathic posture, is the source of our wish to apologize. It is the failure of understanding that reflects our mistakes, and it is our own grandiose fantasy that we can completely understand someone else that evokes an apology for our failure to fully do so.

The other position that eschews apology assumes implicitly that the patient will work through the distortions of the transference to a reality that the analyst possesses. This is not something that occurs *after* we understand the patient, since understanding is always operant and transference interpretations are seen as evidence that we understand the patient. There is no place for apology in this transaction, because there are no natural or expectable errors, only accidents of technique. The analyst who is expected to apologize sees this as transference and treats it as such. The analyst who appropriately apologizes can only do so if he has made a move that deviates from community standards. Usually he would not apologize, because for the most part the world that he sees is more attuned to reality. Such a posture is equally in error. We simply do not know the right ways to consider things; our norms are likewise negotiated issues. It takes work on my part to see what that Christmas tree means to the patient, just as every bit of knowing a patient demands some alteration in our judgments and convictions. Analytic work does not deal with fixed and unalterable facts and truths as much as it does with agreed upon states of affairs. To refuse to admit a mistake and apologize is to refuse to acknowledge that we can be more than we are. Just as our grandiosity forces us to apologize, our defects do not allow us to do so. In an abbreviated and perhaps unsatisfactory solution of the problem, we may say that we apologize when we try to be more than we can be, and we fail to apologize when we insist on being less.

DISCUSSION

Psychoanalysis considers psychopathology to derive from developmental problems. They range in concept from a Kleinian viewpoint, which sees the child's intense drives to be the primary source of difficulty, to one espoused by Kohut and Winnicott, who tend to attribute the problems to parental failures. Freud, posed a complemental series for the combination of mismatches that lead to neuroses. Over the years psychoanalysts have tended to align themselves with one or another of these camps. Allegiance to a theory of psychopathology forces a corresponding posture of treatment. Thus, if one feels that the drives need to be tamed, interventions are directed to aiding the ego to control the id and superego with insight that effects neutralization. If, on other hand, one lays childhood traumatic experiences at the core of adult disorders, treatment tends to be directed at experiences that correct or undo or, at a minimum, allow normal development to proceed.

If an analyst believes that the patient's wishes and fantasies wreak havoc with his psyche, then the role of interpretation is to transfer these unconscious products to conscious control. In a sense this is a limited ambition, because such intervention is in itself limited to repressed psychic contents. Of course, most analyses are felt to consist of much more in the way of gains achieved in the analytic relationship, but as a model of treatment this form of analysis is confined to a small set of neurotic disorders.

If an analyst believes that the patient suffers because of childhood traumas that have not allowed normal development to proceed, then the interpretations that are made are felt to ameliorate the trauma. This can readily be seen to be a much more ambitious approach, since we are constrained only by our capacity to understand that patient and so to prepare the groundwork that the thwarted development can now utilize and so prosper. There need, therefore, be no inherent limitation to helping severely disturbed patients save that of our own personal failings. Such an approach tends to promote rescue fantasies and to foster a therapeutic megalomania.

Its counterpart is the humble and narrow stance of one who can deal only with certain circumscribed disorders that lend themselves to cure by insight. This approach tends to promote a profound therapeutic pessimism as well as an elitist view of treatment. These therapists hardly ever apologize, because they expect so little of themselves; the ambitious ones tend readily to apologize, because they expect so much of themselves.

The clinical example that was described aimed to show that apologies can be of several sorts. For one, they can have a special transference meaning that must be elucidated, as in this patient's experience of his father's inappropriate apology. Second, the therapist's wish to apologize probably reflects his own need to be better or smarter or more empathic than he is able to be. Third, the act of apologizing always resets the relationship and is experienced by the patient as a reparative effort that may or may not be appropriate. It does seem to forestall a more comprehensive meaning of the transference, as noted in the patient's recall of the mother's mistreatment of him. There is no doubt, however, that this does have a place at certain times in certain treatments. But this is not to say that one cannot form a general rule about the place of apology in treatment. Such a rule will not tell us when to apologize but rather will alert us to what apologizing may mean. To the degree that our own narcissistic therapeutic zeal determines our attitude to a patient, we will embrace our mistakes. Thus, every impetus to admit our errors is a potential indulgence of our grandiosity. But lest we, on the contrary, never expect to help anyone very much or to expand our capacity to help more people, then we can never readily say that we are sorry.

18

Post-Termination

This chapter is about what happens after termination, but its intent is not to carve out and delineate a period of time during a following psychoanalysis wherein a certain set of characteristics can be observed and responded to accordingly. Although we may wish for such conveniently sequential categories in our work, we are too often frustrated in this regard. The therapeutic or working alliance, which should begin a treatment, at times becomes the whole of the work. The transference neurosis, which should be the hallmark of successful analytic efforts, on occasion is seen at the start of an analysis. And the termination period, which should usher in the culmination of treatment, either may never be seen or may dominate the entire course of treatment. Thus post-termination should be viewed more as a focus of scrutiny and inquiry than as a time characterized by certain salient features. However, it should not, as happened so often, be ignored in our literature, our case studies, or our curriculum. It may be that we overlook issues that could be helpful in the overall evolution of the psychoanalytic enterprise. Things do happen to us and to our patients after an analysis is ended, and most of these go unnoticed and unrecorded. Except for chance meetings, follow-up studies, reanalyses, or returns for specific indications, we are usually ignorant of what happens to patients after they leave and equally uninformed about what happens to their analysts.

We will define *post-termination* as a period that begins immediately after analyst and patient no longer meet. It has no endpoint. One cannot correlate the length of the post-termination period with either suc-cess or failure—some analytic failures are quite profound and long lasting in terms of post-termination phenomena, just as some analytic successes are. Interrupted treatments should be included in the general area of concern. We do assume that a well-conducted and well-terminated analysis should yield a different set of reactions than one that is considered more or less a failure, but as long as we concern ourselves with a set of issues rather than a normative program, there is no need to separate failures from successes. To be sure, we will need some criteria to ascertain that the analytic process was well enough along to qualify for a place in our concern. Here is a clinical illustra-tion.

I was called by an out-of-town psychiatrist about a former patient who needed some information from me about a legal problem. My records were adequate to answer the request, but I felt troubled per-sonally because I could not remember the patient, whom I had seen briefly in psychotherapy; in particular, I could not conjure up an im-age of her. I asked the inquiring psychiatrist to describe her to me, but his description had no effect on my memory lapse. Yet there was no indication from him or from my records that there had been anything untoward about the treatment. She had told the other doc-tor that she had benefited from our time together, and I saw no sign in myself of conflict regarding her. I puzzled over why I could manage no recall of her and decided that she meant either very little or very much to me. I never did resolve my quandary, but it seems to me now that we simply did not have that much of an involvement. Thus, the case qualifies as one that was dismissed easily from memory because of its minimal significance (or its opposite).

In sharp contrast, another woman ended a long analysis, again on a positive note, but I was quite unable to forget her. I thought a great deal about her and had a seemingly undiminished curiosity about what had become of her. I found myself hoping for some good turn of for-tune for her and imagined a life course that would fulfill the best of her dreams and fantasies. I had no great wish to see her again; rather I had had a strong desire to know what her life was like. I had a pro-gram for her future development that I very much wanted to see fulfill-ed.

It is far too easy to explain these contrasts by saying that some pa-tients mean more to us than others or by claiming that unresolved transference and countertransference issues are responsible. Without denying these points, it remains an open question just what "meaning more or meaning less" really says. It is also much too general to claim the problem is answered under the rubric of transference or counter transference. Can we possibly delineate better just why some patients haunt us after treatment while others hardly matter? Can these same points help to explain the *variety of postanalytic contacts* that seem so prevalent and problematic in our profession? And, above all, is there some proper analytic perspective on post-termination that can be separated from normative procedures and the realistic moral issues that we will note?

REVIEW OF LITERATURE

There is a small corpus of writings on issues after analysis, but most of it has to do with patient, rather than analyst, reactions. Statements about the analysis continuing after leaving the analyst (Alexander, 1940) are sometimes illustrated with some patient anecdotes (Hart, 1972). There is some feeling that postanalytic contacts with patients delay the achievement of the requisite equilibrium (Buxbaum, 1950). For the most part, it is felt that the work of mourning needs to be carried out by the patient after the analysis (Klein, 1950) and that this permits further progress in analytic insight. The resolution of the transference is thought to occur after termination (Bibring, 1954). Some analysts suggest seeing the patient about a year after termination (MacAlpine, 1950), and some propose avoiding any contact with the patient until a long enough period of time has elapsed to allow the mourning reaction to unfold without disruption (Weigert, 1955). There is no doubt that after termination memories and fantasies emerge that were never noted during treatment, and case reports of this are notable (Hendrick, 1958). In sharp contrast to those who advise complete abstinence, some analysts encourage periodic visits by the patient. There is some agreement that postanalytic information is sparse. Follow-up studies on terminated analyses seem to indicate that the transference can be reactivated in a few interviews long after the analysis is over (Robbins and Schlessinger, 1983). The outstanding case of postanalytic material or follow-up is that of the Wolf Man (Freud, 1918), but it would be injudicious to generalize about that person, since the payment of a stipend to him, as well as his treatment by other therapists, seems to have contaminated the case for purposes of our inquiry.

In a very courageous paper about the end of an analysis, Johnson (1951) makes a case for the female therapist ultimately to accept the male patient as "on the same level as that of her husband." Johnson claims that the therapist resolves the oedipal transference by her own renunciation "much as we expect the patient to renounce his own oedipal fantasies." She states: "At a point in the analysis it is an evasion, a condescension, an arbitrary prohibition for the analyst to say: 'I love my husband . . . I am not in love with you.' '' Thus she accepts her reciprocal feelings toward the patient. She later claims that the real reason for the analysis ending as it does is that nature of what is shared in an analysis makes it so unique that the two persons could never have continued their relationship.

Fleming (1951) discusses that paper by pointing to a subtle seduction of the patient by the analyst, likening her to a covertly seductive parent. Fleming appears to differentiate the sexual component of the transference from the caring component. She claims that analysis ends on a note not of frustration, but of resolution, and that what is renounced is the unrepeatable relationship rather than the memory of a great love and the hope of its fulfillment. Fleming seems to conclude that the analyst's feeling of loss and her own sense of disappointment with an unfulfilled fantasy are all signs of failure of the analysis.

There is little doubt that one reaction to Johnson's paper is that it is the analyst's way of working out her own post-termination problems with a particular patient. She tries to generalize these points in order to see a form of acting-in all analyses that involve heterosexual issues, but there seems no reason to limit it to this form. Fleming responds by noting either an irrational countertransference or else, interestingly enough, no transference at all. I take this last as a pointer to the real relationship's overriding transference issues. Essentially the paper and the discussion open up the problem of the emotional investment of the analyst in the patient and the subsequent efforts to resolve or rationalize it. It points to a fact of life in analyses that is not well handled in the literature: the analyst in relation to the post-termination time of treatment.

A recent contribution covering 71 cases (Hartlaub, Martin, and Rhine, 1986) surveyed recontact with analysts and determined that they satisfied needs for (1) continuing deidealization of the analyst, (2) the reactivation of the self-analytic function, and (3) the restructuring of self- and object representations by reporting accomplishments to the analyst. This paper is in contrast to that of Johnson, who shares with us her own struggle with ending. This last contribution once again focuses on the patient's needs and ignores those of the analyst.

SOME THEORETICAL POSITIONS

It is generally taught that termination is a species of mourning, this being the task the patient takes on as the analysis ends, requiring time for full engagement and working through. The patient is to gradually decathect the representation of the analyst and, over time, to resolve the ambivalent feelings that are evoked in any form of mourning, from the most benign loss involving a favored pet to the most malignant loss involving an unresolved psychological conflict. The desired endpoint in the mourning process is a relative decathexis, wherein the lost object can be viewed neutrally and unambivalently or can be dispensed with in terms of infantile needs and fantasies. It goes without saying that the analyst would proceed through a reciprocal sort of personal mourning process. To be sure, no mourning is total, and thus no relationship is completely resolved or laid to rest. But the resumption of a relationship after successful mourning would be characterized by a diminution of the strong unconscious components that may have previously been dominant. That is why certain contact with patients outside the treatment setting are sanctioned; that is, on the basis of the relationship's being more like a new or neutral one. This position of mourning the termination of analysis, however, presumes an absence of any sort of involvement with patients after the end. Thus questions of such involvement that are addressed later are all to be considered in the light of some lack of resolution of the mourning work. All contacts with patients, as well as fantasies about patients, are, with this model, examples of unresolved transference or countertransference. The exceptions are those few that satisfy the maxim of the patient's being equivalent to any other person in the analyst's environment and thus being free of any residue of the analysis. The same would hold for the patient: the analyst is now like any other friend or business associate or rival.

An alternative theory offered by psychoanalytic self psychology claims that the selfobject transferences activated by psychoanalysis are resolved not in the sense of independence or freedom but in the sense of maturation. One need not be free of the relationships of old, but rather these relationships should have changed from archaic to mature. Thus, the patient's intense need for mirroring from the analyst becomes internal pride and greater deployment of alternate selfobjects. This change would allow a continued relationship with the former analyst, who is now but one of a series of mature relationships. It may be that there is merely a change in emphasis in this theoretical outlook, since mature selfobjects and objects after ambivalence is resolved may not be immediately distinguishable save theoretically. However, the self psychologist leans in the direction of continuing relationships, as there is no inherent value of independence, whereas the other theoretical approach would appear to stress the growing move away from the analyst in any form whatsoever. Both theories make room for the deleterious effects of unresolved transferences as noted in the inability to complete a reasonable termination. Both would question the variety of devices—some of which we delineate below—used to make post-termination less than ideal.

MODES OF CONDUCT IN POST-TERMINATION

The following areas of inquiry are not easily categorized either as symptomatic acts or as rational and acceptable behaviors. Clearly they may be both. Nor can one see them as wholly belonging to the analyst, although this will be the major emphasis. One can easily see any of the actions to be discussed as indicative of unresolved analytic issues, ranging from gross and even unethical conduct on the part of the analyst to subtle forms of uninterpreted transference material. But one can also present the most sensible and rational reasons for their existence. To deny the validity of such conduct after an analysis would be the most rigid and unprofessional stance imaginable. Somewhere between the forbidden and the necessary is where most of us practice, so this is where our inquiry should be directed. As any behavior is capable of analytic rationalization, we must exercise caution in either condemning or condoning what follows.

Once-a-Week Therapy

Some analyses seem unable to end. They become transformed sooner or later into some variant of continuing treatment, often called supportive. The form usually involves the patient's moving from the couch to the chair, sitting up instead of lying down. The reasons range far and wide but usually are said to lie in the patient's inability to leave for good and forever. The anxiety generated by the idea of ending is considered intolerable, so the analyst compromises with the patient by way of this once-a-week solution, for a shorter or longer time, extending to an interminable experience of treatment, if that word can be applied here . Some of these never ending treatments are looked upon as a form of companionship, and, over time, efforts really to effect termination are abandoned.

If the original prescription for analysis was valid, then it is hard to reconcile the cessation of analytic treatment being transformed to a weekly, sitting-up form. At one extreme, there might be a monetary reason to continue the treatment, or a wish on the analyst's part to hold on to the relationship with the patient. At the other would be a mistaken early evaluation, with the patient turning out to be more severely ill than believed in the initial diagnosis. Even those cases, however, merit our attention because interminable treatment seems to be a rare occurrence. Here is a clinical example of the problem.

A woman in analysis wondered about ending her treatment in a gradual way, a sort of a weaning to once-a-week treatment with an open-ended, final finishing point. She compared her planned state to that of a friend who had been in once-a-week therapy for many years. That person said that she enjoyed her weekly sessions with her analyst and saw no reason to give them up as long as she could afford this indulgence, and it did no harm. I felt personally antagonistic to this purely utilitarian approach and aimed to see if we could find just what an extended course of weekly treatment meant to my patient. In so doing, I assumed a stance that might be considered rigid, in that I did not acquiesce to the request. The patient had severe separation anxiety and saw the end of analysis as an abandonment that seemed equated with the end of her life. Staying connected meant some sort of a lifeline to her, and the "renunciation" that was seemingly required was tantamount to death. The analysis proceeded on to termination with a definite end, with no plans for further contact.

I consulted a colleague, who suggested that my own preconceived program about analytic endings and my prejudice against the sort of arrangement that my patient's friend enjoyed were possibly being imposed on this patient without my considering that was in her best interests. When the patient later called to be seen and soon thereafter asked about coming regularly, I was nowhere near so adamant in my position as I had been. Her weekly returns failed to lead very far, and we soon decided to terminate for good. Some time later she wrote a letter saying that she felt the major gain from her return was the simple recognition that it was possible. She, as of this writing, has not been heard from again for some time.

I think that case represents the problem of termination as often lying with the analyst and his convictions. I was able to gain a little freedom from my preconceptions by way of a consultation. I do not mean to present the case as indicative of a good or bad ending, but rather as one that merits attention in an area that is not well delineated. I suspect that many post-terminations drift into supportive psychotherapy because of a certain indolence on the part of analysts in pursuing just what continuation of treatment means. It is a happening that is well cloaked in the best of intentions, as opposed to the next category, which is often seen as a highlight of impropriety.

Gifts

Partings are often marked by presents, and analytic partings are no exception. The gift-giving surrounding analytic endings is notoriously one sided. The question of gifts during the analysis is a separate one that itself has a substantial literature (Hart, 1972). That of gifts at ending is less well studied, but an exemplary article by Calef and Weinshel (1983) considers the gift as an expression of "unfinished business." Without denying its expression of conscious gratitude, they claim there is also in the gift the patient's wish to claim that no further consummation is necessary and that is as far as we will go; it is not necessary to consummate wishes in reality. For these authors, the wish for sexual consummation is often a dissatisfaction with the mere interpretation of treatment and shows hidden lack of resolution of the transference. Such patients indicate a need to return to analysis in the future and then, perhaps, to be fulfilled. The authors also say the gift is a bribe to the analyst not to hope for consummation; that is, it defends against the patient's own wish. One would presume that accepting the gift would prevent a completed analysis, although the authors only indicate what the gesture *may* represent.

If we put aside the more blatant and pernicious behavior of analysts' soliciting gifts, as well as those incidents of analysts being named in wills or suggesting bequests in their name, we can study what the more benign manifestations of gift giving do to the period after termination. Though the direction of most gifts is usually from patient to analyst, it is true that some few analysts do give gifts to patients, especially to adolescents, usually in the form of books, which appear to rank as nonconflictual presents (Glover, 1955). If we pursue the Calef and Weinshel (1983) point, we may claim that every analysis is unfinished, and a significant number end on a note indicating that they are not a completed event, although not many terminate with the prominent feeling of dissatisfaction that seemed to dominate the treatment in that article. If gift giving means gratefulness, it also means dissatisfaction, and this dissatisfaction may lie either in the analysand or the analyst. Here is a clinical example:

A professional man in his mid-forties came to analysis because of a recurrence of perverse behavior that threatened the safety of his social and professional position. He had had two previous analyses without much help with his symptoms. He recalled that in those treatments the emphasis had been on a superego defect that allowed for expression of some infantile sexual fantasy. His present analysis was conducted along a different theoretical line, one stressing a disorder of the self, and was remarkably successful. The patient gained insight into his perverse behavior, entered into a happy and gratifying marriage, and terminated with a good deal of gratitude. At the last session he gave me a gift of a small brass box. I thanked him and he left.

Over the year I have learned through other sources that he has done well, and he has never returned for treatment. In reflecting on his gift, I cannot help but wonder if we both saw that I felt that I deserved more than the fee that I was paid, something special, more than the other analysts had gotten. Although this patient was not dissatisfied in his analysis with me, dissatisfaction was alive in each of us for his previous treatments, and I wonder if it was not realized in the gift.

Regardless of the correctness of that conjecture, *many gifts continue the analytic relationship beyond the date of termination*. They make us think about patients, they open doors for the return of patients, they carry fantasies of libidinal or narcissistic import, and they are probably never confined to expressions of conscious gratitude.

Social Contacts

Lawrence Kubie (1957) took an unrelenting stand against all social contacts between patient and analyst. He bolstered his position on theoretical grounds, feeling it a disservice to the patient to allow any extra-analytic contacts to occur. In today's analytic world, there seems no unanimity of opinion in this regard. One hears of analysts who will stay away from any social gathering at which a patient my be present. Most explain this as being for the benefit of the patient, although some few admit that it is often due to a personal discomfort. I know of others who feel that they would never construct their comings and goings around the possible presence of a patient. They claim that one should be able to manage one's personal feelings, while those of the patient can be readily analyzed in ensuing sessions. It does seem true that a patient's fantasy that he or she can keep you away from a social situation can be just as powerful and significant as one that arises within the social situation itself. But even with the diehard group of social avoiders, there is often a distinction that occurs when the analysis is finished. After analysis is over, there is much more license allowed for social relationships. Whether or not that is a valid position is an open question.

Again putting aside the more blatant examples of social interaction, we find that the problem is intertwined with ethical and moral issues, such as the gift issue. If one can tease apart those activities involving exploitation of the patient, there remains the fact that an analytic relationship that predates a friendship or any other form of social interaction contaminates it in a very unique way. Here is an example:

> Many years after my analysis, I was invited to a party at my analyst's house because of his more recent friendship with my wife. It was a pleasant evening, and over the ensuing years there had been many such oc-

casions. Once we were at a very small gathering, and I happened to mention something about my brother. Much to my surprise, disappointment, and, probably, deep consternation, my former analyst seemed not to "know" that I had a brother. It is true that I had never mentioned my sibling to my newly found friend during the time of our new friendship, but my blood relative certainly had been a vivid presence in my analysis. I had a strange feeling that this indeed was a new relationship.

Over the years I have asked a few other analysts who are caught up in these situations, about this phenomenon, and this feeling of new relationship has been independently confirmed. I have no idea how prevalent it is, but it does direct attention to differences between analytic and social interactions. It lends some support to the feasibility of postanalytic social contact, although this remains a very problematic area.

Professional Contacts

Our professional lives rarely allow the ideal or optimal forms of post-termination, if such do exist, mostly because the size of the analytic community—"tight little islands"—forces a great deal of contact between analysts and ex-analysands. There is a great deal of evidence (unpublished) that splits within analytic institutes occur along lines determined by allegiance to a training analyst, that cliques develop on the same basis, and that the experience of being with one analyst rather than another becomes a measure of narcissistic enhancement or its opposite. There seems no easy way to diminish these lingering transferences within a professional group. For example, journal articles that are referred for publication can be stripped of author identification and so be considered anonymously on their intrinsic merit. This practice is not followed in psychoanalytic circles but is not uncommon elsewhere, for instance in chemistry or physics. More than as an avenue for social contacts, we see the ending of an analysis as a ticket to a change in the nature of the relationship, sometimes without a time period elapsing, as if a graduation had occurred that made for a new status and position. There may even be a premium within our professional lives to know the lineage of our colleagues in terms of the identification of their analysts. So too there may be some sort of familial claims that descend from analyst to patients long after the treatment has ended.

The unconscious claims that patients make on analysts is reciprocated. Analysts who need patients for their own psychic equilibrium communicate this in a myriad of ways and so enhance the fantasies of patients who remain tied to their ex-analyst. They protect and comfort their teachers and mentors and parental surrogates in a manner that mirrors what they feel was adequately or inadequately done for them. How long this goes on and how deleterious it may be is a proper question to ask about post-termination.

THE PERIOD OF VULNERABILITY

The time immediately after the cessation of treatment is felt to be an especially vulnerable period for an analysand as well as for the analyst. Rangell (1966) would put this in a limited time framework, but such determinations depend on the analyst's theoretical stance. A theory of termination as mourning would lend itself to an analogous path of griefwork leading to a new object relationship. Another viewpoint, one of maturation of selfobjects, would point to a less infantile tie to the analyst but one that would not, or need not, resolve. The vulnerable period might, in this viewpoint, be of a longer duration. The Shanes (1984), as well as others, have suggested seeing analysis as a developmental process, and from this vantage point one could envision a trajectory of future development that lives in the analyst's mind. The period of vulnerability would be dependent on the particulars of developmental needs that are relevant to a given patient. If we pursue this last orientation, then we have some sort of guideline or map for post-termination, a series of expectations derived from the analyst's concepts of development and its probable course in a patient. In a sense, every analyst has some sort of program of possibilities for a patient. When termination occurs, there usually is a plan that outlines options for the patient's lifecourse. Certainly much of this plan is implicit, may even lie outside of conscious awareness, but most analysts can speak of what might happen to a patient over time. My own impression is that this is usually addressed in terms of social phenomena and not by way of analytic theory and its terminology. I suspect that here may lie the answer to why some patients remain with us after treatment.

According to the program of expectations, analytic curiosity and concern will be greater in one patient than in another. A complex mix of transference and countertransference feelings toward the patient, concern about doing a competent job, or worry about the incompleteness of the analytic work, as well as certain aspects of personality organization of the analyst, all contribute to the persistence of concern about the patient. For example:

An analyst was planning to visit a foreign country and recalled a patient who had gone to live there after her analysis. She had left treatment with an invitation to the analyst to contact her if he ever found himself planning a visit to her new homeland. As the analyst thought about such a contact, he imagined that it would be awkward. Where could they go? Should the two of them meet alone or could he bring his family? Should they have a drink together or would that seem terribly seductive? He happened to mention his dilemma to a colleague, who asked how long ago the patient had departed. It was several years. Then the analyst realized that he had frozen her in time and had not allowed for the likelihood this his ex-patient had pursued her own development. His musings led him to realize that he thought the patient's analysis had still had a way to go; and since he felt the termination was premature, he was not able to put her fully to rest.

THE ANALYST'S CONTRIBUTION TO POST-TERMINATION

As a candidate in a termination seminar many years ago, I heard Dr. Maxwell Gitelson tell the class of occasionally receiving a phone call with no sound or voice on the other end of the line. He would say "hello," there would be silence, and he would hang up. He told us that he was convinced that this was an ex-patient who wanted to know if he was still alive. He used this to illustrate patients' needs to stay in touch with their analysts. Aside from the obvious possibility that the call had simply been a wrong number, I was impressed with how Gitelson left himself and his own needs out of the equation and so ignored his own wish to have his ex-patient continue to need him. The incident is a nice example of a *projective test*, like a TAT, and, as such, allows us to inquire more into how analysts participate in the post-termination experience.

Let us consider two clusters of analysts and their attitudes toward patients after termination. Each of these clusters represents a group exhibiting a particular personality organization that can be considered pathological at one end of the spectrum and normal at the other. The first group fairly readily stands apart from involvement with patients both during the analysis and afterward. It includes analysts who are almost phobic about extra-analytic patient contact and those who feel only a minimum of concern about a patient's fate after termination. It is with the postermination psychology that we are most concerned, but no doubt there are significant and lasting links to ongoing analytic behavior. For the time after termination, these analysts show little curiosity and a great deal of forgetting. When asked about an ex-patient, they may have a cognitive grasp of the course of the analysis and their analysand's possible future course, but they are seldom preoccupied with such issues. It may also be that this stance reflects a theoretical bias—that is, termination is like mourning and analysis can be finished—as well as reflecting overall personality. These analysts conduct their lives in a rather independent and isolated manner.

The second group comprises, at the abnormal pole, those analysts who are excessively involved with, even exploitative of, their patients. It includes those who remain steadfastly interested and involved. Such analysts seem to remember much about ex-patients, to have clear ideas of what they would like to happen to them over their life's course, and even to maintain some contact with them. This group's posture is supported by its own theory and is characterized as involved in networking or staying in touch. A variety of rationalizations is employed for this continued contact, sometimes using a theory of resolving mourning, sometimes saying it is for the patient's continued benefits, but rarely noting its significance for the analyst's own psychic equilibrium.

Clearly, neither cluster represents a normative route of behavior about the period after termination. Rather, at the end of every treatment both patient and analyst imagine a future course. They participate in a silent negotiation like that discussed in chapter 14. Such ideas are more often implicit than explicit, but for the analyst there is his assessment of the analysis, his unresolved involvement with the patient, his theoretical predilections, and his general personality configuration in terms of the durability of relationships. The period after termination thereby requires a periodic consideration and evaluation at every point of possible contact with a patient. Life would perhaps be more comfortable if analyses were experiences that could be finished, but they well may be for life.

CONCLUSION

Perhaps in an ideal world the end of an analysis would be composed of the patient's proceeding through life with periodic self-analysis while the analyst invests his time and energy in a new patient. This certainly does happen, but it is not the whole of the matter. The changes that occur in patients following termination seem to support the idea that the work that analysis began continues indefinitely either in the form of self-analytic efforts or as the unfolding of a developmental track. Thus, all analyses are unfinished business. For his part, the analyst does not emerge without his own unfinished task. The change effected in analysts by their patients has ramifications in a variety of results ranging from alterations in their theoretical ideas to different social and professional conduct. Behavior is explained by theoretical assumptions that may have no more basis in fact than do personal preferences. This is primarily because post-termination is a neglected and unstudied area that can become an arena for unprofessional conduct in the sense of being outside of our dominant set of rules. There is no doubt that different analysts do things differently, without subscribing to a "right way" for post-termination. And here remains a wide area for expanding our understanding of the phenomena that do occur.

Just as post-termination points out to us that the work of anlaysis is unfinished, so, too, do I hope that this book evokes the same sort of reaction. Our science of psychoanalysis is not a finished product, nor will it probably ever be. We have too many ways to look at clinical material and too many questions that remain unanswered. If psychoanalytic self psychology accomplishes nothing more than rousing us from a state of contentment to force us to look at our field afresh, then it will have been worth all the effort attached to it. Such fresh looks at familiar vistas are a basic requirement for the continued vigor of any field of study.

References

Adler, G., & Buie, D. (1979), Aloneness and borderline psychopathology: The possible relevance of child development issues. *International Journal of Psycho-Analysis*, 60:83–96.

Alexander, F. (1940), Psychoanalysis revised. In: *The Scope of Psychoanalysis*. New York: International Universities Press.

Arlow, J., & Brenner, C. (1964), *Psychoanalytic Concepts and the Structural Theory*. New York: International Universities Press.

Atwood, G., & Stolorow, R. (1984), *Structures of Subjectivity: Explorations in Psychoanalytic Phenomenology*. Hillsdale, NJ: The Analytic Press.

Barnes, B. (1982), *Kuhn and Social Science*. New York: Columbia University Press.

_____ & Bloor, D. (1982), Relativism, rationalism, and the sociology of knowledge. In: *Rationality and Relativism*, ed. M. Hollis & S. Lukes. Cambridge: MIT Press.

Barratt, B. (1984), *Psychic Reality and Psychoanalytic Knowing*. Hilldsale, NJ: The Analytic Press.

_____ (1985), Further notes on the epidemic and the ontic in psychoanalytic transformations. Unpublished manuscript.

Basch, M.F. (1975), Toward a theory that encompasses depression: A revision of existing causal hypotheses in psychoanalysis. In: *Depression and Human Existence*, ed. E.J. Anthony & T. Benedek. Boston: Little, Brown, pp. 485–534.

_____ (1981), Psychoanalytic interpretation and cognitive transformation. *International Journal of Psycho-Analysis*, 62(2):156–176.

_____ (1983), Empathic understanding: A review of the concept and some theoretical considerations. *Journal of the American Psychoanalytic Association*, 31:101-126.

Beebe, B., & Lachmann, F. (1987), Mother-infant mutual influences and precursors of psychic structure. In: *Frontiers in Self Psychology: Progress in Self Psychology, Vol. 3, ed. A. Goldberg. Hillsdale, NJ: The Analytic Press.*

Bellin, E. (1984), The psychoanalytic narrative: The push-pull of a Mareutic text. *Bulletin of the Association for Psychoanalytic Medicine*, 23(4).

Bettelheim, B. (1982), *Freud and Man's Soul*. New York: Knopf.

Bevenuto, B., & Kennedy, R. (1986), *The Works of Jacque Lacan: An Introduction.* London: Free Association Books.

Bibring, G. (1954), The training analysis and its place in psychoanalytic training. *International Journal of Psycho-Analysis,* 35:169–173.

Bird, B. (1972), Notes on transference: Universal phenomenon and hardest part of analysis. *Journal of the American Psychoanalytic Association,* 20(2):267–301.

Bornstein, M., Silver, D., & Poland, W. ed. (1985), The mirror: Psychoanalytic perspectives. *Psychoanalytic Inquiry,* 5(2).

Boesky, D. (1983), The problem of mental representation in self and object theory. *Psychoanalytic Quarterly,* 52:564–583.

Bowlby, J. (1984), Psychoanalysis as a natural science. *Psychoanalytic Psychology,* 1(1):7–22.

Bradlow, P., & Coen, S. (1984), Mirror masturbation. *Psychoanalytic Quarterly,* 53:267–285.

Brazelton, T.B., Kowloski, B., & Main, M. (1974), The origins of reciprocity. In: *The Effect of the Infant on the Caregiver,* ed. M. Lewis & L. Rosenblum. New York: Wiley-Interscience.

Breger, L. (1981), *Freud's Unfinished Journey.* London: Routledge & Kegan Paul.

Brenner, C. (1968), Psychoanalysis and science. *Journal of the American Psychoanalytic Association,* 16:675–696.

———— (1979), The components of psychic conflict and its consequences in mental life. *Psychoanal. Quart.,* 48:547–567.

———— (1980), Metapsychology and psychoanalytic theory. *Psychoanalytic Quarterly,* 49:207

———— (1982), *The Mind in Conflict.* New York: International Universities Press.

Brown, H.I. (1977), *Perception, Theory and Commitment.* Chicago: University of Chicago Press.

Bruner, J. (1984), Narrative and paradigmatic modes of thought. Address to Division 1, American Psychological Association, Toronto, August 1984.

———— (1986), *Actual Minds, Possible Worlds.* Cambridge, MA: Harvard University Press.

Bubner, R. (1981), *Modern German Philosophy.* Cambridge: Cambridge University Press.

Buie, D. (1981), Empathy: Its nature and limitations. *Journal of the American Psychoanalytic Association,* 29(2):281–308.

Buxbaum, E. (1950), Technique of terminating analysis. *International Journal of Psychoanalysis,* 31:185–190.

Calef, V. & Weinshel, E. (1979), The new psychoanalysis and psychoanalytic revisionism. *Psychoanalytic Quarterly,* 48: 470–491.

———— & ———— (1983), A note on consummation and termination. *Journal of the American Psychoanalytic Association,* 31:643–650.

Cath, S. H. (1986), Review of *Annual of Psychoanalysis, Vol. II* in *International Journal of Psycho-Analysis,* 67:379.

Dahl, E. (1983), The therapist as decoder: Psychotherapy with toddlers. In: *Infants and Toddlers,* ed. S. Provence. New York: International Universities Press.

Demos, V. (1987), Affect and the development of the self: A new frontier. In: Frontiers in Self Psychology; *Progress in Self Psychology* Vol. 3, ed. A. Goldberg. Hillsdale, NJ: The Analytic Press.

Eagle, M. (1984), *Recent Developments in Psychoanalysis.* New York: McGraw Hill.

Edelson, M. (1984), *Hypothesis and Evidence in Psychoanalysis.* Chicago & London: University of Chicago Press.

Eisenberg, R. (1984), Membranes and channels. In: *Membranes, Channels and Noise,* ed. R.S. Eisenberg, M. Frank, & C.F. Steven. New York: Plenum Press.

Eisnitz, A. (1980), The organization of the self-representative and its role in pathology. *Psychoanalytic Quarterly*, 49:361–393.

Eissler, K. (1953), The effect of the structure of the ego on psychoanalytic technique. *Journal of the American Psychoanalytic Association*, 1:104–143.

Elkisch, P. (1957), The psychological significance of the mirror. *Journal of the American Psychoanalytic Association*, 5:235–244.

Feigelson, C. (1975), The mirror dream. *The Psychoanalytic Study of the Child*, 30:341–355. New Haven: Yale University Press.

Fenichel, O. (1945), *The Psychoanalytic Theory of Neurosis*. New York: Norton.

Feyerabend, P. (1975), *Against Method*. London: New Left Books.

Fleming, J. (1951), Discussion of A. Johnson's paper on heterosexual transference and countertransference. Presented at meeting of Chicago Psychoanalytic Society.

Flew, A. (1979), *A Dictionary of Philosophy*. New York: St. Martin's Press.

Freud, A. (1965), *Normality and Pathology in Childhood: Assessments of Development*. New York: International Universities Press.

Freud, S. (1909a), Analysis of a phobia in a five-year-old boy. *Standard Edition*, 10:5–149. London: Hogarth Press, 1955.

———— (1909b), Notes upon a case of obsessive neurosis. *Standard Edition*, 10:155–318. London: Hogarth Press, 1955.

———— (1913), On beginning the treatment. *Standard Edition*, 12:123–144. London: Hogarth Press, 1958.

———— (1915), Mourning and melancholia. *Standard Edition*, 14:243–258. London: Hogarth Press, 1957.

———— (1916), Some character types met with in psycho-analytic work. *Standard Edition*, 14:309–333. London: Hogarth Press, 1957.

———— (1916–17), Introductory lectures on psycho-analysis. *Standard Edition*, 15 & 16. London: Hogarth Press, 1963.

———— (1917), Mourning and melancholia. *Standard Edition*, 14:243–258. London: Hogarth Press, 1957.

———— (1918), From the history of an infantile neurosis. *Standard Edition*, 17:3–122, 1955.

———— (1923a), The ego and the id. *Standard Edition*, 19:12–59. London: Hogarth Press, 1961.

———— (1923b), A short account of psycho-analysis. *Standard Edition*, 19:191–209. London: Hogarth Press, 1961.

———— (1933), New introductory lectures on psycho-analysis. *Standard Edition*, 22:5–182. London: Hogarth Press, 1964.

———— (1937), Analysis terminable and interminable. *Standard Edition*, 23:216–253. London: Hogarth Press, 1964.

Furman, R. & Furman, E. (1984), Intermittent decathexis: A type of parental dysfunction. *International Journal of Psycho-Analysis*, 65:423–434.

Furth, H.G. (1981), *Piaget and Knowledge*, 2nd ed. Chicago: University of Chicago Press.

Gadamer, H.G. (1975), *Truth and Method*. New York: Seabury Press.

Gedeman, H.K. (1982), Special review: *Loss, Sadness and Depression* by John Bowlby. *Psychoanalytic Review*, 69(3).

Gedo, J. & Goldberg, A. (1973), *Models of the Mind*. Chicago: University of Chicago Press.

Gelinas, D. J. (1983), The persisting negative effect of incest. *Psychiatry*, 46:312–322.

Gellner, E. (1974), *Legitimation of Belief*. London: Cambridge University Press.

Gibson, J.J. (1966), *The Senses Considered as Perceptual Systems*. Boston: Houghton Mifflin.

Gill, M. (1982a), *Analysis of Transference, I*. New York: International Universities Press.

———— (1982b), *Analysis of Transference, II*. New York: International Universities Press.

_____ (1984), Psychoanalysis and psychotherapy: A revision. *International Journal of Psycho-analysis*, 11:161–179.

Glasser, M. (1986), Identification and its vicissitudes as observed in the perversions. *International Journal of Psycho-Analysis*, 67:9–17.

Glover, E. (1955), *The Technique of Psychoanalysis*. New York: International Universities Press.

Goffman, E. (1974), *Frame Analysis*. New York: Harper Calaphon Books.

Goldberg, A. (1975), A fresh look at perverse behavior. *International Journal of Psycho-Analysis*, 56:335–342.

_____ (ed.) (1978), *The Psychology of the Self: A Casebook*: New York: International Universities Press.

_____ (1981), Self psychology and the distinctiveness of psychotherapy. *International Journal of Psychoanalytic Psychotherapy*, 8:57–70.

_____ (1983), Self psychology and alternatives to internalization. In: *Reflections on Self Psychology*, ed. J. Lichtenberg & S. Kaplan. Hillsdale, NJ: The Analytic Press.

_____ (1984), The tension between realism and relativism in psychoanalysis. *Psychoanalysis and Contemporary Science*, 7:367–386.

_____ (1985), Translation between psychoanalytic theories. In: *Annual of Psychoanalysis*, 12. New York: International Universities Press, pp. 121–135.

_____ (1986), The wishy-washy personality. *Contemporary Psychoanalysis*, 22:357–373.

_____ & Marcus, D. (1985), Natural termination: Some comments on ending analysis without setting a date. *Psychoanalytic Quarterly*, 54:46–65.

Goodman, N. (1978), *Ways of Worldmaking*. Indianapolis, in: Hackett.

Gould, S. (1984), Review of *Not in Our Genes: Biology, Ideology and Human Nature* by R.C. Lewontin, S. Rose & L. J. Kamen. In *New York Review of Books*, August 16, 1984, pp. 30–32.

Grossman, W.I. (1982), The self as fantasy: Fantasy as theory. *Journal of the American Psychoanalytic Association*, 30:919–937.

Grünbaum, A. (1982), Can psychoanalytic theory be cogently tested "on the couch"? *Psychoanalysis and Contemporary Thought*, 5(2–3):311–436.

_____ (1983), *The Foundations of Psychoanalysis: A Philosophical Critique*. Berkeley: University of California Press.

Grundy, R.E., ed. (1973), *Theories and Observations in Science*. Englewood Cliffs, NJ: Prentice-Hall.

Guttman, S. (1985), The psychoanalytic point of view: Basic concepts and deviant theories. *International Journal of Psycho-Analysis*, 66:167–170.

Habermas, J. (1971), *Knowledge and Human Interest*. Boston: Beacon Press.

_____ (1978), *The Critical Theory of Jurgen Habermas*, tr. McCarthy. Cambridge, MA: MIT Press.

Hart, H. (1972), *Conceptual Index to Psychoanalytic Technique and Training*. North River Press.

Hartlaub, G., Martin, G., & Rhine, M. (1986), Recontact with the analyst following termination: A survey of seventy-one cases. *Journal of the American Psychoanalytic Association*, 34(4):895–910.

Harre, R. (1972), *The Philosophies of Science*. Oxford: Oxford University Press.

Hartmann, H. (1927), Understanding and Explanation. In: *Essays on Ego Psychology*. New York: International Universities Press, pp. 369–403, 1964.

_____ (1939), Psychoanalysis and the concept of health. In: *Essays on Ego Psychology*. New York: International Universities Press, 1964.

_____ (1951), Technical implications of ego psychology. In: *Essays on Ego Psychology*. New York: International Universities Press, 1964.

_____ (1964), *Essays on Ego Psychology*. New York: International Universities Press.

_____ & Loewenstein, R. M. (1962), Notes on the superego. *Psychological Issues* Monogr. 14. New York: International Universities Press.

Hempel, K. (1942), The function of general laws in history. In: *Theories of History*, ed. P. Gardener. New York: Free Press.

Hendrick, I. (1958), *Facts and Theories of Psychoanalysis*. New York: Knopf.

Hesse, M. (1978), Theory and value in the social sciences. In: *Action and Interpretation*, ed. C. Hookeway & P. Petit. Cambridge: Cambridge University Press.

_____ (1980), *Revolutions and Reconstruction in the Philosophy of Science*. Bloomington: Indiana University Press.

Hoffman, I. (1983), The patient as interpreter of the analyst's experience. *Contemporary Psychoanalysis*, 19:389–422.

Husserl, E. (1960), *Cartesian Meditations*. tr. Dorion Cairas. The Hague: Nighoff.

Jacobson, E. (1964), *The Self and the Object World*. New York: International Universities Press.

James, W. (1950). *The Principles of Psychology*. New York: Dover Press. Chapter X.

Johnson, A. (1951), Heterosexual transference and countertransference. Presented to the Chicago Psychoanalytic Society, February.

Kant, I. (1781), *Critique of Pure Reason*. London: Macmillan, 1929.

Kaye, K. (1982), *The Mental and Social Life of Babies*. Chicago: University of Chicago Press.

Kernberg, O. (1970), A psychoanalytic classification of character pathology. *Journal of the American Psychoanalytic Association*, 18:800–822.

Klein, G. (1968), Psychoanalysis: Ego psychology. In: *International Encyclopedia of the Social Sciences*. New York: Free Press, pp. 11–31.

Klein, Melanie (1950), On the criteria for the termination of an analysis. *International Journal of Psycho-Analysis*, 31:78–80.

_____ (1952), Some theoretical conclusions regarding the emotional life of the infant. In: *Developments in Psychoanalysis*, ed. J. Riviere. London: Hogarth Press, pp. 198–236.

Klein, M. & Tribeck, (1981), Kernberg's object-relation theory: A critical evaluation. *International Journal of Psycho-Analysis*, 62:10–29.

Kohut, H. (1959), Introspection, empathy and psychoanalysis. *Journal of the American psychoanalytic Association*, 7:459–483.

_____ (1971), *The Analysis of the Self*. New York: International Universities Press.

_____ (1973), Psychoanalysis in a troubled world. *The Annual of Psychoanalysis*, 1:3–25. New York: International Universities Press.

_____ (1977), *The Restoration of the Self*. New York: International Universities Press.

_____ (1979), The two analyses of Mr. Z. *International Journal of Psychoanalysis*, 60:3–27.

_____ (1984), *How Does Analysis Cure?* Chicago: University of Chicago Press.

Kramer, S. (1979), The technical significance and application of Mahler's separation-individuation theory. *J. Amer. Psychoanal. Assn.*, 27 (suppl.):251.

Kris, A. (1983), Determinants of free association in narcissistic phenomena. *The Psychoanalytic Study of the Child*, 38:439–458. New Haven: Yale University Press.

Kubie, L. (1957), *Practical and Theoretical Aspects of Psychoanalysis*. New York: International Universities Press.

_____ & Israel, H. A. (1955), "Say you're sorry." *The Psychoanalytic Study of the Child*, 10:289–299 New York: International Universities Press.

Kuhn, T. S. (1970), *The Structure of Scientific Revolution*. Chicago; University of Chicago Press.

_____ (1977), *The Essential Tension*. Chicago: University of Chicago Press.

Laing, R. D. (1967), *The Politics of Experience*. New York: Pantheon.

Lana, R. E., & Georgoride, M. (1983), Causal attributions: Phenomenological and Dialectic aspects. *Journal of Mind and Behavior,* 4:479–490.

Langes R. (1982), *The Psychotherapeutic Conspiracy.* New York: Aronson.

Laplanche, J., & Pontalis, J.B. (1973), *The Language of Psychoanalysis,* trans. D. N. Smith. London: Hogarth Press.

Lichtenstein, H. (1964), The role of narcissism in the emergence of a primary identity. *International Journal of Psycho-Analysis,* 45:49–56.

Lipton, S. (1983), Further observations on the advantages of Freud's technique. Presented to the Chicago Psychoanalytic Society, October 25, 1983.

Luborsky, L. & Spence, D. (1978), Quantitative research of psychoanalytic theory. In: *Handbook of Psychotherapy and Behavior Change,* ed. S. Garfield & A. Bergin. New York: Wiley.

MacAlpine, I. (1950), The development of the transference. *Psychoanalytic Quarterly,* 19:501–539.

Mahler, M. (1968), *On Human Symbiosis and the Vicissitudes of Individuation.* New York: International Universities Press.

———— (1972), On the first three subphases of the separation-individuation phase. *International Journal of Psycho-Analysis,* 53:333–338.

————, Pine, F., & Bergman, A. (1975), *The Psychological Birth of the Human Infant.* New York: Basic Books.

Mahoney, P. (1982), *Freud as a Writer.* New York: International Universities Press.

Malcolm, J. (1983), Review of *Narrative Truth and Historical Truth* by D. Spence. *The New Yorker,* Jan. 29, pp. 95–106.

May, R. (1976), Simple mathematical models with very complicated dynamics. *Nature,* 261:459–462.

McCarthy, T. (1973), On misunderstanding understanding. *Theory and Decision,* 3:351–370. Dordrecht, Holland: D. Rudel.

McDougall, J. (1982), *Plea for a Measure of Abnormality.* New York: International Universities Press.

Merleau-Ponty, M. (1962), *Phenomenology of Perception.* New York: Humanities Press.

Modell, A. (1984), In: *Psychoanalysis: The Vital Issues,* Vol. II, ed. G. H. Pollock & J. Gedo. New York: International Universities Press.

Moore, B. (1981), Book Notice: *The Psychology of the Self: A Casebook.* In: *Journal of the American Psychoanalytic Association,* 2991:249–252.

Newman, K. (1985), Countertransference—Its role in facilitating the use of the object. Presented to the Chicago Psychoanalytic Society, November, 1985.

Niederland, W. (1951), New York: Three notes on the Schreber case. *Psychoanalytic Quarterly,* 20:579–591.

Peterfreund, E. (1983), *The Process of Psychoanalytic Therapy.* Hillsdale, NJ: The Analytic Press.

Piaget, J., & Inhelder, B. (1969), *The Psychology of the Child.* New York: Basic Books.

Pine, F. (1985), *Developmental Theory and Clinical Process.* New Haven: Yale University Press.

Poland, W. (1975), Tact as a psychoanalytic function. *International Journal of Psycho-Analysis,* 56:155–163.

Popper, K. (1959), *The Logic of Scientific Discovery,* rev. New York: Harper & Row, 1968.

———— (1963), *Conjectures and Refutations.* New York: Harper & Row.

———— (1972), *Objective Knowledge: An Evolutionary Approach.* Oxford: Clarendon Press.

Provence, S., ed. (1983), *Infants and Toddlers. Clinical Case Reports.* New York: International Universities Press.

Pruett, K. D. (1983), Babies everywhere: Assessing and treating a toddler's pervasive developmental disorders. In: *Infants and Toddlers*, ed. S. Provence. New York: International Universities Press.

Putnam, H. (1982), The philosophy of science. In: *Men of Ideas*, ed. B. Magee. Oxford: Oxford University Press, pp. 194–208.

Quine, W. V. (1969), *Ontological Relativity and Other Essays*. New York: Columbia University Press.

_____ & Ullean, J. S. (1978), *The Web of Belief*, 2nd ed. New York: Random House.

Racker, H. (1968), *Transference and Countertransference*. New York: International Universities Press.

Ragland-Sullivan, E. (1986), *Jacque Lacan and the Philosophy of Psychoanalysis*. Urbana: University of Illinois Press.

Rangell, L. (1966), An overview of the ending of an analysis. In: *Psychoanalysis in the Americas*, ed. R. E. Litman. New York: International Universities Press, pp. 141–165.

_____ (1981), From insight to change. *Journal of the American Psychoanalytic Association*, 29:119–141.

_____ (1985), On the theory of theory is psychoanalysis and the relation of theory to psychoanalytic therapy. *Journal of the American Psychoanalytic Association*, 33:59–92.

Ravitch, R. A. & Dunsten, H. D. (1965), "Say you're sorry": A ten-year follow-up. *American Journal of Psychotherapy*, 20(4):615-623.

Richards, A. (1981), Self theory, conflict theory, and the problem of hypochondriasis. *The Psychoanalytic Study of the Child*, 36:319–338. New Haven: Yale University Press.

Ricoeur, P. (1970), *Freud and Philosophy: An Essay on Interpretation*. New Haven: Yale University Press.

_____ (1977), The question of proof in Freud's psychoanalytic writings. *Journal of the American Psychoanalytic Association*, 25:833–871.

_____ (1981), *Hermeneutics and the Human Sciences*, ed. & trans. J. B. Thompson. Cambridge: Cambridge University Press.

_____ (1984), *Time and Narrative*. Chicago: University of Chicago Press.

Robbins, F., & Schlessinger, N. (1983), *A Developmental View of the Psychoanalytic Process. Emotions and Behavior*. Monogr. I. New York: International Universities Press.

Robitscher, J. (1980), *The Powers of Psychiatry*. Boston: Houghton Mifflin.

Rorty, R. (1982a), *Consequences of Pragmatism*. Minneapolis: University of Minnesota Press.

_____ (1982b), *Philosophy: The Mirror of Nature*. Princeton, NJ: Princeton University Press.

Rosenblatt, A. & Thickstun, J. (1977), *Modern Psychoanalytic Concepts in a General Psychology*. New York: International Universities Press.

Rothstein, A. (1979), Toward a critique of the self. Unpublished.

Sandler, J. (1976), Actualization and object relations. *Journal of the Philadelphia Association for Psychoanalysis*, 3:59–70.

Saussure, F. de (1916), *A Course in General Linguistics*. New York: Philosophical Library.

Schneiderman, S. (1980), *Returning to Freud. Clinical Psychoanalysis in the School of Lacan*. New Haven: Yale University Press.

_____ (1983), *Jacque Lacan: The Death of an Intellectual Hero*. Cambridge, MA: Harvard University Press.

Sellars, W. (1963), *Science, Perception and Reality*. London: Routledge & Kegal Paul.

Shane, E. (1984), Self psychology: A new conceptualization for the understanding of learning-disabled child. In: *Kohut's Legacy*, ed. P. Stepansky & A. Goldberg. Hillsdale, NJ: The Analytic Press.

_____ & Shane, M. (1984), The end phase of analysis. *Journal of the American Psychoanalytic Association*, 32:739–772.

Shengold, L. (1974), The metaphor and the mirror. *Journal of the American Psychoanalytic Association*, 22:97–115.

Sherwood, M. (1969), *The Logic of Explanation in Psychoanalysis*. New York: Academic Press.

Silverman, M. (1985), Countertransference and the myth of the perfectly analyzed analyst. *Psychoanalytic Quarterly*, 54:173–199.

Simon, H. (1977), Models of discovery. *Boston Studies in the Philosophy of Science*, 54. Dordrecht, Holland: Raidel.

Sonnenschein, S. (1984), How feedback from a listener affects childrens' referential communication skills, *Developmental Psychology*, 20:287–292.

Spence, D. (1982), *Narrative Truth and Historical Truth*. New York: Norton.

Spitz, R. (1964), The derailment of dialogue: Stimulus overload, cycles, and the completion gradient. *Journal of the American Psychoanalytic Association*, 12:752–775.

Spruiell, V. (1983), The rules and frames of the psychoanalytic situation. *Psychoanalytic Quarterly*, 52:1–33.

Steiner, G. (1975), *After Babel*. London: Oxford University Press.

Stern, D. (1985), *The Interpersonal World of the Infant*. New York: Basic Books.

Stevens, J. (1980), Review of *Advances in Self Psychology* in *Journal of the Philadelphia Psychoanalytic Association*, 7:208–212.

Stroud, B. (1984), *The Significance of Philosophical Scepticism*. Oxford: Clarendon Press.

Suppe, F. (1974), *The Structure of Scientific Theories*. Urbana: University of Illinois Press.

Tolpin, P. (1986), On understanding dreams. Presented to Chicago Psychoanalytic Society, June 24, 1986.

Toulmin, S. (1974), *Encyclopedia Brittanica Macropedia*, Vol. 16. Chicago: Encyclopedia Britannica, p. 389.

_____ (1982), The construal of reality criticism in modern and postmodern science. *Critical Inquiry*, 9:93–111.

Tower, L. (1956), Countertransference. *Journal of the American Psychoanalytic Association*, 4:224–255.

Tyson, R. L., & Tyson, P. (1982), A case of "pseudonarcissistic" psychopathology: A re-examination of the developmental role of the superego. *International Journal of Psycho-Analysis*, 63:283–294.

Von Eckhardt, B. (1981), Why Freud's research methodology was unscientific. *Psychoanalysis and Contemporary Thought*, 5:549–574.

_____ (1982), The scientific status of psychoanalysis. In: *Introducing Psychoanalytic Theory*, ed. L. Gilman. New York: Brunner/Mazel, pp. 139–180.

Waelder, R. (1930), The principle of multiple function. *Psychoanal. Quart.*, 5:45–62.

_____ (1962), Psychoanalysis, scientific method and philosophy. *Journal of the American Psychoanalytic Association*, 10:617–637.

Wallerstein, R. (1981), The bipolar self: Discussion of alternative perspectives. *Journal of the American Psychoanalytic Association*, 29(2):377–394.

_____ (1983), Self psychology and "classical" psychoanalysis: The nature of their relationship. In: *The Future of Psychoanalysis*, ed. A. Goldberg. New York: International Universities Press.

Weigert, E. (1955), Special problems in connection with termination of training analysis. *Journal of the American Psychoanalytic Association*, 3:314–322; 63–64.

Wilden, A. (1972), *System and Structure*. London: Tavistock.

Williams, M. (1977), *Groundless Belief*. New Haven: Yale University Press.

Winnicott, D.W. (1953), Transitional objects and transitional phenomena. *International Journal of Psycho-Analysis*, 34:89–97.

_____ (1965), *The Maturational Processes and the Facilitative Environment*. New York: International Universities Press.

_____ (1974), Mirror role of mother and family in child development. *Playing and Reality*. New York: Penguin.

Wittgenstein, L. (1950), *On Certainty*. ed. G. E. M. Anscomb & G. H. Von Wright. Oxford: Basil Blackwell, 1969.

Wittgenstein L. (1922), *Tractatus-Logico-Philosophicus*. (Trans. by Ogden & Richards.) London: Routledge & Kegan Paul.

Author Index

Subject Index